Beyond Repair?

Constitutional Conflicts

A Series with the Institute of Bill of Rights Law

at The College of William and Mary

Series Editors: Neal Devins and Mark Graber

BEYOND REPAIR? America's Death Penalty

Edited by Stephen P. Garvey

DUKE UNIVERSITY PRESS *Durham and London 2003*

© 2003 Duke University Press
All rights reserved
Printed in the United States of America on acid-free paper ∞
Typeset in Trump Mediaeval by Keystone Typesetting, Inc.
Library of Congress Cataloging-in-Publication data
appear on the last printed page of this book.

For Carolyn

CONTENTS

ACKNOWLEDGMENTS

I'd like to thank my colleagues in the Cornell Death Penalty Project for the work they do and for their friendship, the contibutors to this volume for their scholarship, and two of my former students, Robert B. Black (Cornell '01) and Jonathan N. Francis (Cornell '02), both of whom provided service above and beyond the call. I'd also like to thank Valerie Millholland, the editor at Duke who shepherded the book through the publication process, and Neal Devins, the general editor of the series in which the book appears, for his insight, advice, and encouragement along the way. Finally, I'd like to thank my wife, for everything.

INTRODUCTION

Stephen P. Garvey

Few decisions are more profound than that of a state faced with the question of taking a life. The United States has been living with capital punishment now for more than twenty-five years. Capital punishment has, of course, been around for much longer, but the modern era in the United States dates back only to 1976, when the Supreme Court of the United States resolved the then-extant doubts about the death penalty's constitutionality. Death, the Court finally said, was not an unconstitutionally cruel and unusual punishment, provided that it was administered in a manner free from arbitrariness, caprice, and discrimination.

Thus began America's modern experiment with death. Much has changed between then and now. More states have added themselves to the roster of those that authorize death as a sanction for murder, even as more nations of the world have taken themselves off. We have, as of July 1, 2002, seen 784 men and women put to death in the United States. Texas and Virginia lead the way with 360 executions between them.[1] We have seen the electric chair and the gas chamber gradually give way to lethal injection; and we have seen the first execution under federal authority since 1963: on June 11, 2001, the United States executed Timothy McVeigh for the 168 deaths he caused with the 1995 bombing of the Murrah Federal Building in Oklahoma City. The second federal execution followed eight days later. Meanwhile, the Supreme Court has worked to keep the penalty of death functioning within the limits, as it sees them, of the rule of law.

But even as the numbers on death row continue to grow, the doubts that have long surrounded the death penalty continue to grow as well. Can we really

---

1. See Death Penalty Info. Ctr., "Executions," available at http://www.deathpenaltyinfo.org/facts.html.

administer a system of capital punishment fairly, without arbitrariness, without mistake, without regard to race, and consistent with evolving international norms?

Questions such as this are once again attracting serious public concern. A recent issue of *Newsweek* magazine carried the headline "Rethinking the Death Penalty" on its cover.[2] Within the last year and a half, two justices of the United States Supreme Court have publicly raised questions about the fairness of the death penalty's administration.[3] Indeed, the prospect of a national moratorium on executions is no longer just the wishful thinking of abolitionists. In Illinois, for example, Governor George Ryan put a halt to executions after the thirteenth innocent man walked off that state's death row; at the same time, he appointed a special commission to investigate the causes of these miscarriages and, if possible, to identify ways to prevent any more of them in the future.[4]

The essays collected here focus on a variety of recent developments, ranging from changes in the legal processes for administering the death penalty to new information about how those processes actually work and to the emerging international consensus against death as a punishment for crime. Each chapter provides the insight and analysis necessary for informed debate.

Public opinion. Since the mid-1980s public support for the death penalty has been surprisingly stable, hovering between 70 and 80 percent. But recent polls show signs of change. According to one of the latest, a Gallup poll conducted in February 2001, the percentage of respondents nationwide who expressed generalized support for the death penalty was down to 67 percent.[5] In Chapter 1, Professors Samuel Gross and Phoebe Ellsworth examine in detail the nature of public support for the death penalty today and the reasons behind the recent drop. They end with some thoughts on what this change means for the future. Is it a blip, or is it a harbinger of a larger and more enduring shift in public opinion?

Habeas corpus. Most of the men and women on the death rows across the United States arrived there under state authority. The courts of those states are

2. See Jonathan Alter, "The Death Penalty on Trial," *Newsweek*, June 2000, at 24; see also John Harwood, "Death Reconsidered," *Wall St. J.*, May 22, 2001, at A1.

3. See Ken Armstrong and Steve Mills, "O'Connor Questions Fairness of Death Penalty," *Chi. Trib.*, July 4, 2001 (Justice Sandra Day O'Connor); "Death Penalty Moratorium Backed," *Houston Chron.*, Apr. 10, 2001 (Justice Ruth Bader Ginsburg).

4. See Ken Armstrong and Steve Mills, "Ryan Suspends Death Penalty," *Chi. Trib.*, Jan. 31, 2000.

5. See Jeffrey M. Jones, "Two-Thirds of Americans Support the Death Penalty," available at http://www.gallup.com/poll/releases/pr010302.asp (reporting results of poll conducted on February 19–20, 2001).

obliged to guarantee that no death sentence is carried out unless it was obtained in accord not only with state law but also with the federal Constitution. However, every capital defendant sentenced to death under state authority is entitled to petition a *federal* court, through a process known as habeas corpus, to review the constitutional validity of his conviction and sentence. As a recent and widely reported study has shown,[6] federal habeas corpus is a vitally important part of the process by which the legal system detects and remedies unconstitutionally obtained death sentences. Yet, as Professor Larry Yackle documents and explains in Chapter 2, recent changes in the law of federal habeas corpus jeopardize its ability to perform this all-important function.

Innocence. Learned Hand, one of the nation's most respected federal judges, once called the prospect that an innocent man could be convicted of a crime, let alone a capital crime, little more than a "ghostly phantom," an "unreal" specter "haunt[ing]" the law.[7] But Hand's phantom is real. Thanks in no small part to DNA technology, Hand's phantom has acquired a human face—indeed, several human faces. Since 1973, 101 men have been set free from death row.[8] The faces of the wrongfully condemned have become the driving force behind the movement for a moratorium. But how do such mistakes happen? *Chicago Tribune* journalists Ken Armstrong and Steve Mills conducted an intensive investigation into the operation of the death penalty in Illinois. The resulting five-part series, "The Failure of the Death Penalty in Illinois," appeared in November 1999 and was instrumental in Governor Ryan's subsequent decision to impose a moratorium. In Chapter 3, Armstrong and Mills draw on the Illinois experience to explain how and why the criminal justice system fails in this most fundamental of ways and why mistakes are especially likely when the crime is murder and the potential punishment is death.

Race. Any effort to understand the death penalty in the United States without attending to the influence of race would be incomplete. Those who defend the current system often admit that race once mattered, but they insist that times have changed and that it matters no longer. Yet, as Professor Sheri Lynn Johnson

6. See James S. Liebman et al., "Capital Attrition: Error Rates in Capital Cases, 1973–1995," 78 *Tex. L. Rev.* 1839, 1849 (2000) (finding that federal courts overturned due to serious error 40 percent of the death sentences subject to federal court review during the twenty-three-year study period).

7. See, for example, Di Carolo v. United States, 6 F.2d 364, 368 (2d Cir. 1925) (Hand, J.); United States v. Garsson, 291 F.646, 649 (S.D.N.Y. 1923) (Hand, J.).

8. Death Penalty Info. Ctr., "Innocence: Freed from Death Row," available at http://www.death penaltyinfo.org/Innocentlist.html (current as of July 1, 2002).

explains in Chapter 4, the influence of race persists. All too often the difference between life and death cannot be explained without at some point taking account of race, whether it be the race of the defendant or the race of the victim (or both) or the race of the jurors. The challenge of creating a capital sentencing system free from the pernicious power of race remains unmet. Professor Johnson explains why and assesses the prospects for meeting that challenge.

Capital juries. Sentencing in capital cases is different in many ways. One significant difference is the fact that, while judges do most of the sentencing in noncapital cases, in most capital cases jurors—the conscience of the community—decide the defendant's fate. But how do jurors decide between life and death? In Chapter 5, Professors John Blume and Theodore Eisenberg and I describe some of the most recent empirical investigations into the behavior of capital sentencing juries. The results are disquieting. Far too many unqualified jurors end up serving; many capital jurors fail to understand the basic constitutional principles on which their deliberations should proceed; unfounded anxieties about the defendant's future dangerousness distort their decision making; and a defendant's fate can turn not just on the facts and circumstances of his case but also on the race of the jurors who sit in judgment of him.

International law. We live in an increasingly global world, and the international community increasingly insists that every nation of the world respect human rights. Most of the countries with which the United States prefers to keep company have abolished the death penalty. Indeed, most of them now see capital punishment as a human rights violation. In this respect, we are left in the company of nations whose records on human rights we regard with contempt. But what exactly does existing international law say about the status and legitimacy of the death penalty? In Chapter 7, Professor William Schabas surveys contemporary international law. He analyzes the variety of legal instruments, from treaties and conventions to declarations and resolutions, that constitute the international law of the death penalty. He then assesses how those instruments might affect the future course of law and politics here at home.

As capital cases go, *Callins v. Collins*[9] was fairly typical. Callins, the defendant in the case, was convicted and sentenced to death in Texas. He appealed his conviction and sentence on various grounds through the state courts of Texas and then through the federal courts. His next step was to petition the United States Supreme Court to hear his case. The Court declined, as it does in most of the cases that come before it, and Callins was eventually executed in the spring

9. 510 U.S. 1141 (1994).

of 1997. This otherwise common case nonetheless provided the occasion for an uncommon exchange between two of the Court's members, an exchange that frames the debate over the future of capital punishment.

Dissenting from the full Court's decision not to hear Callins's appeal, Justice Harry Blackmun examined the Court's long struggle to make good on the promise it made many years before that the death penalty had to be administered fairly or not at all.[10] For Justice Blackmun, that promise remained unfulfilled, not for want of trying, but because the promise itself was impossible to keep. Convinced that mere mortals could never come up with a system of capital punishment capable of being both just and even-handed, Justice Blackmun made the following pronouncement: "From this day forward, I no longer shall tinker with the machinery of death."[11] Accordingly, he voted, until his retirement three years later, to reverse every capital sentence that came before the Court for review.

Justice Antonin Scalia, concurring in the Court's decision not to hear Callins's appeal, took a different view.[12] According to Justice Scalia, the notion that capital punishment and the Constitution were on a collision course rested on a misunderstanding of the Constitution itself. The Constitution does not, he said, require the impossible. On the contrary, its text clearly countenances the punishment of death; consequently, any reading of the Constitution that foreclosed death was a mistaken reading. The Constitution demanded no further tinkering with the machinery of death. Indeed, according to Justice Scalia, the Court had tinkered too much already.

Is America's death penalty beyond repair? My hope is that the chapters to follow will help readers decide for themselves.

[Editor's note: All chapters in this volume were substantially complete by early summer 2001. Several important developments have taken place since then: the terrorist attacks of September 11, 2001; the decisions of the U.S. Supreme Court proscribing the execution of the mentally retarded and requiring that a jury, not a judge, find any fact necessary to render a defendant eligible for the death penalty; the decision of a New York federal district judge declaring the federal death penalty unconstitutional; a moratorium on executions imposed by the governor of Maryland; and the exoneration of at least three more innocent men sentenced to death.]

10. See id. at 1144 (Blackmun, J., dissenting from the denial of certiorari).
11. Id. at 1145.
12. See id. at 1141–43 (Scalia, J., concurring in the denial of certiorari).

1 : SECOND THOUGHTS: AMERICANS' VIEWS ON THE DEATH PENALTY AT THE TURN OF THE CENTURY

Samuel R. Gross & Phoebe C. Ellsworth

American public opinion on the death penalty has turned a corner. From the early 1980s through the mid-1990s, support for capital punishment reached record highs. Public support for the death penalty is still strong, but between 1996 and 2000 it declined significantly from the extraordinary levels that we saw just a few years ago. Why this has happened is less clear, although not for lack of plausible explanations. What will happen next is even more in doubt. If this is Act II, in which America's love affair with the death penalty loses much of its passion, Act III could go in various directions: breakup, renewed infatuation, long-term ambivalence, or indifference. But the very fact that we don't know is news. For the first time in decades, the future popularity of this long-time favorite is in doubt.

We begin this chapter by presenting the evidence for a steady decline in American support for capital punishment since 1996. We then attempt to identify the factors that made change possible. Our analysis proceeds on two levels, the individual and the contextual. On the individual level, we draw on basic psychological research on attitudes and decision making to provide a general account of the conditions that might make it possible for deep-seated attitudes to change. On the contextual level, we examine the social and political trends and events that could have created those conditions over the past decade.

The authors thank Katherine Barnes, William Bowers, Richard Gonzalez, Reid Hastie, Yale Kamisar, Donald Kinder, William McGuire, Richard Petty, Michael Radelet, and Lee Ross for help and for comments on an earlier draft of this chapter, and Les Adler, Barbara Brown, and Karen Rushlow for their assistance in completing this project.

Public opinion polls have asked Americans about their attitudes toward the death penalty on a reasonably steady basis since the mid-1950s. Looking back over the accumulated data, it's easy to see the long-term trends. Thus, in 1994 we reported that "support for capital punishment declined through the 1950s to a low of 47% in 1966; increased steadily from 1966 through 1982; and has remained roughly stable since 1982, in the range of 70%–75%."[1] Spotting a change while it is in progress is another matter entirely. In an update in 1998—looking at data through 1997—we said that there had been no change in the level of support for capital punishment since 1994.[2] In retrospect, it now seems that by then support had actually begun to decline, although at that point there was no way to distinguish a real downward trend from a short-term fluctuation. By now, we can see that the decline is real.

From 1936 through 1971 the Gallup organization had a virtual monopoly on death penalty questions in national polls.[3] They never asked about the death penalty more than once a year and sometimes not at all. In 1972 death penalty attitudes became a regular item on the General Social Survey (GSS), the most extensive and highest quality general-purpose periodic survey of the American population, conducted by the National Opinion Research Center at the University of Chicago. Since 1973 the Harris organization has also been asking death-penalty-attitude questions on a reasonably regular basis, and from 1977 on other polling organizations and the news media have gotten into the act as well.[4] The

1. Phoebe C. Ellsworth and Samuel R. Gross, "Hardening of the Attitudes: Americans' Views on the Death Penalty," 50 *J. Soc. Issues* 19, 21 (1994).

2. Samuel R. Gross, "Update: American Public Opinion on the Death Penalty—It's Getting Personal," 83 *Cornell L. Rev.* 1448, 1448–49 (1998).

3. We know of only one exception, an October 1964 poll by the National Opinion Research Center in Chicago that asked: "Do you think having the death penalty for the worst crimes is a good idea, or are you against the death penalty?" Fifty-one percent said the death penalty for the worst crimes is a good idea; 43 percent were opposed; and 6 percent were undecided.

4. See Ellsworth and Gross, supra note 1, app. at 50–52; appendix at the end of this chapter. Most of the polls in these appendices can be found in a computerized database that is maintained by the Roper Center for Public Opinion Research at the University of Connecticut. Unless otherwise attributed, the polls we discuss are taken from that Roper database and can be accessed through Lexis or Westlaw. In these notes, we refer to polls from the Roper database by the name of the survey organization and the month and year in which the survey was completed (for example, "Gallup, 10/74"); if that information is already included in the text, no further reference is included. For the two periodic academic surveys that we use, the General Social Survey

frequency of these surveys has varied from year to year—primarily in response to issues in the news—but in general it has increased over time, especially in the past few years. There were, for example, at least twelve national surveys that asked about general death penalty attitudes in the first nine months of 2000.[5]

The reported levels of support for the death penalty fluctuate a good deal from survey to survey. In December 1982 an ABC News poll found 76 percent in favor; the following month a Harris poll reported 68 percent. Similarly, on successive years the GSS reported 70 percent in favor (1984), 76 percent (1985), and 71 percent (1986). Some of these oscillations are due to sampling error; others are probably caused by real short-term variations in public opinion, such as responses to egregious and heavily publicized murders. But one possible cause can be ruled out as a major contributor. In many other contexts, question wording has a strong influence on the overall levels of response to attitude questions.[6] Not here. On this issue—support for or opposition to the death penalty in general—responses to survey items show no relationship to the form of the question. Since the 1970s almost all Americans have had a position on the death penalty, know what that position is, and give it in response to any question that they interpret as asking for it.[7]

The multiplicity of polls enriches, but also complicates, the process of interpreting temporal trends in death penalty attitudes. We have simplified the clutter by choosing a single poll for each year and drawing a time line through the resulting points. The natural candidate is the GSS, when available; for years when there was no GSS we use the National Election Survey (NES)—another series of academic polls of comparable quality—if one was conducted.[8] The re-

---

(GSS) and the National Election Survey (NES), we omit the reference to the month in which the survey was completed since there is only one such survey per year. See infra note 8.

5. See appendix at the end of this chapter.

6. Norbert Schwarz et al., "Survey Methods," in 1 *The Handbook of Social Psychology* 143–79 (Daniel T. Gilbert et al. eds., 4th ed. 1998).

7. Ellsworth and Gross, supra note 1, at 24–26. The only exception to this rule appears to be that asking about the frequency with which the death penalty is used or should be used affects the proportions of the answers. For example, questions that ask about "mandatory" death penalties attract less support than those that do not include that qualification. See id. at 25.

8. See Ellsworth and Gross, supra note 1, at 21 n.1; Gross, supra note 2, at 1449 n.7. Note that the National Election Surveys we use are listed as occurring in odd-numbered years—1995, 1997, 1999. In each case, these are postelection surveys for the preceding election years, 1994, 1996, and 1998. Because the postelection surveys ran into January of the following year, for our purposes they count as surveys in those later years. See supra note 4.

Figure 1. American Death Penalty Attitudes, 1970–2000

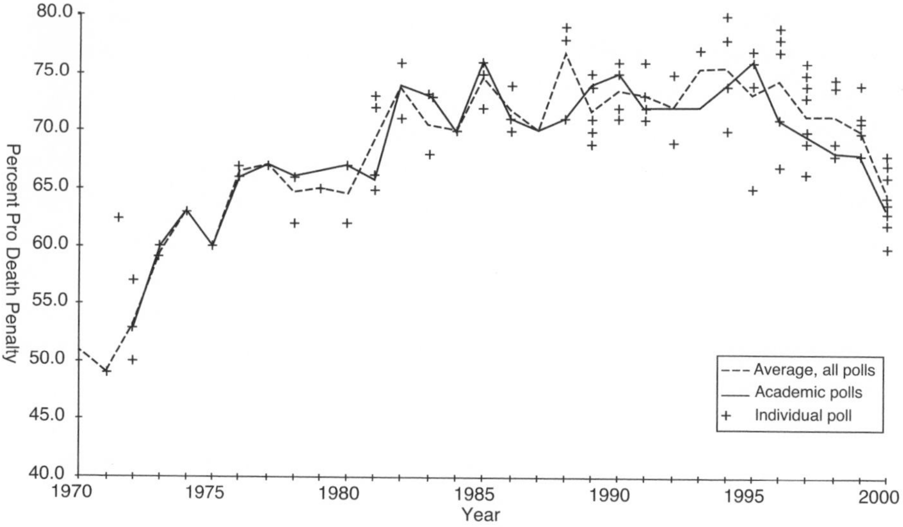

sult is displayed in figure 1, for the period from 1972 (when the GSS first included a general death-penalty-attitude question) through 2000. It shows a decline in support for the death penalty from 76 percent in 1995 to 63 percent in 2000.

The GSS and NES may be more reliable than commercial surveys, but in the short run they can mislead. Between 1982 and 1995, for example, this measure of support for the death penalty goes up or down for two or three successive years several times, but it remains essentially steady over the entire period. In figure 1 we attempt to improve our ability to spot comparatively short-term trends by presenting data from other polls as well, in two ways. First, we plot the results for every survey we could locate that asked respondents whether they favored or opposed the death penalty.[9] Second, for each year from 1970 through 2000, we calculate the average support across all polls, including the academic polls conducted that year, and draw a line through those points.

The two time lines in figure 1 are very similar. Their most conspicuous diver-

9. The surveys we included are those with questions that required the respondent to take a position in favor of or in opposition to the death penalty in general, including several surveys in which respondents were asked to state the strength of their support or opposition. The questions that meet this criterion are those in the "Standard Questions" and "Scale-Answer Questions" categories in Ellsworth and Gross, supra note 1, at 50–51, and similar questions on later surveys. The polls we used, and the wording of the death-penalty-attitude questions they asked, may be found in the appendix at the end of this chapter. The time period covered by this appendix is from 1936 through 2000.

gence is in 1988, when the overall average is almost six percentage points higher than the GSS, 76.7 percent to 71 percent. There may be a story behind that. In September and October of 1988, three polls in succession measured support for the death penalty at unprecedented levels of 78 percent and 79 percent.[10] They may have caught a real spike that was caused by George Bush's notorious "Willie Horton" campaign in the 1988 presidential election, in which he successfully painted his opponent, Michael Dukakis, as a liberal death-penalty opponent who was dangerously sympathetic to vicious criminals.[11] If so, support quickly returned to the usual late-1980s range of 70 percent to 75 percent,[12] and the moment was entirely missed by the GSS polls that bracketed it, several months earlier and several months later. In other words, for better or worse, yearly polls may be blind to short-term effects.

The trend across all polls for the last several years is very similar to the GSS and NES findings: a decrease from an average of 75 percent support for capital punishment in 1996 to 65 percent in 2000. Perhaps the single most striking thing about these recent surveys is the pattern in the year 2000. Each of twelve polls through September of that year measured support for the death penalty at 68 percent or lower. By contrast, only five of fifty polls in the fifteen years from 1982 through 1996 recorded levels of support below 70 percent. In other words, it is now clear that support for the death penalty—as it is measured by these general-attitude questions—has dropped significantly in the past few years. A good estimate is that it has gone down by about six to eight percentage points, from the 70–75 percent range to the 63–68 percent range. This decline erases an increase in support nearly two decades earlier, from 1976 through 1980, when support fluctuated around 65 percent, to 1982, by which time it had stabilized at above 70 percent.

The decline in support for capital punishment should not be overstated. In 1978 about 65 percent of Americans favored the death penalty, and support was considered strong. The same level must still be considered strong support in 2000. But when attitudes are changing the fact of change may be more important than any snapshot taken at a single moment. In 1978, as it turned out, 65 percent was a pause on the way up higher. The long-term context of the current level of support remains to be seen.[13]

10. Gallup, 9/88; Gallup, 10/88; CBS News/N.Y. Times, 10/88.

11. See Ellsworth and Gross, supra note 1, at 43–44.

12. CBS News/N.Y. Times, 1/89.

13. The Roper database, supra note 4, includes twelve more recent polls that asked general

Why has support for the death penalty decreased? Asking people to explain why they changed their minds is unlikely to provide useful information. As far as we know, nobody has tried this technique, but researchers in June 2000 did ask respondents *whether* their attitude toward the death penalty had changed "in recent years."[14] A majority, 58 percent, said their position was unchanged; 24 percent said they supported the death penalty more than before; and only 15 percent said that they supported it less. Yet we know that support for the death penalty has gone down, not up, in the past five years. These results are not surprising. Except for radical conversion experiences, people are rarely aware that their attitudes have changed:[15] they report their current attitudes as attitudes they have held as long as they can remember.[16] Similarly, most people are unable to give an accurate account of the reasons for their attitudes.[17] Finding people who both recognize that their attitudes have changed and can give an accurate explanation for that change is hopeless. Instead, we must use indirect methods, looking for events and circumstances that might help explain the drop in support for the death penalty.

Crime and Perceived Crime

As we noted in 1994, there is a simple commonsensical explanation for aggregate changes in support for capital punishment: that they correspond to changes

---

death-penalty-attitude questions in 2001. These polls, with the levels of reported support for capital punishment, are: Gallup, 2/01 (67 percent); Opinion Dynamics, 4/01 (66 percent); ABC News/Wash. Post, 4/01 (63 percent); Associated Press, 5/01 (71 percent); Techno Metrica Institute of Policy and Politics, 5/01 (61 percent); CBS News, 5/01 (66 percent); Gallup, 5/01 (65 percent); Opinion Dynamics, 6/01 (68 percent); CBS News/N.Y. Times, 6/01 (67 percent); Harris, 7/01 (68 percent); Harris, 7/01 (67 percent); Gallup, 10/01 (68 percent). As a group, these recent polls indicate little change in death penalty attitudes from 2000 to 2001. For the moment, support for the death penalty seems to have stabilized in the range from 65 to 68 percent.

14. Princeton Survey Research Assoc., 6/00.

15. Richard E. Nisbett and Lee Ross, *Human Inference: Strategies and Shortcomings of Social Judgment* (1980).

16. Daryl J. Bem and H. Keith McConnell, "Testing the Self-Perception Explanation of Dissonance Phenomena: On the Salience of Premanipulation Attitudes," 14 *J. Personality & Soc. Psychol.* 23 (1970).

17. Richard E. Nisbett and Timothy D. Wilson, "Telling More Than We Can Know: Verbal Reports on Mental Processes," 84 *Psychol. Rev.* 231 (1977).

Figure 2. Death Penalty Attitudes and Crime Rates, 1953–2000

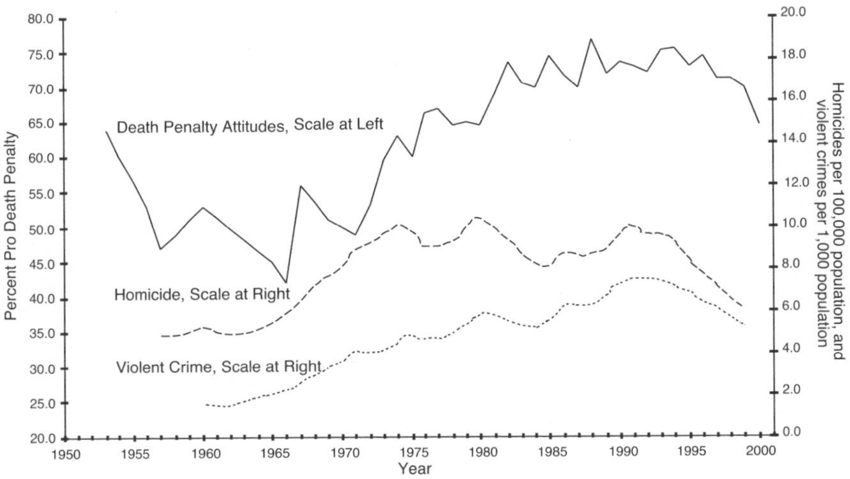

in the rates of violent crime in general and of homicide in particular.[18] We have decent data for both crime rates and death penalty attitudes from 1960 on, and they are generally consistent with this hypothesis. As we see in figure 2, support for the death penalty decreased from the late 1950s through 1966, when crime rates were low; increased from 1966 through 1982 as crime and homicide rates rose sharply; remained roughly stable from 1992 through 1996; and decreased starting in 1997 as crimes rates have fallen.[19]

Figure 2 also shows that death penalty attitudes do not track crime rates perfectly. Crime and homicide rates had been rising for years before support for the death penalty turned upward in 1967; they decreased temporarily from 1980 to 1984, but support continued to move up to record heights; and they fell from 1994 through 1996 with no discernable effect on death penalty attitudes. This should be no surprise. If personal experience with crime shaped death penalty attitudes directly, changes in criminal behavior might have immediate effects. But it doesn't. Many studies have shown that people who have actually been victims of violent crime, or who fear for their personal safety, are no more likely

18. See Ellsworth and Gross, supra note 1, at 40–42; see also Benjamin I. Page and Robert Y. Shapiro, *The Rational Public* 92–94 (1992); Joseph H. Rankin, "Changing Attitudes toward Capital Punishment," 58 *Soc. Forces* 194 (1979).

19. The homicide and violent-crime data in figure 2 are derived from the FBI's Uniform Crime Reports, which tabulate crimes reported to the police; they include national homicide statistics starting in 1953 and national statistics on violent crime from 1960 on. The death-penalty-attitude data are the mean percentage of support for each year, across all polls, as used in figure 1.

to support the death penalty than those who are more fortunate or less fearful.[20] Instead, as in many other contexts, public opinion is not shaped by events themselves but by public perception of those events, and public perception of crime has a complex and indirect relationship to crime itself.

For the most part, Americans learn about crime through the mass media, especially television. Television news programs do report crime statistics; but even when crime is low, they devote far more time to stories of death and violence, murders if possible,[21] and the fictional worlds of television and film are rife with killing and mutilation. The public is aware that the media overemphasize violence. In a 1996 Harris poll, for example, 90 percent recognized that the media were more likely to report "terrible violent crimes" than "[g]ood news [that] violent crime [is] decreasing."[22] And they are aware that their knowledge about crime comes from that untrustworthy source. Nonetheless, their attitudes are more affected by gruesome crime stories than by encouraging statistics showing that crime is on the wane. In April 1998, for example, after four years of declining crime rates, 68 percent of the respondents in a national Harris poll said that violent crime in this country was "increasing," and 44 percent said it was "increasing a lot." In an ABC News poll in June 2000, 80 percent of respondents said that the crime problem in this country was "bad" or "very bad"; of those who took that position, 82 percent said that their opinion was based on the news media, and 17 percent said it was based on personal experience.

Since the perception of increasing crime is driven by the media rather than by experience, its focus is always elsewhere—somewhere other than the place the respondent actually knows. In an October 1993 national Gallup poll, for example, 57 percent of respondents said that their neighborhood had less crime than the national average, and 27 percent said it had none at all; only 10 percent said their neighborhood had an average amount of crime, and a mere 5 percent said it had more than average. In Lake Woebegone all children are above average; in America, all neighborhoods are safer than average. A May 1980 poll by Research and Forecasts got very similar results, and on several national polls strong majorities said simultaneously that while crime in the nation was "bad" or "very bad," crime in their own communities was "not too bad" or "not bad at all."[23]

Eventually, however, the good news gets through, at least in part. In figure 3

20. See Ellsworth and Gross, supra note 1, at 42.

21. Gross, supra note 2, at 1449–50; Center for Media and Public Affairs, "Crime Most Common Story on Local Television News," available at http://www.cmpa.com/archive/healthtv.htm.

22. Gross, supra note 2, at 1450 n.15.

23. See Polling Report.com, "Fear of Crime/Fighting Crime," available at http://www.pollingreport.com/crime.htm (reporting ABC News polls for 5/96, 6/97, and 6/00).

Figure 3. Respondents Who Say There Was Less Crime Than the Year Before, 1989–1998

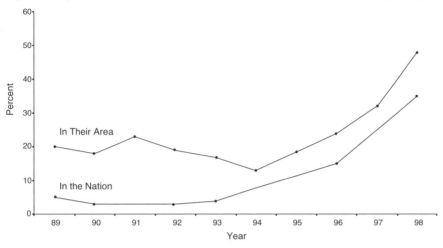

we tabulate the percentages of Gallup poll respondents, from 1989 through 1998, who said that there was less crime than the year before, either in the United States as a whole or in their own areas. As expected, across all years people are prone to think that crime is worse than it really is, and are more likely to believe that it's dropping locally than that it's dropping nationally. But there is a clear change over time: starting in 1996 there has been a sharp increase in the proportion of respondents who believe that crime rates are going down. The change is particularly dramatic for the perception of crime nationally—an increase from 3 percent to 5 percent in the early 1990s, to 35 percent in 1998—but the absolute size of the shift is similar for the perception of local crime, roughly 30 percent. To be sure, most people had not changed their views on crime rates by 1998, but the 30 percent or so who did change could accommodate three or four times the group that switched from favoring the death penalty to opposing it between 1996 and 2000.

National crime rates for a given year are not reported until late the following year, and they may not be noticed for some time after that, if at all.[24] Even then, a well-informed and rational public would wait before responding to reported changes, since they do not necessarily last. The decline in crime in the early 1980s, for example, was short-lived. Therefore, any attempt to explain death penalty attitudes by crime rates must assume a time lag of one to several years between the crimes reported and their impact on public opinion. In a recent

24. The crime data we use—the FBI Uniform Crime Reports—have the advantage of being the most widely reported national crime statistics and therefore those most likely to influence public perception of crime rates.

paper, Katherine Barnes of the University of Michigan reports a set of time-series analyses that attempt to predict death penalty attitudes from crime rates. She finds that the national violent crime rate is a good predictor of support for the death penalty. With a lag of either one or two years, that crime rate explains approximately 70 percent of the yearly variation in the percentage of people who supported the death penalty from 1965 through 2000.[25]

So far we have argued that falling crime rates probably contribute to the recent decrease in support for capital punishment. That does not mean that crime rates explain this change, much less that they are a complete explanation. For one thing, the relation between crime and death penalty attitudes need not be symmetrical. Rising crime is in itself an argument for harsh penalties: it puts crime and punishment on the public agenda and suggests the need for severe punitive measures in order to reduce crime, or for retributive purposes, or both. But falling crime rates might not have the opposite effect. Less crime, on its own, is no more of a reason to reject the death penalty than warm weather is a reason to tear out insulation, and the fact that crime is down can as easily suggest that the death penalty has been effective as that it is unnecessary. Dropping crime rates may undercut a major source of pressure to support the death penalty, but they are probably insufficient, by themselves, to change strongly held views.

Of course, if people had been ambivalent about the death penalty all along, voicing stronger support than they actually felt, the decrease in crime might be enough to move them toward opposition. Thus, for example, many people who support affirmative action feel some reservations because they think it compromises their commitment to racial equality; given that ambivalence, they may change their minds quickly if they come to believe that affirmative action is no longer necessary to provide opportunities to members of groups that have suffered long-standing discrimination. Death penalty attitudes seem different. At least until recently, there has been little evidence of ambivalence in American support for capital punishment; it has been enthusiastic. There is substantial evidence that those who support capital punishment will agree with almost

25. Katherine Y. Barnes, "Do Crime Rates Explain American Attitudes toward the Death Penalty?" (University of Michigan Law School, Law and Economics Working Paper, 2002). Barnes used the FBI Uniform Crime Reports, supra note 19, for crime data. Her death-penalty-attitude measure for the analyses discussed in the text is the average percentage of support for the death penalty across all polls for each year, as displayed in figures 1 and 2. Barnes also found that the criminal homicide rate predicted about two-thirds of the yearly variance in support for capital punishment, with either a three- or four-year time lag.

any plausible argument for that position,[26] and the great majority of those who favor the death penalty say that they do so "strongly." On the 1989 National Election Survey, for example, 79 percent of the 70 percent who supported the death penalty—55 percent of the total—were strongly in favor, and on the 1995 National Election Survey 78 percent of the 76 percent in favor were strong supporters.

Given this apparent enthusiasm, there are two mechanisms that might explain a drop in support for the death penalty.

First, strength of support is not uniform. On every survey that has asked about the strength of support, some respondents who favored the death penalty said that they did not support it "strongly"—usually between 15 percent and 25 percent of the total. Many people in this intermediate group may indeed be ambivalent about the death penalty and may be prepared to abandon it if it is no longer necessary. If this is the explanation, the current decline in support will soon flatten out as susceptible death-penalty supporters become increasingly rare. But the drop looks too steep for this to be the main cause. A decrease in crime, by itself, would not make the death penalty enough of a public issue to attract the attention that could generate a rapid change in public opinion.

Moreover, there is no evidence that weak supporters of the death penalty are becoming less common. On the 1995 National Election Survey, 57 percent said they favored the death penalty "strongly" and 17 percent said they favored it but "not strongly"; on the 1999 National Election Survey the comparable proportions were 50 percent and 18 percent. In fact, two recent surveys suggest that weak support may be becoming *more* common. In an August 2000 poll by Peter Hart Research Associates, almost half of those who supported the death penalty—28 percent out of 60 percent—had at least some "doubts and reservations," and in a June 2000 Gallup poll a majority of those who supported the death penalty, 37 percent out of 65 percent, did so "with reservations." From the look of it, support for the death penalty is eroding across the spectrum. Of those who supported it strongly, some now have doubts; of those who supported it with reservations, some now oppose it.

Second, the drop in crime may have created an opening for affirmative arguments against the death penalty. It may operate as an enabling condition, making it easier for people to reconsider their positions in light of new concerns.

26. Phoebe C. Ellsworth and Lee D. Ross, "Public Opinion and Capital Punishment: A Close Examination of the Views of Abolitionists and Retentionists," 1983 *Crime and Delinq.* 116, 145–57.

This explanation is consistent with recent opinion polls, and also with recent history. Over the past few years, the public image of the death penalty has been complicated by serious problems that had long been ignored. And, as we see in the next section, by the late 1990s support for the death penalty may have become more vulnerable than before for reasons apart from the drop in crime.

The State of Death Penalty Attitudes as of 1996

The steep rise in support for the death penalty began in the early 1970s. It is important to remember that in the early 1970s the role of the death penalty in America was very different from what it had become by the 1990s. It was unusual; it was controversial; and many people believed that America had evolved to a stage where it would soon be abolished. The public was much more evenly divided on the issue, with about 50 percent in favor and about 40 percent opposed. Since 1964 there had only been ten executions in the entire country. From 1968 until 1977 there were none at all. In 1972, in *Furman v. Georgia*,[27] the Supreme Court held that the death penalty, as then administered, was unconstitutional.

At about the same time, as homicide and other violent crime began to increase dramatically, more people ranked crime or violence as the most serious problem in America.[28] "Law and order" became an important theme in political campaigns. Americans were frustrated at the apparent helplessness of the criminal justice system to control the explosion of crime and called for harsher penalties as a solution, including the death penalty. It had become an issue that people cared about, an emotional issue of powerful symbolic significance.[29] The response to the *Furman* decision was swift and unequivocal. By 1976, when the Supreme Court affirmed the constitutionality of capital punishment,[30] thirty-five states had passed new death penalty laws, and two-thirds of the population were in favor of capital punishment. But the death penalty in practice was still uncommon and contested. As of January 1980, there had only been three executions under the new laws, each one attracting a great deal of publicity.

In the mid-1990s the picture was entirely different. The death penalty was uncontroversial, and executions were common and not particularly newsworthy. Capital punishment had become a long-standing fixture in the criminal

27. Furman v. Georgia, 408 U.S. 238 (1972).
28. Tom W. Smith, "America's Most Important Problem—A Trend Analysis, 1948–1976," 44 *Pub. Opinion Q.* 164 (1980).
29. Ellsworth and Ross, supra note 26.
30. Gregg v. Georgia, 428 U.S. 153 (1976).

justice system, a background element of American life, provoking little discussion. Support for capital punishment had been strong and unwavering for a dozen years, consistently over 70 percent since 1982. The idea that the Supreme Court might even *consider* abolishing the death penalty was inconceivable. Support for the death penalty, it seemed, was widespread, deeply entrenched, and enduring.

In addition, the nature of people's opinions on capital punishment seemed to contribute to their stability. Death penalty attitudes were linked to many other values and beliefs about crime and the criminal justice system,[31] so much so that they are sometimes used as a shorthand indicator of attitudes toward crime and punishment in general. Attitudes that are linked to many other attitudes, beliefs, and values have long been considered particularly resistant to change[32] because change would either require reconsideration of the whole set of related attitudes or would result in an uncomfortable cognitive inconsistency. Finally, we and others have argued that death penalty attitudes came to have a powerful symbolic significance, support for the death penalty representing an ideological self-definition of the person as unyielding in the war on crime, unwilling to coddle criminals, firm and courageous.[33] Most supporters were strongly committed to their position, and commitment has long been recognized as a major obstacle to attitude change.[34] Changing an attitude of this sort might be seen as a sign of personal weakness, of capitulation.

And yet, by 1996 support for the death penalty in America may have become

31. Robert Fitzgerald and Phoebe C. Ellsworth, "Due Process vs. Crime Control: Death Qualification and Jury Attitudes," 8 *Law and Hum. Behav.* 31 (1984); Tom R. Tyler and Renee Weber, "Support for the Death Penalty: Instrumental Response to Crime, or Symbolic Attitude?" 17 *Law and Soc'y Rev.* 20 (1982); Kimberly Gross and Donald R. Kinder, "Ethnocentrism Revisited: Explaining American Opinion on Crime and Punishment," paper presented at the annual meeting of the American Political Science Association, Washington, D.C. (Aug. 2000) (unpublished manuscript, on file with the authors).

32. *Attitude Organization and Change* (Milton J. Rosenberg and Carl I. Hovland eds., 1960); Richard E. Petty and Duane T. Wegener, "Attitude Change: Multiple Roles for Persuasion Variables," in 1 *The Handbook of Social Psychology*, supra note 6, at 323–90.

33. Jan Górecki, *Capital Punishment: Criminal Law and Social Evolution* (1983); Ellsworth and Gross, supra note 1; Ellsworth and Ross, supra note 26; Gross, supra note 2; Philip W. Harris, "Oversimplification and Error in Public Opinion Surveys on Capital Punishment," 3 *Just. Q.* 429 (1986); Tyler and Weber, supra note 31; D. H. Wallace, "Bloodbath and Brutalization: Public Opinion and the Death Penalty," 12 *J. Crime and Just.* 51 (1989).

34. William J. McGuire, "The Nature of Attitudes and Attitude Change," in 3 *Handbook of Social Psychology* 136–314 (Gardner Lindzey and Elliot Aronson eds., 2d ed. 1969); Petty and Wegener, supra note 32.

more vulnerable than it appeared. In the 1970s capital punishment was a live issue in people's minds. After the Supreme Court struck down all existing death penalty laws in 1972, there was a period of doubt that capital punishment would ever be restored. At the same time, crime seemed to be rising uncontrollably, and people were losing faith in the idea that criminals could be rehabilitated. Retribution began to gain favor as an acceptable goal of punishment, and many Americans who had not thought about it much before came to believe in the death penalty—and to care about it. Support for the death penalty was a new attitude for many of them, one that needed to be defended, given its ambiguous status and the existence of substantial opposition. By the 1990s most people had favored the death penalty for decades; their position was normal for them and normal for the country as a whole. There was no particular need to think much about it, much less to defend it, since the opposition had dwindled to insignificance and the death penalty had become a fixed fact of American life.

By 1996 support for the death penalty had been so strong and so widespread for so long that it came to be taken for granted. It began to resemble what McGuire[35] has called a "cultural truism." According to McGuire, cultural truisms are beliefs that are widely held and never questioned. People have little practice in defending such beliefs and little motivation to do so. The person "is unpracticed because he has never been called upon to defend the truism. He is unmotivated to start practicing because he regards the belief as unassailable."[36] Because these beliefs are so taken for granted that they need no defense, they are actually quite vulnerable to attack.

Belief in the death penalty is not exactly like the cultural truisms studied by McGuire, truisms such as "It's a good idea to brush your teeth after every meal." Supporters have always known that there were opponents, and they were probably familiar with most of their opponents' arguments. But when there were very few opponents, they could be dismissed as naive, sentimental, fanatical, or saintly—in any case, not normal. No new arguments against the death penalty had come along for quite a while, and the old familiar ones had been rejected long ago: It is not wrong for the state to take a life if the person deserves to die. It doesn't matter that the death penalty is no better a deterrent than a life sentence—murderers deserve it, and besides maybe it deters *some* people. Poor people and minorities may be sentenced to death more often than rich white

35. William J. McGuire, "Inducing Resistance to Persuasion: Some Contemporary Approaches," in 1 *Advances in Experimental Social Psychology* 192–229 (Leonard Berkowitz ed., 1964).
36. McGuire, supra note 35, at 201.

people, but that just means we should try to execute more rich white people, not abolish the death penalty. The risk of executing an innocent person is minuscule. A life sentence won't work because only death will *guarantee* that the murderer will never get free.

By 1996 arguments against the death penalty had not been salient in American public discourse for almost two decades. Over that period, support for the death penalty may have become something like a cultural truism—widely shared, settled, and unquestioned. Unaccustomed for so long to defending their attitudes, or even to thinking much about them, supporters of the death penalty may have become more vulnerable to new information that challenges their beliefs—especially in a period of decreasing crime.

Recent Developments

Of course, there are no really new issues on this topic. Comic writers sometimes say that the last original joke was written by Aristophanes, and in this respect at least the debate about capital punishment is similar: the last new argument against the death penalty may have been made by Cesare di Beccaria in 1764.[37] Certainly no novel issues have surfaced since 1970.[38] But old issues can take on new life, and that has happened in the past few years. In part, there has been real news—not about new problems but about new events that have revived old ones. And in part, the media and the public are paying attention to problems they ignored for decades.

Nineteen ninety-seven is a convenient starting point. On February 3 of that year the American Bar Association (ABA) House of Delegates passed a resolution calling for a moratorium on executions in the United States.[39] The ABA did not oppose capital punishment as such, except as applied to juveniles or mentally retarded offenders. Instead, it called for a halt until procedures are in place that ensure the fair and impartial administration of the death penalty and that minimize the risk of executing innocent defendants. Specifically, the ABA called on death penalty jurisdictions to implement a series of earlier ABA resolutions, dating back to 1979, that called for competent capital defense counsel, thorough review of capital cases by state and federal courts, the elimination of racial

37. Cesare di Beccaria, *On Crimes and Punishment* (Henry Paolucci trans., 1963) (1764).

38. See, e.g., Brief of Amici Curiae NAACP Legal Defense Fund et al., Boykin v. Alabama, 345 U.S. 238 (1969) (No. 642); Brief for Petitioner, Aikens v. California, 406 U.S. 813 (1972) (No. 68–5027).

39. American Bar Ass'n, "Report with Recommendation No. 107 (Feb. 1997)," available at http://www.abanet.org/irr/rec107.html.

discrimination in capital sentencing, and the end of capital punishment for defendants who are mentally retarded or who were condemned for crimes committed before they turned eighteen.

Of the issues addressed in the ABA resolution, the most potent turned out to be the danger of executing innocent defendants. Between 1970 and 1997 at least seventy defendants had been released from death row because of innocence; four of them were cleared in part through the use of the newly available technology of DNA identification of blood or semen.[40] Over the years, the stories of the more notorious cases of erroneous death sentences had received significant attention from the media, usually when the defendant was released,[41] but individual stories could be interpreted as isolated events, or even as evidence of the success of the system of review of capital cases. In November 1998, at a well-publicized conference on wrongful convictions in capital cases at Northwestern University Law School in Chicago, thirty of the inmates who had been sentenced to death for murders they did not commit shared the stage in a dramatic demonstration that this was a systemic problem.[42] And it kept happening. In 1999 eight more innocent prisoners were released from death rows across the country.[43]

The stories of these wrongful capital convictions had several common threads. In most cases the defendants had inadequate if not incompetent defense attorneys at trial; in many, if not most, the prosecution and the police had conducted shoddy investigations, concealed evidence that might have exonerated the defendant, or both; in some cases the police had obtained false confessions by threats and psychological coercion; and in some the authorities had simply manufactured evidence against innocent defendants. By late 1999 these stories were becoming regular items on the news. In November 1999 the *Chicago Tribune* published a series of articles describing the death penalty system in Illinois in excruciating detail.[44] Among other things, the newspaper reported

40. Death Penalty Info. Ctr., "Innocence: Freed from Death Row," available at http://www.death penaltyinfo.org/Innocentlist.html.

41. This was true, among others, for Walter McMillian, who was released from death row in Alabama in 1993, and for Rolando Cruz and Alejandro Hernandez, who were released in Illinois in 1995.

42. See, e.g., Don Terry, "Survivors Make the Case against Death Row," *N.Y. Times*, Nov. 16, 1998, at A14.

43. Death Penalty Info. Ctr., supra note 40.

44. Ken Armstrong and Steve Mills, "Death Row Justice Derailed," *Chi. Trib.*, Nov. 14, 1999, at 1. This was the first of a five-part series of articles that appeared in the *Chicago Tribune* from

that dozens of capital defendants had been represented by attorneys who were later suspended from practice or disbarred and that dozens of death sentences had been obtained using the unreliable testimony of jailhouse informants.

On January 31, 2000—two weeks after the thirteenth innocent inmate had been released from death row in Illinois—Governor George Ryan imposed a moratorium on executions.[45] In the preceding year, the legislatures in at least six states had considered moratorium resolutions. In Illinois such a resolution was approved by the house of representatives but died in the state senate. In Nebraska the legislature passed a moratorium bill, but the governor vetoed it.[46] Governor Ryan actually put a moratorium into effect. He explained that he was doing it because of the obvious danger of executing an innocent defendant and because his confidence in the fairness of the system of capital prosecutions had been undermined by the findings of the *Chicago Tribune* study.

The Illinois moratorium changed the shape of the national debate over capital punishment. A campaign for a national moratorium on executions that had been under way since 1998 accelerated rapidly, with hundreds of organizations and dozens of local governments passing moratorium resolutions in the eight months following Governor Ryan's action.[47] A moratorium on executions became an obvious option in any context in which the death penalty was in contention. At the same time, other newspapers followed the lead of the *Chicago Tribune* and editorialized against capital punishment or conducted investigations of the process of administering the death penalty in their states.[48]

Nov. 14 to Nov. 18, 1999; they can be found at http://www.chicago.tribune.com/news/metro/chicago/ws/0,,37842,00.html.

45. Dirk Johnson, "Illinois, Citing Faulty Verdicts, Bars Executions," *N.Y. Times*, Feb. 1, 2000, at A1.

46. Ken Armstrong and Steve Mills, "Ryan Suspends Death Penalty; Illinois First State to Impose Moratorium on Executions," *Chi. Trib.*, Jan. 31, 2000, at 1.

47. Claudia Kolker, "Death Penalty Moratorium Idea Attracts Even Conservatives," *L.A. Times*, Aug. 29, 2000, at A5; Sara Rimer, "Support for a Moratorium in Executions Gets Stronger," *N.Y. Times*, Oct. 31, 2000, at A18.

48. Ames Alexander et al., "Uncertain Justice, the Death Penalty on Trial: Errors, Inequities Often Cloud Capital Cases in the Carolinas," *Charlotte Observer*, Sept. 10, 2000, at 1A (first of five-part series); Jennifer Autrey and Miles Moffeit, "Futile Arguments: In Texas Highest Criminal Court, Innocence Is an Elusive Concept," *Fort Worth Star-Telegram*, Oct. 8, 2000, at 1; "Defense Called Lacking for Death Row Indigent: But System Supporters Say Most Attorneys Effective," *Dallas Morning News*, Sept. 10, 2000, at 1A; "Taking a Step back from the Death Penalty," *The Tennessean*, Feb. 14, 2000, at 14A (editorial).

Many of these investigations focused on southern states, where the vast majority of American executions take place. Attention to the death penalty in Texas was particularly intense, both because Texas leads the country in executions and because the Republican governor of that state, George W. Bush, was running for president. Governor Bush was repeatedly forced to express his confidence that none of the 146 prisoners executed under his administration was innocent. In a June 2000 national Gallup poll, 26 percent agreed with the governor that this had never happened; 46 percent said that an innocent person had been executed under Governor Bush's authority; and 28 percent had no opinion. The issue came to a head in June 2000, with the heavily covered execution of Texas prisoner Gary Graham, despite strong claims that he was innocent.[49]

In June 2000, researchers at Columbia University released a widely publicized study of the several thousand capital cases that had been processed by American courts since 1975.[50] They found that at least 68 percent of death sentences, or the convictions on which they were based, were reversed on review. In September 2000, the Department of Justice released a report showing strong racial and geographic disparities in federal capital prosecutions.[51] Like the problem of miscarriages of justice in capital cases, these were not new issues. But the new reports documented them in detail, and they fell on fertile ground. Overall, in the year 2000 the news media devoted an unprecedented amount of attention to the death penalty, and—even more unprecedented—much if not most of it was critical.[52]

In the past several years the death penalty has also become an increasingly common theme in the entertainment media. In 1995 Sister Helen Prejean's book *Dead Man Walking* was made into a partly fictionalized popular movie. The protagonist in the movie is unquestionably guilty of a vicious double murder; the question is whether it is right for the state to kill him nonetheless. This basic moral issue became much more vivid in 1998 at the time of the real-life execution of Karla Faye Tucker, a slight and attractive woman who admitted committing two pick-ax murders while high on drugs in 1984, but who, by the

49. Frank Bruni and Jim Yardley, "With Bush Assent, Inmate Is Executed," *N.Y. Times*, June 23, 2000, at A1.

50. James S. Liebman, Jeffrey Fagan, and Valerie West, "A Broken System: Error Rates in Capital Cases, 1973–1995 (June 12, 2000)," available at http://justice.policy.net/jpreport/index.html.

51. U.S. Dep't of Justice, *The Federal Death Penalty System: A Statistical Survey (1988–2000)* (2000).

52. See, e.g., Center for Media and Public Affairs, "Networks Set Record Pace for Green Mile," available at http://www.cmpa.com/pressrel/deathpenalty.htm.

time of her execution, had become a devout, soft-spoken Christian.[53] In 1999 and 2000 the conviction of innocent defendants became a prominent theme in movies[54] and in television dramas.[55] The change should not be exaggerated—there are still many more films and television shows in which the death (if not the execution) of a criminal is presented as the appropriate and satisfying conclusion—but it is a shift. The entertainment industry now regularly presents the death penalty as a debatable topic.

The new atmosphere that surrounds capital punishment has probably been created as much by the people and organizations that have expressed doubts or opposition as by any news about the penalty itself. The American Bar Association was not the first major centrist national institution to take a position against capital punishment; that honor belongs to the Catholic Church. Starting in 1974, the United States Conference of Catholic Bishops has issued a series of increasingly strong statements in opposition to capital punishment,[56] but the church's position received relatively little attention until 1999. On January 28 of that year Governor Mel Carnahan of Missouri commuted the death sentence of a man who was scheduled to be executed two weeks later, after Pope John Paul II, on a pastoral visit to St. Louis, condemned the death penalty in strong

53. See, e.g., Sam Howe Verhovek, "As Woman's Execution Nears, Texas Squirms," *N.Y. Times*, Jan. 1, 1998, at A1.

54. *True Crime* (Warner Bros. Studios 1999); *The Green Mile* (Warner Bros. Studios 1999); *The Hurricane* (Universal Studios 1999).

55. Sharon Waxman, "Hollywood Pleads Its Case," *Wash. Post*, May 7, 2000, at G10.

56. See United States Conference of Catholic Bishops, Archbishop Joseph L. Bernardin, "Statement on Capital Punishment (Jan. 26, 1977)," available at http://www.nccbuscc.org/sdwp/ national/criminal/death/uscc89.htm; U.S. Catholic Conference, "Statement on Capital Punishment (1980)," available at http://www.nccbuscc.org/sdwp/national/criminal/death/uscc 80.htm; Administrative Board of the U.S. Catholic Conference, "A Good Friday Appeal to End the Death Penalty (Apr. 2, 1999)," available at http://www.nccbuscc.org/sdwp/national/ criminal/appeal.htm. Although absolute opposition to the death penalty is not a doctrinal position of the Catholic Church, the church has become increasingly outspoken on this issue. Thus the current Catholic catechism states that while "the traditional teaching of the Church does not exclude recourse to the death penalty, if this is the only possible way of effectively defending human lives against the unjust aggressor," because of the possibility of indefinite imprisonment in modern states, "cases in which the execution of the offender is an absolute necessity 'are rare, if not practically non-existent.'" See United States Conference of Catholic Bishops, "The Death Penalty and the Catechism," available at http://www.nccbuscc.org /sdwp/national/criminal/ cappunishment.htm. In fact, American Catholics favor the death penalty about as much as other religious groups do.

terms and appealed personally to the governor to halt the upcoming execution—
an event that received nationwide publicity.[57]

The pope's strenuous opposition to capital punishment may have been unknown to most Americans, but it was not new. Other prominent voices, however, have expressed changes of heart. In 1998 the Reverend Pat Robertson, head
of the conservative Christian Coalition and a death penalty supporter, cham-
pioned the cause of Karla Faye Tucker and apparently was deeply affected by her
execution.[58] The following year he spoke out against the unfairness and discrimination that has infected the use of the death penalty and condemned the
"culture of death" that leads to the execution of many who should be spared;[59]
in April 2000 he called for a national moratorium on executions because of
discrimination in the use of the death penalty against poor people and minorities.[60] That same month George Will, a prominent conservative columnist and
longtime supporter of capital punishment, wrote a column describing in some
detail several cases of innocent defendants who had nearly been executed, prais-
ing the moratorium in Illinois and reminding fellow conservatives that "Capital
punishment . . . is a government program, so skepticism is in order."[61] And these
are only the most conspicuous examples. In the past two years scores of colum-
nists, editorial boards, and former and present judges and prosecutors have written or spoken publicly about their concerns about the death penalty, usually to
say that its administration is unacceptable.

But by far the most important recent new voice on the death penalty has been
that of Governor George Ryan of Illinois. Governor Ryan is a Republican and a
lifelong supporter of capital punishment who had authorized an execution just
ten months earlier. And yet he not only imposed a moratorium on executions in
order to avoid the risk of killing an innocent defendant; he also unsparingly
condemned the defects in the system that produced thirteen erroneous death
sentences in his state. He made it impossible to dismiss critics of the death
penalty as bleeding-heart liberals. It is difficult to estimate the scope of the
effect of Governor Ryan's action. For example, in September 2000 Governor

57. Gustav Niebuhr, "Governor Grants Pope's Pleas for Life of a Missouri Inmate," *N.Y. Times*,
Jan. 29, 1999, at A1.
58. Teresa Malcolm, "Tucker's Death Affected Robertson Views," *Nat'l Cath. Rep.*, Apr. 23,
1999, at 4.
59. Id.
60. Brooke A. Masters, "Pat Robertson Urges Moratorium on U.S. Executions," *Wash. Post*, Apr.
8, 2000, at A1.
61. George F. Will, "Innocent on Death Row," *Wash. Post*, Apr. 6, 2000, at A23.

John Engler of Michigan told a reporter that he opposed the death penalty on moral and pragmatic grounds, adding that "We're pretty proud of the fact that we don't have the death penalty [in Michigan]."[62] Although Governor Engler was long known to those around him as an opponent of the death penalty, he had apparently never spoken publicly on the issue before. Did he break his silence because Governor Ryan had made it safe for Republican politicians who oppose capital punishment to come out of the closet? Certainly Governor Ryan has made it much easier for other public figures to reassess their views on the death penalty, and that has played a major role in a conspicuous realignment of positions by conservative leaders.

A New Script

For years there was a single story or script that death penalty supporters relied on more or less unquestioningly.[63] The perception was that death penalty cases were treated with exceptional care, that death sentences were scrutinized far more painstakingly than other legal decisions, that they were examined over and over again for any possible error through an interminable series of appeals, while the victims' families spent years in agony waiting for closure. Vicious killers got more help than they deserved from do-gooder lawyers intent on finding legal technicalities and creating endless delays. They lived on and on, eating free meals and watching TV at public expense, while disingenuous liberals succeeded in obstructing justice through meticulous attention to irrelevant details.

People did recognize that death sentences were far more frequent for poor people than for rich people[64] and more common for blacks than for whites,[65] but this was abstract background knowledge. Stories about grisly murders and the suffering families of the victims were more prevalent and more vividly described in the media than stories of unfair convictions. Statistical evidence of arbitrariness and discrimination did not arouse people's emotions.

People were also aware of the theoretical possibility of mistaken death sentences, and supporters regarded the possibility of wrongful executions as the

62. Raymond Bonner and Ford Fessenden, "Absence of Executions, a Special Report: States with No Death Penalty Share Lower Homicide Rates," *N.Y. Times*, Sept. 22, 2000, at A1.

63. Robert P. Abelson, "The Psychological Status of the Script Concept," 36 *Am. Psychol.* 715 (1981).

64. Ellsworth and Gross, supra note 1; Ellsworth and Ross, supra note 26; Gross, supra note 2; Gallup, 2/99.

65. Gallup, 2/99.

strongest argument against capital punishment.[66] Once in a while they would be confronted by a vivid example, such as *The Thin Blue Line*, a 1988 movie about Randall Dale Adams, an innocent man sentenced to death in Texas. But these cases were regarded as very rare—the exceptions that proved the rule—and could even be taken as evidence that the extreme care in the administration of the death penalty meant that mistakes were discovered in time: Adams, after all, was eventually released. The execution of an innocent person remained a remote, hypothetical possibility that did not move people.

Over the last few years an alternative script has emerged and gained strength. Stories of capital defense lawyers who hardly spoke to their clients before trial, who were later suspended or disbarred, who dozed through the trial or showed up drunk are common, and they contradict the image of capital cases as paragons of legal scrupulousness. Stories of prosecutors who failed to follow up plausible leads on other suspects once they had someone in custody, who relied on obviously perjured testimony from snitches guaranteed immunity, or who concealed crucial evidence are also widespread, and they raise serious doubts about the accuracy of the criminal justice system's identification of the truly guilty. The new story is one of a system full of blunders and deception, a bureaucracy hustling people toward death row without proper concern for whether the right person has been condemned. Thoughtful proponents of capital punishment have justified their position on the ground that the most heinous criminals deserve the ultimate punishment. They want justice. The idea that those who are sentenced to death are the victims of incompetent police work, sloppy lawyering, discrimination, or deliberate deception is deeply troubling to them. They regard themselves as tough but fair, not bloodthirsty.

In addition, the new evidence against the death penalty was no longer purely abstract and statistical. The old script had been bolstered by shocking stories of callous killers, and by heart-rending stories about the victims and their families, real people overcome by pain and outrage. This sort of emotional imagery engages our attention, and a single vivid example has often been shown to have a far greater influence on attitudes than disembodied statistical evidence that is much more probative.[67] The new script was supported by individualized stories of a new kind of victim—Hurricane Carter, Anthony Porter, and the others who spent years of their lives unjustly imprisoned and came close to being unjustly

66. Gross, supra note 2.
67. Richard E. Nisbett et al., "Popular Induction: Information Is Not Always Informative," in 2 *Cognition and Social Behavior* 227 (John S. Carroll and John W. Payne eds., 1976); Nisbett and Ross, supra note 15.

killed. The case of Anthony Porter, who came within a couple of days of execution, and whose innocence was proved by undergraduates in a journalism class, raised grave doubts about the competence—or honesty—of the prosecutor's office. If a bunch of college kids could find the truth when the legal establishment had been unable or unwilling to do so, that was a problem worth worrying about. A new script had become available, and it seemed as though everywhere they looked people encountered further evidence to confirm it.

Strongly held attitudes are most susceptible to change when people believe that there is genuinely new information.[68] Being able to point to genuinely new information may really change attitudes, but it also provides a way to save face for people who do not want to be seen as weak willed. A change in attitude does not reflect weakness, but an intelligent adjustment based on important new information. Best of all is a "scientific breakthrough": olive oil is now good for you because it increases good cholesterol, and polyunsaturated fats are no longer a panacea because they don't; estrogen replacement is good one month and bad the next; and so on. People change long-standing habits on the basis of such real or apparent "scientific breakthroughs."

DNA testing is the scientific breakthrough that justifies a change in support for the death penalty. It provides scientific proof that the criminal justice system makes serious mistakes, even in cases of life and death. This "scientific breakthrough" became a fixture in the public's view of criminal investigations as a result of the unprecedented media coverage of the O. J. Simpson murder trial in 1995. That trial also brought national attention to lawyers Barry Scheck and Peter Neufeld, who, with others, publicized DNA identification as a means of exonerating the innocent.[69] The picture that emerged by the end of 1999 was this: (1) An uncomfortably large number of people scheduled for execution were released because it turned out that they did not commit the killings for which they were condemned; (2) DNA identification—a new scientific test—was involved in this rash of exonerations. The fact that only eleven of the ninety-nine people who have been released from death row since 1970 were actually exonerated on the basis of DNA mismatches[70] would no doubt come as a great surprise to most of the public.

68. Eugene Burnstein and Amiram Vinokur, "What a Person Thinks upon Learning That He Has Chosen Differently from Others: Nice Evidence for the Persuasive-Arguments Explanation of Choice Shifts, 11 *J. Experimental Soc. Psychol.* 412 (1975).

69. See Jim Dwyer, Peter Neufeld, and Barry Scheck, *Actual Innocence: Five Days to Execution and Other Dispatches from the Wrongly Convicted* (2000).

70. Death Penalty Info. Ctr., supra note 40.

Inconsistencies and Contradictions

For almost a quarter of a century, support for the death penalty was strong, stable, and passionate. It was central to people's image of themselves as adamant in their stand against intolerable crime rates and to a whole network of attitudes about crime and the criminal justice system. Attitudes like this, linked to many other beliefs and attitudes, do not change all at once, and there is likely to be a period of inconsistency during which some beliefs have changed and others have not. Eventually, these inconsistencies approach resolution, sometimes in favor of a new attitude, sometimes in favor of the old.

The new script has made salient issues that used to be ignored and has changed some beliefs related to death penalty attitudes. Most conspicuously, most Americans now believe that innocent people are sometimes sentenced to death and executed. A 1995 Gallup poll found that 82 percent of the public believed that an innocent person had been sentenced to death in the past twenty years; by 2000 the percentage had risen to 91 percent. A Harris poll conducted in July 2000 found that almost everyone agreed that "innocent people are sometimes convicted of murder" (94 percent); when asked, "For every one hundred people convicted of murder, how many would you guess are actually innocent?" their average estimate was thirteen. And most people no longer believe that the criminal justice system has been able to discover and correct these miscarriages of justice. Three different polls conducted in 2000 found that 80 percent or more of the respondents believed that innocent people had actually been executed.[71]

These numbers are not surprising. As we have seen, the death penalty received extraordinary media exposure in 2000, and a large proportion of the stories focused on mistaken death sentences and the power of DNA testing to identify innocent people who would otherwise have been executed. In August 2000, 54 percent of those surveyed said that they had seen, heard, or read something about the death penalty in the past few months, most frequently information about DNA testing and the discovery of dozens of innocent people convicted and sentenced to die.[72]

The growing uneasiness about mistaken capital convictions is reflected in the support for Governor Ryan's decision to declare a moratorium on execution in Illinois. The moratorium was a radical move, the first of its kind, yet public

71. Gallup, 6/00 (80 percent say it happened in the past five years); Princeton Survey Research Assoc., 6/00 (82 percent); *L.A. Times*, 7/00 (83 percent).
72. Hart Research Assoc., 8/00.

support was strong and immediate: 66 percent of Illinois voters approved of the governor's decision.[73] Nationally, 37 percent of those surveyed said that other states should follow the lead of Illinois and suspend executions, while about 50 percent said executions should continue.[74] Although more people oppose a moratorium than support it, the issue has been reframed. Ten years earlier, for example, 64 percent of the population favored "restricting the rights of those convicted of murder to appeal their sentencing so that they can be executed more promptly," while only 33 percent opposed it.[75] At that time opposition to speeding up executions presumably meant maintaining the status quo, since slowing down the pace had not been mentioned and a moratorium was on nobody's agenda.

Still, the new script has not entirely replaced the old one. Despite the continuing decline in violent crime, crime is still an important issue in people's minds, and there is still a sense that criminals should be dealt with more severely. In 1994 the percentage of people who said that they thought crime was the most important problem facing the country ranged from 28 percent[76] to 52 percent,[77] far ahead of any other problem. In 2000 crime was only mentioned by 12 percent of the population and was roughly tied with education (11 percent) and health care (10 percent),[78] but it was still the most commonly mentioned problem.

Support for the death penalty is still at about 65 percent and remains strong. In July 2000 an ABC/Washington Post survey found that 75 percent of those polled said that the death penalty was important to them in deciding how to vote in the presidential election, with 40 percent saying that it was "very important." For some, this concern might have reflected new-found doubts about the death penalty, but not for most: 60 percent of the respondents in a Gallup poll in February 2000 said that the death penalty was not imposed often enough.[79] And in a 2000 Harris poll two-thirds of the respondents favored either no change in the rate of executions (31 percent) or an *increase* in "the number of convicted criminals who are executed" (36 percent). The number of people who want more

73. *Chi. Trib.*, 2/00.

74. Fox News, 2/00 (47 percent said executions should continue); Princeton Survey Research Assoc., 2/00 (50 percent said continue).

75. Harris, 7/90.

76. Gallup, 10/94.

77. Gallup, 8/94.

78. Gallup, 6/00.

79. In the same poll, 26 percent of respondents said the death penalty was imposed too often. In 1999 the comparable figures were 64 percent and 25 percent. Gallup, 2/99.

executions has declined—from 53 percent in 1997 and 43 percent in 1999[80]—but it remains high, especially since executions were taking place at a faster pace than at any time since the early 1950s. Likewise, in June 2000 after the extraordinary press coverage of the near-fatal errors in capital convictions and of the Illinois moratorium, almost half of the population still endorsed the idea that death row inmates are given "too much help and opportunity to appeal their cases and prove their innocence"; only 19 percent thought that they needed more help.[81] The old script—the picture of obviously guilty murderers living on and on at public expense, prolonging the nightmare of the victims' families—coexists uneasily with the new concern about wrongful convictions.

Either one of these scripts can be activated depending on the context. The question about death row inmates getting "too much help" triggers the old script, suggesting long delays while lawyers dredge up technicalities to postpone the execution that will finally provide closure for grieving relatives. But the new script can be triggered by asking the question in a different way, most conspicuously by mentioning the magic phrase "DNA testing." In recent polls almost everyone wants to allow convicted prisoners access to DNA testing.[82] Simply mentioning DNA testing in an opinion poll question produces tremendous shifts toward sympathy and concern for people sentenced to death. We have just seen that only 19 percent of the population thought that death row inmates should be given more assistance in proving their innocence when the question is asked in a general way. In the same month a similar question was embedded in a series of questions about DNA, and 82 percent of those polled agreed that "states should make it easier for death row inmates to introduce new evidence that might prove their innocence, even if it might result in delays in the death penalty process."[83] Mentioning DNA testing also produces huge increases in support for a moratorium. As we noted above, 37 percent of the population favored a moratorium in response to a question that mentioned Governor Ryan and the execution of innocent people.[84] But when respondents were reminded that "there have been several instances in which criminals sentenced to be executed have been released based on new evidence or new DNA testing," support for a moratorium soared to 63 percent.[85]

80. Harris, 6/97; Harris, 7/99; Harris, 7/00.

81. Opinion Dynamics, 6/00. The exact breakdown was as follows: too much help, 48 percent; about the right amount, 23 percent; not enough help, 19 percent; not sure, 10 percent.

82. Gallup, 3/00 (92 percent favor); *Newsweek*, 2/00 (95 percent favor for death row inmates).

83. Princeton Survey Research Assoc., 6/00.

84. Fox News, 2/00.

85. NBC News/*Wall St. J.*, 7/00.

Several aspects of American public opinion on the death penalty have remained largely unchanged over the past five years, even as support has dropped. Race and gender remain the major demographic predictors of death penalty attitudes.[86] As before, men support the death penalty more than women—74 percent to 63 percent on the 1998 General Social Survey, 73 percent to 60 percent in a February 2000 Gallup poll—and whites support it more than blacks, by a wide margin, 72 percent to 49 percent and 70 percent to 43 percent on those two polls, respectively. And, as in past decades, more Republicans than Democrats support the death penalty, 77 percent to 62 percent in the 1998 General Social Survey.

Retribution remains the major reason that people give for supporting capital punishment. In a June 1991 Gallup poll, in answer to an open-ended question asking why they favored the death penalty, 50 percent of respondents were coded as saying "a life for a life," and an additional 3 percent are listed as saying "judicial system is too lenient." The next most common response ("keeps them from killing again") was far behind, at 19 percent. In response to the same question in a March 2000 Gallup poll, 40 percent said "an eye for an eye," "they took a life," or "punishment fits the crime," and an additional 13 percent of responses were coded as "fair punishment," "they deserve it," or "serve[s] justice." The next most common response ("save[s] taxpayers money") drew only 12 percent. On the other hand, in a June 1997 survey that asked, "Do you think the desire for vengeance or retribution is a legitimate reason for having capital punishment and putting a murderer to death, or don't you feel that way?" 34 percent said "yes," and 60 percent said "no, don't feel that way." Apparently, most Americans support the death penalty for retributive reasons but do not like the word "retribution," at least not when it is coupled with "vengeance."[87]

What about other reasons for supporting the death penalty? In a presidential debate in October 2000, both candidates, the Democrat Al Gore and the Republican George Bush, said that they favored the death penalty because it deters murder and that it would be wrong to execute people otherwise. Perhaps they had been told that "retribution" and "vengeance" were unpopular themes and didn't realize they could talk about retribution as "justice" or "fair punishment." In any event, deterrence is not a common reason offered by the public at large; only 13 percent of death penalty supporters mentioned it in 1991,[88] and

86. Ellsworth and Gross, supra note 1, at 21–22; Gross, supra note 2, at 1451.

87. Ellsworth and Ross, supra note 26, at 155.

88. Gallup, 6/91.

8 percent in 2000.[89] Part of the reason may be that most Americans (unlike candidates Bush and Gore, if they are to be taken at their word) do not believe the death penalty does deter homicide. In a July 1999 Harris poll, for example, 47 percent said that "executing people who commit murder deters others from committing murder," and 49 percent said that "executions don't have much effect." In July 2000, 44 percent believed there was a deterrent effect, and 50 percent thought there was not.[90] The nonbelievers are right; there is a wealth of evidence that the death penalty does not deter murder more effectively than life imprisonment.[91] Not surprisingly, most supporters of capital punishment say that they would not change their position even if "new evidence showed that the death penalty does not act as a deterrent to murder." In 1991, 69 percent of death penalty proponents expressed that view; in 1999, it was 77 percent.[92]

When asked why they personally support the death penalty, people rarely mention incapacitation. In 1991, 19 percent of supporters said that they favored the death penalty because it "keeps them from killing again";[93] in February 2000, the equivalent reason—without capital punishment "they will repeat their crime/[the death penalty] will keep them from repeating it"—drew a mere 4 percent.[94] On the other hand, 74 percent of respondents on a 1997 survey said that the fact that the death penalty "removes all possibility that the convicted person can kill again"[95] is one of "the best reasons to support the death penalty"; the next most popular choice—deterrence—was far behind at 53 percent. Although it does not figure strongly in their *own* decision to favor or oppose capital punishment, most people think that incapacitation is the pro–death penalty argument most likely to convince others.[96] Judging from studies of capital-jury deliberations, their intuition is right. In that life-or-death decision-

89. Gallup, 2/00, available at http://gallup.com/poll/indicators/inddeath_pen.asp.

90. Harris, 7/00.

91. See, e.g., William C. Bailey and Ruth D. Peterson, "Murder, Capital Punishment, and Deterrence: A Review of the Literature," in *The Death Penalty in America: Current Controversies* 135 (Hugo Adam Bedau ed., 1997).

92. Gallup, 6/91; Gallup, 2/99 (71 percent favored death penalty on general death-penalty-attitude questions; 55 percent favored death penalty on assumption that it does not deter murders; .55/.71=.77).

93. Gallup, 6/91.

94. Gallup, 2/00, available at http://gallup.com/poll/indicators/inddeath_pen.asp.

95. Princeton Survey Research Assoc., 6/97.

96. See Gross, supra note 2, at 1454–55 and 1460.

making context, the possibility that the defendant might someday be released and kill again is used frequently and effectively to persuade reluctant jurors to return a sentence of death.[97]

Since 1985, a series of polls have asked, "What should be the penalty for murder—the death penalty or life imprisonment with absolutely no possibility of parole?" As an alternative to the death penalty, life without parole (or "LWOP") obviously speaks to the desire to permanently incapacitate convicted murderers, but it may satisfy retributive impulses as well. Most Americans believe (falsely) that murderers who are not sentenced to death are likely to be released in twenty, ten, or even seven years.[98] Such sentences may seem too light for murder, regardless of any future danger the defendant might pose; if so, life without parole may right the retributive balance. In any event, it is now well established that offering life without parole as an option decreases support for capital punishment considerably. On twelve national surveys that asked this question from 1985 through 1998, support for the death penalty fluctuated between 45 percent and 61 percent, with no apparent temporal pattern.[99] In 2000, in four additional polls through September that asked essentially the same question, support for the death penalty was in the same range—from 45 percent to 52 percent—but perhaps marginally lower than in previous years. Support for life imprisonment may have changed slightly more—it averaged over 42 percent in 2000, while before that year it had never exceeded 38 percent—but so far, any change is slight.[100]

Americans overwhelmingly believe that the death penalty should be applied equally to men and to women.[101] On the other hand, a large majority opposes the use of the death penalty for "mentally retarded persons,"[102] which is sadly

97. See William J. Bowers and Benjamin D. Steiner, "Death by Default: An Empirical Demonstration of False and Forced Choices in Capital Sentencing," 77 *Tex. L. Rev.* 605, 701–2 (1999).

98. Richard C. Dieter, Death Penalty Info. Ctr., *Sentencing for Life: Americans Embrace Alternatives to the Death Penalty* 8 (1993); Sally Costanzo and Mark Costanzo, "Life or Death Decisions: An Analysis of Capital Jury Decision Making under the Special Issues Sentencing Framework," 18 *Law and Hum. Behav.* 151, 163–64 (1998).

99. See Bureau of Just. Stat., Dep't of Just., *Sourcebook of Criminal Justice Statistics 1998* 131 tbl.2.52 (Kathleen Maguire and Ann L. Pastore eds., 1999); Gross, supra note 2, at 1456; Fox News, 2/98; CBS News, 2/98.

100. ABC News, 1/00; Gallup, 2/15/00; Gallup, 2/21/00; Gallup, 9/00. The increase in the percentage of respondents who favored life imprisonment without parole in 2000 largely reflects a corresponding decrease in the percentage who answered that they didn't know or weren't sure.

101. Princeton Survey Research Assoc., 5/91; Fox News, 1/98.

102. Harris, 9/88; Yankelovitch, 6/89; Tarrance Group and Greenberg Lake, 3/93. Apparently, there are no more recent polls on this issue.

ironic: since 1977, five women have been executed in the United States, and thirty-five mentally retarded people have suffered the same punishment.[103] Americans, however, do support executions for teenagers, apparently in increasing numbers. In 1989, 57 percent favored the death penalty for sixteen- and seventeen-year olds, a sharp increase from previous findings;[104] in 1994, 61 percent said that teenagers should not be spared the death penalty because of their age;[105] in 1999, 75 percent agreed that "teens who kill other teens should face the possibility of the death penalty,"[106] more than supported the death penalty itself in any poll taken that year. This trend probably reflects the continuing demonization of teenage criminals in American popular culture, especially in the wake of the massacre by two students at Columbine High School in Colorado and other school killings by young students.[107]

Finally, as we have noted in the past, Americans have deep reservations about the fairness of the death penalty.[108] In the two most recent polls on this issue, most respondents agreed that "a black person is more likely than a white person to receive the death penalty for the same crime"—50 percent to 46 percent—and that a poor person is more likely to be sentenced to death than one "of average or above average income"—65 percent to 32 percent;[109] they divided equally on whether the death penalty is applied fairly or unfairly, at 42 percent for each response.[110] These findings are essentially unchanged from years past.

103. Death Penalty Info. Ctr., supra note 40.

104. Yankelovitch, 6/89.

105. Gallup, 9/94.

106. Opinion Dynamics, 4/99.

107. A June 2000 NBC News/Wall Street Journal poll asked respondents if they favored "lowering the age at which the death penalty can be applied to juveniles under the age of fourteen." Fourteen percent "strongly favored" this proposal, and 12 percent "favored" it. To be sure, 68 percent were opposed—50 percent strongly—but it is telling that this idea is even taken seriously. Executing people for crimes committed before they turned eighteen is prohibited in most countries that use the death penalty. And even in the United States—which appears to account for a majority of all executions of juvenile offenders in the world since 1990 (see Richard C. Dieter, Death Penalty Info. Ctr., "International Perspectives on the Death Penalty: A Costly Isolation for the U.S. (1999)," available at http://www.deathpenaltyinfo.org/international report.html)—the death penalty is unavailable and probably unconstitutional for crimes committed before the age of sixteen. See Thompson v. Oklahoma, 487 U.S. 815 (1988).

108. Ellsworth and Gross, supra note 1, at 35–36; Gross, supra note 2, at 1458–59.

109. Gallup, 2/99.

110. NBC News/Wall St. J., 7/00.

Speculations

In this section, we summarize, integrate, and elaborate the social and individual themes we have developed, focusing on the new concrete scripts, the new political climate, and the moratorium as a new alternative to favoring or opposing the death penalty. We then go on to speculate about possible futures.

The Power of Concrete Cases

In his concurring opinion in *Furman v. Georgia*, Justice Marshall articulated what became known as the "Marshall hypothesis." He asserted that an essential test for the constitutionality of capital punishment is "whether people who were fully informed as to the purposes of the [death] penalty and its liabilities would find the penalty shocking, unjust, and unacceptable."[111] He then summarized well-established findings about the death penalty in operation: that it does not deter homicide more effectively than life imprisonment but does cost a lot more; that it is not necessary to prevent murderers from committing future crimes; that it is applied arbitrarily and used discriminatorily against the poor and against racial and ethnic minorities; and that innocent defendants are likely to be executed. Unfortunately, according to Justice Marshall, "American citizens know almost nothing about capital punishment."[112] However, if they did know "all facts presently available regarding capital punishment, the average citizen would, in my opinion, find it shocking to his conscience and sense of justice."[113]

The Marshall hypothesis has not fared well. When he presented it in 1972, Justice Marshall argued that because "[s]o few people have been executed in the past decade . . . capital punishment is a subject only rarely brought to the attention of the average American"; and that this lack of exposure led to "indifference and ignorance."[114] In the decades that followed, the death penalty was frequently brought to the attention of the American people; it became a major social and political issue. By the mid-1980s executions were regular events; by the mid-1990s they were common. But public opinion did not turn against capital punishment; quite the opposite. In addition, several studies have shown that few death-penalty supporters change their minds when given factual infor-

111. 408 U.S. 238, 361 (1972).
112. Id. at 362.
113. Id. at 369 (footnote omitted).
114. Id. at 361 n.145.

mation about the problems that Justice Marshall described.[115] And, as we have mentioned, surveys repeatedly show that many Americans believe that the death penalty does not deter murder, that it is administered unfairly, and that it is used in a manner that discriminates against minorities and poor people—but they support it nonetheless.

But Justice Marshall may have been more right than we thought. In the past few years, public support for the death penalty has been undercut by growing experience with one of the problems that Marshall addressed, if not the others— that innocent defendants are convicted and sentenced to death for crimes they did not commit. The power of this issue may reflect the fact that people respond more strongly to concrete cases than to abstract concepts. In the context of the death penalty, this cuts both ways. On one side, advocates of capital punishment point to specific examples of terrible murders to generate support for the death penalty. On the other, there is evidence, from studies and from capital trials alike, that many people who support the death penalty in theory are reluctant to apply it in practice to an individual defendant with a life, a name, and a face.[116]

By 1995, 82 percent of Americans agreed that an innocent person had been sentenced to death in the preceding twenty years, but support for the death penalty remained as high as ever.[117] Several years later, mounting experience with the death penalty in operation has shown that these tragic errors are far more common than most people would have believed. The same could be said for other problems in the administration of capital punishment. Mounting evidence also indicates that this penalty does not deter[118] and that it is costly,[119] arbitrary, and discriminatory.[120] Those issues, however, are inherently abstract.

115. See Ellsworth and Gross, supra note 1, at 33–35.

116. Charles D. Lord et al., "Typicality Effects in Attitudes toward Social Policies: A Concept-mapping Approach, 66 *J. Personality and Soc. Psychol.* 658 (1994); Phoebe C. Ellsworth, "Attitudes towards Capital Punishment: From Application to Theory," paper presented at the annual meeting of the Society for Experimental Social Psychology, Stanford University (Nov. 1978) (unpublished manuscript, on file with the authors).

117. Gallup, 5/95.

118. See supra note 92; Bonner and Fessenden, supra note 62.

119. See, e.g., Philip J. Cook and Donna B. Slawson, *The Costs of Processing Murder Cases in North Carolina* (1993).

120. See, e.g., Samuel R. Gross and Robert Mauro, *Death and Discrimination: Racial Disparities in Capital Sentencing* (1989); U.S. Gen. Acct. Off., *Death Penalty Sentencing: Research Indicates Pattern of Racial Disparities* (1990); David Baldus et al., "Racial Discrimination and

They are aspects of the system as a whole rather than features of particular cases. With wrongful convictions, the general argument is attached to specific people, victims of our system of justice, human beings whose ruined lives we can picture and whose terror we can imagine. Their stories have generated a new script for death penalty cases: the botched capital prosecution, with the defendant as innocent victim.

So Justice Marshall seems to have been at least partly right. In the context of concrete cases, learning about the operation of the capital punishment in practice does sometimes shock people's conscience and offend their sense of justice. It helps that the issue that did it—capital convictions of innocent defendants—is identified in the public mind with DNA evidence. Because DNA identification is new, it is an attractive basis for changing long-held views, and it can provide virtually irrefutable scientific proof of innocence. DNA has not played a role in 90 percent of the cases of death row inmates who have been exonerated, but that goes unnoticed.

Concrete cases are not always influential. Innocence condemned is only one of several recurring themes in the recent spate of unflattering publicity about the death penalty. We have also heard about defense attorneys who fell asleep in capital trials[121] or sabotaged their own clients' cases,[122] prosecutors who concealed or manufactured evidence,[123] and police officers who chose murder suspects simply because they were black.[124] These too are dramatic stories with familiar villains: the disloyal, dishonest, or amoral lawyer; the arrogant or corrupt government official. Such images certainly reinforce the belief that our system is likely to make fatal errors, but it is not clear how much independent effect they have beyond that. Would many Americans care if they learned that a death row inmate who was in fact guilty of a vicious multiple murder had a defense attorney who never talked to him, or a prosecutor who lied, or was arrested because of his race? Or would they feel that fouls and errors happen in every game and that the only real question is the accuracy of the final outcome?

the Death Penalty in the Post-*Furman* Era: An Empirical and Legal Overview, with Recent Findings from Philadelphia," 83 *Cornell L. Rev.* 1638 (1998).

121. See Diane Jennings, "Judges Say Sleeping Lawyer May Not Have Harmed Case," *Dallas Morning News*, Oct. 28, 2000.

122. "Lawyer Admits Sabotaging Client's Appeal," *USA Today*, Nov. 3, 2000.

123. See Thomas Frisbie and Randy Garrett, *Victims of Justice* (1998) (discussing cases of Rolando Cruz and Alejandro Hernandez).

124. Michael L. Radelet, Hugo Adam Bedau, and Constance E. Putnam, *In Spite of Innocence* 119–36 (1992) (discussing case of Clarence Brandley).

It may be that a memorable story only makes a claim of injustice more powerful if the injustice claimed is one the audience cares about in the first place.

And what about the most basic question in the debate over capital punishment—the morality of execution? Would support suffer if more people knew the faces and the stories behind this issue? In 1960 Caryl Chessman was executed in California. In twelve years on death row, he had published a novel and three autobiographical books, one of which was made into a movie, and had become a celebrity.[125] His story and his execution were the focal points of opposition to capital punishment in America in the 1950s and early 1960s. The execution of Karla Faye Tucker in 1998 had some of the same impact for a short while. Will other death row prisoners capture the public imagination in the same way and transform the image of the condemned murderer from featureless monster to human being? In a country with several thousand people on death row, such stories are always available. It may be that the attention they sometimes get is more a symptom than a cause of ambivalence and opposition to the death penalty. That would explain, for example, why some interesting and attractive prisoners under sentence of death in America are far better known in Europe;[126] and it suggests that if support for the death penalty continues to wane, more prisoners will be given human faces.

A New Context

It's usually pretty easy to explain an accomplished fact. By now, it's not hard to figure out that people react strongly to stories of innocent defendants sentenced to death: we've seen it happen. The harder question, in retrospect, is why it did not happen earlier. Forty-three innocent defendants had been released from death row by the beginning of 1990; fifty-nine were released before 1995. Some of their stories received extensive publicity, but support for the death penalty did not budge. Why did it take several more years for the issue to hit home?

Part of the reason may simply be the intolerable accumulation of numbers. By 1998, when the Chicago Conference on Wrongful Convictions in Capital Cases was held, the count stood at seventy-five; in January 2000, when Governor Ryan announced a moratorium in Illinois, it was eighty-five.[127] But this is not a very

---

125. See Frank J. Parker, *Caryl Chessman: The Red Light Bandit* (1975); Note, "The Caryl Chessman Case: A Legal Analysis," 44 *Minn. L. Rev.* 941, 996–97 (1960).

126. See, e.g., "European Network to Free Mumia Abu-Jamal," available at http://www.xs4 all.nl/~tank/spg/mumia-eu/. This is one of dozens of European Web sites devoted to the cause of a death row prisoner in Pennsylvania.

127. Death Penalty Info. Ctr., supra note 40.

convincing explanation. Forty, fifty, and sixty cases are already large numbers of potentially fatal miscarriages of justice, and the overall pattern had long been clear—to anyone who was paying attention. The skill of the organizers of the Chicago conference probably made a difference, and the increasing prominence of DNA identification was certainly influential. But the overriding reason, in our view, is the context in which this issue came to the fore. To put it simply, the time was ripe. To explain why requires a short digression back in time.

Crime became a major item on the national political agenda in 1968, when Richard Nixon made "law and order" a prime focus of his campaign for president.[128] At the time, that meant an attack on "lenient" penalties and on "liberal" judges who "coddled" criminals—notably the Supreme Court under the leadership of Chief Justice Earl Warren. This was a smart political move. In 1968 both crime and public concern about crime were rising rapidly. By claiming to take the lead in fighting crime, and by identifying liberalism as a cause of crime, Republican politicians were able to gain a significant electoral advantage. The death penalty was not part of this strategy at its inception; the focal point was *Miranda v. Arizona*,[129] the Supreme Court's 1966 decision regulating police interrogations. In 1968 a national moratorium on executions had only just started, the legal status of capital punishment was just coming under systematic attack, and public support for the death penalty was near its all-time low.

128. Nixon was not the first to make crime an issue in a presidential campaign. Republican candidate Barry Goldwater did so in his unsuccessful campaign in 1964, and the concept of a "War against Crime" originated in the second Johnson administration, 1965–1969. Even in the 1968 presidential campaign, the "law and order" issue was advanced first by George Wallace, who ran as a third-party candidate. But Nixon and John Mitchell, his campaign manager and later his attorney general, picked up the theme and made it more central and prominent than did any politicians who preceded them. The 1968 presidential campaign overlapped with congressional consideration of the Omnibus Crime Control and Safe Streets Act of 1968 ("Omnibus Crime Act"), and the anticrime debates went on simultaneously in both settings and fed off each other. The anticrime fervor of 1968 was also fed by several major incidents that occurred that year, including the assassinations of Robert Kennedy (on the day the House of Representatives began debating the Omnibus Crime Act) and of Martin Luther King Jr. and a series of race riots that followed the King assassination. For an excellent summary of these debates, focusing on the Omnibus Crime Act, see Yale Kamisar, "Can (Did) Congress 'Overrule' Miranda?" 85 *Cornell L. Rev.* 883, 887–90 (2000). It is also important (but beyond the scope of this chapter) that in this period violent crime in America was increasingly seen as a black problem. See generally Francis A. Allen, *The Decline of the Rehabilitative Ideal: Penal Policy and Social Purpose* 36–40 (1981); Page and Shapiro, supra note 18, at 90–93; James Vorenberg, "The War on Crime: The First Five Years," *Atl. Monthly*, May 1972.

129. 384 U.S. 436 (1966).

Capital punishment became a national issue in its own right in 1972, when the Supreme Court declared all existing death penalty laws unconstitutional.[130] Thirty-five states responded by passing new death penalty laws within a few years; in 1976 the Court upheld the constitutionality of capital punishment and approved several of the new laws that were enacted after 1972.[131] In the late 1970s and 1980s the death penalty became an increasingly prominent theme in the politics of crime in state and local elections around the country, and in 1988 the Republicans made it a central issue in their presidential campaign. From the point of view of the Republican candidate, George Bush, the timing was ideal. Violent crime and support for the death penalty were both as high as ever, and his Democratic opponent, Michael Dukakis, was a lifelong opponent of capital punishment. Dukakis's opposition to capital punishment was a central element in a campaign that painted him as "soft on crime." It worked. Bush beat Dukakis 53 percent to 45 percent in what had once been seen as a close contest. In an exit poll, voters chose "the candidates' positions on the death penalty" as an issue that was "very important" to them more often than any other issue except abortion.[132]

Bill Clinton changed all that when he ran for president as a Democrat in 1992. The basic strategy was simple and had already been used by many Democrats in local and state elections: defuse crime as an issue by being as punitive as the local Republicans, or more so. In his presidential campaign against George Bush, Clinton accomplished this primarily by making it clear that he was as much in favor of the death penalty as anybody. As the sitting governor of a death penalty state, he had a positional advantage, and he used it conspicuously by presiding over two executions during the presidential campaign. It worked. In stark contrast to 1988, the death penalty did not surface as an issue in 1992, and Clinton won. Once in office, he continued to make sure that he would not be outflanked by Republicans on crime. His legacy includes the Federal Death Penalty Act of 1994,[133] which greatly expanded the scope of the federal death penalty, and the Antiterrorism and Effective Death Penalty Act of 1996,[134] which expanded the reach of the federal death penalty even farther and greatly reduced the power of federal courts to review the fairness of state capital prosecutions—both of which passed Congress with solid bipartisan support.

130. Furman v. Georgia, 408 U.S. 238 (1972).
131. Gregg v. Georgia, 428 U.S. 153 (1976).
132. ABC News, 11/88; see also Ellsworth and Gross, supra note 1, at 23.
133. Pub. L. No. 103–322, 108 Stat. 1959 (1994).
134. Pub. L. No. 104–132, 110 Stat. 1214 (1996).

By 1992 the death penalty was no longer a national political issue in America because there was essentially only one position. In the 1970s and 1980s death penalty attitudes in America were an aspect of self-definition. People favored the death penalty as part of a commitment to be "tough on crime," to do something about rising crime and social disorder. They defined themselves by this attitude in opposition to those who opposed the death penalty or who were seen as "soft on crime" in general. It was the genius of Republican and conservative politicians to align themselves with this popular position, but it could not last. By 1992 everybody had joined the winning side. After Mario Cuomo lost his bid for a fourth term as governor of New York in 1994, there was not a single political officeholder of national stature who was known to oppose capital punishment. The victory for the advocates of the death penalty seemed complete. But did the very completeness of this triumph make it vulnerable? As a matter of individual psychology, the one-sidedness of public opinion may have undermined support for the death penalty by making it reflexive, conventional, unthinking—something like a "cultural truism," as we have discussed above. At the same time, a parallel process seems to have been operating at the level of political identification.

It is not easy to define oneself by an attitude that no one disagrees with. Being against crime or for the death penalty has little content unless there is someone with an opposing position. When almost everybody is on one side of an issue, the differences among those on that side become more noticeable—in this case, the distinctions among supporters of capital punishment. In some political campaigns in the 1980s and early 1990s, candidates tried to compete with each other by trumpeting their enthusiasm for putting prisoners to death, but it was not always a successful strategy.[135] Increasingly, as in the Clinton-Bush race in 1992, the death penalty dropped out of political contests. By the late 1990s, another major change had taken hold: the crime rate had fallen substantially, and the public had noticed. In that setting—with the death penalty no longer a live political question and increasingly irrelevant as a basis for political identification, with crime and concern about crime both down—the issue of wrongful capital convictions took hold.

135. See Samuel R. Gross, "Romance of Revenge: Capital Punishment in America," 13 *Stud. in Law, Pol. and Soc'y* 71, 91–92 (1993) (California Democratic gubernatorial primary of 1990 in which winning candidate Diane Feinstein ran as the only candidate who *truly* favored capital punishment); Richard Lacayo, "The Politics of Life and Death," *Time*, Apr. 2, 1990 (Texas Democratic gubernatorial primary of 1990, in which extreme pro–death penalty campaigns by losing candidates Mark White and Jim Mattox apparently backfired).

This is not a one-way street. So far we have argued that stories of innocent defendants on death row have been very influential in the last four years in large part because of changes in the social and psychological context in which they are heard. But the causal link in the opposite direction is even clearer: the attention that this issue has received has changed the context in which the death penalty is seen. In this direction as well, the process operates at two levels: individual psychology (which we have discussed), and social and political ideology.

In the past, politicians were attacked for not being sufficiently strong in their support for capital punishment. Now, at least in some races, the danger is on the other side: a politician can be hurt by appearing too willing to use the death penalty, as we saw in the race for president in 2000. Both candidates for president in 2000, Republican George Bush and Democrat Al Gore, supported the death penalty. This was no surprise; so has every serious contender for a major party nomination for president or vice president since the Dukakis debacle in 1988. This time, however, neither candidate campaigned on this issue, and neither said anything more about the death penalty than was absolutely necessary. In Gore's case, that meant saying pretty much nothing at all. Bush, however, was haunted by the issue. As governor of Texas he had presided over 146 executions—more than any other governor in modern American history—in a state that had more than its share of publicity for incompetence and callousness in the administration of capital punishment. Many people who supported the death penalty themselves saw Bush as overly eager to kill and insufficiently concerned about accuracy and fairness. He was the butt of countless jokes on this score.[136]

To be sure, more voters supported than opposed Governor Bush's position on the death penalty.[137] But these were people who had been likely to vote for him all along. The important question was how this issue would play among

136. For example, the following joke circulated toward the end of the 2000 presidential campaign: "I heard that George Bush postponed three executions to the week after the election. I guess he wants to make sure he has enough time to really enjoy them." See generally Marshall Sella, "The Stiff Guy vs. the Dumb Guy," N.Y. Times Mag., Sept. 24, 2000, at 72. (In fact, there were three executions in Texas in the eight days following the November 2000 election and six in the thirty days following the election, compared to one execution in the thirty days before election day.)

137. E.g., L.A. Times, 7/00 (49 percent say Bush "would do a better job of handling the death penalty"; 30 percent say Gore); ABC News/Wash. Post, 7/00 (50 percent approve of Bush's handling of the death penalty as governor of Texas; 28 percent disapprove).

those who had a hard time choosing. One week before the election, 3 percent of undecided voters mentioned Bush's stand on the death penalty in response to the question "What about George W. Bush makes you unsure about voting for him?" No similar responses were registered for Al Gore.[138] Several days before the election, 28 percent of a sample of registered voters said that "criticism about Bush's handling of the death penalty and the number of executions in Texas" was a "serious problem," and 21 percent said it was "somewhat of a problem"; for Gore, the question was not asked.[139] This is not to say that the death penalty was a major issue in the 2000 campaign; we do not believe it was. But the direction in which it pushed was unmistakable.

The near political unanimity on the death penalty in the early 1990s may have had another effect as well. For decades, the death penalty was viewed as an issue that partly defined a person's position in the political world: liberals were opposed; conservatives were in favor. The collapse of any serious political opposition to the death penalty removed the issue from the normal left-to-right spectrum of American politics, which may have made it easier for opposition and doubts to crop up in unexpected quarters. Now that the death penalty is not seriously contested, it is no longer an issue that conservatives must embrace to prove their credentials. Maybe that is why the most conspicuous new voices criticizing the use of the death penalty in the United States come from prominent conservatives: columnist George Will, the Reverend Pat Robertson, Governor John Engler of Michigan, and, of course, Governor George Ryan of Illinois. Perhaps the depoliticization of the death penalty that resulted from the overwhelming political victory of the right has made possible a much broader coalition in opposition than could be imagined ten years ago—assuming, of course, that other factors favor a further shift in public opinion.

A New Option

So far, we have discussed three interrelated factors that favor change, each one serving both as an incentive and as a justification for reconsideration of long-unquestioned attitudes. The first is new information. Information about the exoneration of innocent people by means of DNA testing *is* new; it is interesting; and it revives attention to the issues. The new information is reinforced by a second element, the existence of a new script that incorporates it into a coherent story with villains, victims, and heroes. The third is the altered context,

138. Princeton Survey Research Assoc., 10/00.
139. Id.

with lower crime, reduced political salience, and new voices expressing doubts about the death penalty. And these three have resulted in a fourth factor conducive to a shift in public opinion: a new option.

As long as survey researchers have measured attitudes toward the death penalty, the question has been framed as one that involves only two options: either you favor the death penalty or you oppose it. (Of course, people could say that they were undecided, but that just meant that they had not yet made up their minds about which camp to join.) With only two choices on an ideological issue, changing one's attitude means joining the enemy. Now there is a new option: a moratorium on executions while the flaws in the system are investigated.

The existence of a third choice makes a difference. First, bolstered by the new information that stimulated the call for a moratorium in the first place, it provides a way to reopen discussion. In the early 1990s it seemed as though there was nothing left to talk about: proponents and opponents of the death penalty had heard each other's arguments over and over again and had rejected them long ago. Support for the death penalty was a part of people's self-definition as resolute in the crackdown on crime, and reversing this position was unthinkable. A moratorium is something to talk about: Is it warranted? Should it last until everyone on death row has had a DNA test? What about the possibly innocent people who can't be tested because there is no DNA sample? What kind of investigation should be conducted? What should be done if the investigation shows high levels of error and discrimination? These are new issues, fresh air in a debate that had grown stale.

Second, new information and a new script might have been sufficient to reopen discussion of the death penalty, but a third option does something more. Research in cognitive science suggests that when a "wait-for-new-information" option is added to a yes-or-no choice, a substantial proportion of people choose to wait.[140] This is true even when the information that comes at the end of the waiting period would have made no difference if people had known about it beforehand; when a difficult choice has to be made, deferral is an intrinsically attractive option. Bastardi and Shafir argue that "in making decisions that can influence the fate of others, people would be particularly compelled to defer decision."[141]

---

140. Anthony Bastardi and Eldar Shafir, "On the Pursuit and Misuse of Useless Information," 75 *J. Personality and Soc. Psychol.* 19 (1998); Amos Tversky and Eldar Shafir, "The Disjunction Effect in Choice under Uncertainty," 3 *Psychol. Sci.* 305 (1992).

141. Bastardi and Shafir, supra note 140, at 21.

A moratorium is an especially attractive choice in the death penalty debate because it does not require people to move to the enemy camp or even to give up their old position. Opponents can easily see a moratorium as a first step toward their goal of abolition, as an instrumental move rather than a change in attitude. Proponents can say that they still favor the death penalty; they always favored it because they believed that death was the just punishment for cold-blooded killers. They believe in justice, so of course they would *never* have favored the execution of innocent people. A moratorium is an acceptable position because the current system seems to fall short of justice. A serious investigation is necessary to discover the source of these shortcomings and to devise remedies. For many supporters, a moratorium may seem like a "mend it, don't end it" option. Although they still see themselves as taking a hard line on crime, they are not *brutal*. They do not *enjoy* executions. The death penalty is the ultimate punishment, and, although it is necessary, it should be applied with the utmost caution and integrity. There is no inconsistency in the fact that 64 percent of the population favors a moratorium (at least when DNA is mentioned) and that about the same number favors the death penalty.

Some people, however, actually *have* changed from supporting the death penalty to opposing it. There is evidence from the cognitive science literature that adding a new alternative to a set of choices can actually change the relative attractiveness of the previous choices.[142] If alternative A was preferred over alternative B, the introduction of alternative C should not logically change a person's preference from A to B—but there is considerable evidence that it can. For example, suppose a parent has chosen a preschool where there are twelve children per classroom and the teachers have an average of twelve years of experience over another preschool where there are eight children per classroom but the teachers only have five years of experience. It looks as though length of experience is what matters to this parent. But if a new option is offered, a school where the teachers have twelve years of experience but there are fourteen children per classroom, some people decide that after all they want the school with eight children in a class.[143] Apparently, the new option makes people reconsider the importance of class size. So far, none of this research has been concerned

142. Amos Tversky and Itamar Simonson, "Context-Dependent Preferences," 39 *Management Sci.* 1179 (1993); Douglas H. Weddell and Jonathan C. Pettibone, "Using Judgments to Understand Decoy Effects in Choice," 67 *Organizational Behav. and Hum. Decision Processes* 326 (1996).
143. Weddell and Pettibone, supra note 142.

with deep-seated ideological positions, such as attitudes toward the death penalty, but rather with choices among consumer products or hypothetical gambles. Still, the underlying logic is that adding a new option can change the salience of aspects of the old options, resulting in a change in actual preference, and in principle the same logic could apply to death penalty attitudes.

There are many different considerations that play a role in death penalty attitudes—justice, deterrence, fairness, irrevocability, heinous criminals, suffering relatives, biblical morality, belief in rehabilitation, and more. The moratorium option focuses attention on the issues of discrimination and fairness and especially on the execution of the innocent, issues that were very much in the background ten years ago. Bastardi and Shafir's research[144] suggests that people who decide to wait for more information are likely to be strongly influenced by what they learn: information that emerges after a decision has been postponed is more powerful than the same information would have been if it had been there all along. This suggests that if the investigations carried out during a moratorium show that mistakes and discrimination are common, supporters of the moratorium will be likely to move toward opposition.

It is possible that some former supporters of the death penalty have changed their minds because they already foresee the likely results of the moratorium investigations. They may have concluded that the research undertaken during a moratorium will probably reveal that the problems are real and that so far none of the attempted remedies has managed to solve them. Then there will be proposals for new remedies. Will it be another twenty-five years before their effectiveness can be assessed? Is there any likelihood that new efforts will be any more effective than the existing ones? The problems that have led to a call for a moratorium may now be seen as insoluble, and some people may feel that the end result of a moratorium will be a recognition that a just and accurate system of capital punishment is impossible and that it would be best to give up the death penalty altogether. To the extent that the moratorium option raises these issues, some former proponents may have decided that the eventual solution will probably be abolition and may have changed their attitudes in anticipation of that outcome.

A moratorium on executions is not the only candidate to be a new option. Starting in 1985, several years before the risk of executing innocents attracted public attention, researchers began to give respondents the choice of endorsing "life imprisonment with no possibility of parole" instead of the death penalty.

144. Bastardi and Shafir, supra note 140.

As we have seen, life without parole (LWOP) has been consistently chosen by 30 to 40 percent of the population—reducing support for the death penalty to the 45-to-60-percent range—and it may be gaining popularity.[145]

So far, there is little evidence that the availability of LWOP as a punishment for murder, in theory or in practice, has changed basic attitudes toward the death penalty. When asked a standard death-penalty-attitude question without the LWOP alternative, support remained high and stable until 1998; when the LWOP alternative was included, support for the death penalty was lower but it was also stable over that period. This is not surprising: unlike the moratorium option, choosing a life sentence over the death penalty requires supporters of capital punishment to repudiate their long-standing and strongly felt position.

Even if LWOP has not been sufficient to *cause* a change in death penalty attitudes, it may be an influential factor in reinforcing inclinations to change and in sustaining change once it has begun. Apart from the death penalty, life without parole is the harshest punishment we can impose. Even if it does not fully satisfy many people's desire for retribution, it does address the fear that unless killers are sentenced to death they will be released and free to kill again in a few years. To the extent that a moratorium raises the possibility that the death penalty may be abolished, we must decide what to do next: how will we make sure that murderers are adequately punished and that they will never have a chance to repeat their crimes? LWOP addresses those concerns.

But there is a catch. For LWOP to affect people's attitudes toward the death penalty, it must be available, well known, and credible. The first of these conditions has been met: life without parole is now the dominant sentencing alternative to the death penalty across the United States.[146] The state of the second requirement is less clear. The spread of LWOP in the past decade may have drawn some public attention (for one thing, it is now nearly universal practice to tell capital juries, when it is the case, that LWOP is the alternative to death),[147] but there are no data on this point. The third condition, however, seems to be a

145. See supra notes 99–100 and accompanying text.

146. Thirty-three out of thirty-eight death penalty states now use life without parole as an alternative to the death penalty (the conspicuous exception is Texas), as do the federal government and the U.S. military. See Death Penalty Info. Ctr., "Life without Parole," available at http://www.deathpenaltyinfo.org/lwop.html. In 1993 LWOP was already the most common alternative to a capital sentence—it was available in twenty-three death penalty states—but it was not so nearly universal. See Dieter, supra note 98, at 8.

147. See Brief for Petitioner at app. B, Shafer v. South Carolina, 121 S. Ct. 1263 (2001) (No. 00–5250).

stumbling block. In California, LWOP has long been the only sentencing alternative to the death penalty, and no defendant sentenced to life without parole has
been released in decades. Nonetheless, 64 percent of respondents in a 1990
California poll agreed with the statement "life in prison without possibility of
parole does not really guarantee that a prisoner will not be released," and only 27
percent disagreed.[148] Similarly, in an experiment by Diamond and Casper,[149]
simulated jurors were no less likely to sentence a defendant to death when they
were told that otherwise he would get LWOP than when they were told he would
get an unspecified prison sentence; apparently the subjects did not believe that
no parole means no parole. In other words, it looks as though LWOP has suffered
from a credibility gap that has limited its influence on death penalty attitudes.
That could change. In Florida, when LWOP became the alternative to the death
penalty for murders committed after May 25, 1994, the statewide total of death
sentences fell from an average of thirty-nine a year from 1986 through 1994 to
an average of twenty-two a year from 1996 (when most capital trials began to
come under the new law) through 2000.[150] If the availability of LWOP caused this
drop (and there are no other obvious candidates), it might be a harbinger of
things to come.

Does a moratorium signal the end of the death penalty? Have we taken the
first step toward the abolition of capital punishment? For the first time in a
quarter century, there is a chance for real change. But it is still just that: a
chance. A number of elements have combined to raise the possibility of a major
change in American attitudes toward the death penalty, but it is by no means
inevitable.

Over the last few years, the arguments against the death penalty have picked
up momentum. New stories of exonerations are prevalent; new voices are joining the opposition; and the news media have kept the issue in the public consciousness. Illinois has declared a moratorium, and some municipalities have
passed resolutions endorsing the concept. So far no other state has actually
enacted a formal moratorium, nor has the federal government, although the
U.S. attorney general has called for an investigation of possible racial and geo-

148. William Carlsen, "Support for the Death Penalty—Sometimes," *S.F. Chron.*, Mar. 28, 1990,
at A9 (reporting on a survey by the Field Institute).
149. Shari Diamond and Jay Casper, "Understanding Juries" (2000) (unpublished manuscript, on
file with the authors).
150. Glenn L. Pierce and Michael L. Radelet, "Choosing Those Who Will Die: Race and the
Death Penalty in Florida," 43 *Fla. L. Rev.* 1, 18 (1991); letter from Michael L. Radelet to Samuel
R. Gross (Feb. 11, 2001) (on file with the authors).

graphic discrimination in federal capital prosecutions. There are several competing scenarios for what could happen in the future.

First, another major death-penalty state—or two or three—might follow the lead of Illinois and declare moratoria on executions in the next couple of years. If that happens, the recent increase in opposition to the death penalty will persist and probably grow substantially. The status quo will have changed from a period of regular but barely noticed executions to a period of questioning. States that do not institute moratoria will feel pressure to be more cautious, to look into the possibility of error before carrying out an execution. And the outcomes of investigations carried out during a moratorium are predictable. In any state that used the death penalty regularly in the past, there will be evidence of the very problems of mistakes and discrimination that led to the moratorium in the first place. It is hard to imagine a serious investigation in an active death-penalty state leading to the conclusion that nothing is wrong—and harder still to imagine such a conclusion going unchallenged.

And, if after two or three years of moratoria, the reports come back as expected, saying that the system is deeply flawed, what then? Would we try to improve procedures and provide more resources to make the administration of the death penalty fairer and more accurate? In the abstract, that would not seem to be an attractive choice; that is, after all, what we have already been trying to do since we reinstated the death penalty in 1976 and we have failed. If we haven't succeeded so far, what reason is there to think that the next time around would be any different? Or would we decide to throw in the towel and abolish the death penalty outright?

Historically, moratoria on executions have been the transitional phase to the abolition of capital punishment. In Great Britain a moratorium starting in 1965 led to abolition in 1969;[151] in Canada the moratorium began in 1967, and capital punishment was abolished in 1976.[152] The architects of the legal challenge to the death penalty in the United States in the 1960s—primarily lawyers working with the NAACP Legal Defense and Educational Fund—hoped to achieve the same result here.[153] They succeeded in the first step; there was a moratorium on executions in America from 1968 until 1977, while questions about the constitutionality of the death penalty were argued and resolved in the United States

151. Gross, supra note 135, at 89–90.
152. Franklin E. Zimring and Gordon Hawkins, *Capital Punishment and the American Agenda* 5 (1986).
153. See Michael Meltsner, *Cruel and Unusual: The Supreme Court and Capital Punishment* 106–25 (1974).

Supreme Court. But instead of being abolished the death penalty was reaffirmed, restored, and became common and entrenched. The difference in outcome may be due to differences in the nature and context of these moratoria. The 1967 to 1976 moratorium in the United States was instituted by the courts in response to litigation, at a time of rising concern about crime and rising support for capital punishment. The Canadian and British moratoria were enacted by the elected branches of government; they were in effect during periods when the death penalty was generally popular in these two countries, but support was stable and the issue had little political punch. The moratorium in Illinois, like any new moratoria that might occur in other states, looks more like those in Canada and Britain than like the judicial moratorium in the United States before 1977. Such politically instituted moratoria could lead to the same outcome, if other events do not drive up support for the death penalty once again.

A second scenario is that the moratorium movement could fizzle, leaving Illinois as an isolated case. Other states might decide, disingenuously, that the problems uncovered in Illinois are local and have no implications for the death penalty in general. If this happens, opposition to the death penalty might continue to grow—if new credible sources speak out against it or if new stories of wrongful convictions continue to surface—but it will grow more slowly. It is conceivable that new issues could gain prominence and move people—racial discrimination, for example, or the censure of human rights organizations and the world community—but at this time there is no evidence that any other issue approaches the power of the conviction of the innocent.

A related possibility is that people will get bored with the death penalty, that new issues will push it out of public consciousness. It cannot disappear entirely—the moratorium in Illinois remains unresolved, and other stories will predictably crop up—but it might recede and become just another issue that people hear about from time to time and then forget. If capital punishment fades into the background again, attitudes might stabilize where they are, or they might slowly creep back to their 1995 levels—especially if crime rates start to rise.

Finally, attitudes toward the death penalty might be strongly influenced by singular events. A terrible mass murder, the gruesome acts of a serial killer, or (worst of all) a series of murders by a criminal who had killed and been convicted before and was then released—any of those could produce a sharp increase in support. On the other hand, if a sympathetic prisoner is executed and irrefutable evidence then comes to light that the wrong person was put to death, opposition would increase quickly.

The common wisdom is that the recent decline in support for capital punishment reflects the American people's distress about the escalating number of near-fatal mistakes. A system that once seemed to err on the side of caution now seems hasty, careless, and corrupt. However, innocent people have been released from death row for decades, and there is no evidence that the system for deciding capital cases has deteriorated recently. The problem is not new; what is new is that people notice and care. It has helped that the use of DNA identification in a small number of cases has made this issue *look* new and scientifically undeniable, but the main catalyst is timing. Crime and concern about crime are down; capital punishment is no longer a major item on the political agenda; and support for the death penalty has become increasingly reflexive, a matter of habit rather than passionate concern. Attitudes that remain fixed over a long period without reflection can become vulnerable to new information, especially if that information is brought to life with memorable concrete examples. In this context, stories of innocent people who came within days of execution attract attention and raise doubts about the integrity of the system.

This process has gathered substantial momentum. The moratorium on executions in Illinois further focused public attention on problems in administering the death penalty and publicized the possibility of a moratorium as a new position on the death penalty. That in turn has accelerated a process of political realignment, with new conservative voices expressing doubts or speaking out against capital punishment. If we continue on this course—and especially if the moratorium movement spreads—we could see a major shift in public opinion on the death penalty in the next several years, and very likely a corresponding shift in public policy. Or support for the death penalty, which remains strong despite its recent decline, could level out or rebound. We are in a period of doubt and hesitation. All we can say for certain is that there has been a change, and that further change is more possible than it has been for many years.

Appendix: Surveys on General Death Penalty Attitudes

Date	Organization	Question Code	n	% Favor	% Oppose	% Don't Know/NA
Dec-36	GALLUP	01	1500	61	39	
Dec-37	GALLUP	02	1500	60	33	7
Nov-53	GALLUP	03	1498	64	25	11
Apr-56	GALLUP	03	2000	53	34	13
Sep-57	GALLUP	03	1528	47	34	18
Mar-60	GALLUP	03	1535	53	36	11

Date	Organization	Question Code	n	% Favor	% Oppose	% Don't Know/NA
Jan-65	GALLUP	03	2435	45	43	12
May-66	GALLUP	03	1523	42	47	11
Jun-67	GALLUP	03	1518	54	38	8
Jan-69	GALLUP	03	1503	51	40	9
Nov-71	GALLUP	03	1558	49	40	11
Mar-72	GALLUP	03	1513	50	42	9
Apr-72	NORC	04	1613	53	39	8
Nov-72	GALLUP	03	1462	57	32	11
Apr-73	HARRIS	05	1537	59	31	10
Apr-73	NORC	04	1504	60	35	5
Apr-74	NORC	04	1484	63	32	5
Apr-75	NORC	04	1490	60	33	6
Apr-76	NORC	04	1499	66	30	5
Apr-76	GALLUP	03	1540	66	26	7
Dec-76	HARRIS	05	1459	67	25	8
Apr-77	NORC	04	1530	67	26	6
Mar-78	GALLUP	03	1560	62	27	11
Apr-78	NORC	04	1532	66	28	6
Nov-78	NBC/AP	04	1600	66	25	9
Jul-79	NBC/AP	04	1599	65	27	8
Apr-80	NORC	04	1468	67	27	6
Nov-80	LAT	06	1829	62	29	9
Jan-81	GALLUP	07	1030	65	24	11
Feb-81	GALLUP	03	1609	66	25	9
*Apr-81	LAT	06	1406	72	23	5
May-81	ABC/WASH	03	1533	73	20	8
Apr-82	NORC	04	1506	74	21	6
Jun-82	NBC/AP	04	1597	71	20	9
Dec-82	ABC	03	2464	76	19	5
Jan-83	HARRIS	05	1254	68	27	5
Apr-83	NORC	04	1599	73	22	5
Apr-84	NORC	04	1473	70	24	6
Jan-85	GALLUP	03	1523	72	20	8
Feb-85	LAT	11	2993	75	17	8
Apr-85	NORC	04	1534	76	19	5
Nov-85	GALLUP	04	1008	75	17	8
*Jan-86	GALLUP	04	1570	70	22	8
Apr-86	NORC	04	1470	71	24	5
*Jul-86	LAT	11	2405	74	16	10
Apr-87	NORC	04	1466	70	24	6
Apr-88	NORC	04	1481	71	22	7
Sep-88	GALLUP	04	1001	79	16	5
Oct-88	GALLUP	04	1001	79	16	5
Oct-88	CBS/NYT	04	1518	78	14	8
*Jan-89	NES	04	1775	70	18	13

Date	Organization	Question Code	n	% Favor	% Oppose	% Don't Know/NA
Jan-89	CBS/NYT	04	1533	71	20	9
*Mar-89	LAT	11	3583	69	18	13
Apr-89	NORC	04	1537	74	20	6
Jun-89	YANKCS	08	504	75	17	8
Apr-90	NORC	04	1372	75	19	6
Apr-90	CBS/NYT	04	1515	72	20	8
Jul-90	NBC/WSJ	09	1555	71	20	9
Aug-90	CBS/NYT	04	1422	76	15	9
Apr-91	NORC	04	1517	72	22	6
May-91	NBC/WSJ	09	1508	71	18	11
Jun-91	GALLUP	03	990	76	18	6
Nov-91	GALLUP	10	1011	73	21	6
Apr-92	ABC/WASH	04	1003	75	19	6
May-92	NBC/WSJ	09	1118	69	24	7
*Mar-93	TGGL	04	1000	77	18	5
Apr-93	NORC	04	1606	72	21	7
Aug-93	YANK	08	500	77	17	6
May-94	NORC	04	2992	74	20	6
Jul-94	YANK	08	600	78	17	5
Jul-94	NBC/WSJ	09	1005	70	23	7
Sep-94	GALLUP	03	1022	80	16	4
Jan-95	ABC	04	1024	74	19	8
*Jan-95	NES	04	1795	76	18	6
May-95	GALLUP	03	1000	77	13	10
Sep-95	CBS	04	1536	65	21	14
*Apr-96	CSR	19	2047	67	18	15
May-96	NORC	04	2904	71	22	7
Jun-96	PPRI	03	1085	79	21	
*Jun-96	PSRA	17	1975	78	18	4
Aug-96	ABC/WASH	11	1514	77	19	4
*Feb-97	USN	13	1000	70	23	7
May-97	PSRA	04	502	66	21	13
†May-97	FOX	15	900	76	17	7
Jun-97	YANK	08	1024	74	20	6
Jun-97	CBS	04	1021	67	25	8
Jun-97	HARRIS	05	1000	75	22	3
Jun-97	NBC/WSJ	14	2007	69	23	8
†Jun-97	FOX	15	900	73	18	9
Jan-98	FOX	15	904	74	18	8
Jan-98	FOX	15	906	74	19	7
Jun-98	NORC	04	2832	68	25	8
Aug-98	WASH	04	2025	69	27	4
*Jan-99	NES	04	1281	68	27	6
Feb-99	GALLUP	03	1054	71	22	7
Mar-99	RAS	16	1000	68	20	12

Date	Organization	Question Code	n	% Favor	% Oppose	% Don't Know/NA
Jul-99	HARRIS	05	1015	71	21	8
Aug-99	WASH	04	4614	70	26	4
*Sep-99	PSRA	17	1205	74	22	4
Sep-99	TNSI	18	1005	68	25	7
Jan-00	ABC	04	1006	64	27	9
Feb-00	FOX	04	900	67	22	11
Feb-00	GALLUP	03	1050	66	28	6
†Apr-00	NORC	04	2817	63	28	9
May-00	NBC/WSJ	04	1003	62	22	16
Jun-00	ABC	04	1004	63	27	10
†Jun-00	GALLUP	03	1020	66	26	8
Jun-00	FOX	04	900	68	24	8
Jul-00	HARRIS	05	1010	64	25	11
Jul-00	LAT	06	1058	66	28	6
†Aug-00	HART	04	802	60	21	19
Sep-00	GALLUP	03	1012	67	28	5

*Scale-answer questions (see supra note 9)
†Not in Roper Center database (see supra note 4)

Sources

ABC	ABC News
ABC/WASH	ABC News/*Washington Post*
CBS/NYT	CBS News/*New York Times*
CSR	Center for Survey Research, University of Virginia
FOX	Fox News
GALLUP	Gallup Organization
HARRIS	Louis Harris and Associates
HART	Peter Hart Research Associates
LAT	*Los Angeles Times*
NBC/AP	NBC News/Associated Press
NBC/WSJ	NBC News/*Wall Street Journal*
NES	National Election Survey
NORC	National Opinion Research Center
PPRI	Public Policy Research Institute, Texas A&M
PSRA	Princeton Survey Research Associates
RAS	Rasmussan Research
TGGL	Tarrance Group & Greenberg Lake
TNSI	Taylor Nelson Sofres Intersearch
USN	*U.S. News and World Report*
WASH	*Washington Post*
YANK	Yankelovich, Skelly and White
YANKCS	Yankelovich Clancy Shulman

Questions: Code Numbers and Wordings

01 Do you believe in the death penalty for murder?

02 Do you favor or oppose capital punishment for murder?

03 Are you in favor of the death penalty for persons/a person convicted of murder?

04 Do you favor or oppose the death penalty for persons convicted of murder?

05 Do you believe in capital punishment, that is the death penalty, or are you opposed to it?

06 Do you approve or disapprove of the death penalty?

07 Are you in favor of or opposed to the death penalty for persons convicted of murder?

08 Do you, in general, favor or oppose the death penalty for individuals convicted of serious crimes, such as murder?

09 Do you favor or oppose the death penalty?

10 I'm going to read you some proposals that are being discussed around the country, please tell me whether you would favor or oppose it. . . . A death penalty for persons convicted of murder.

11 Generally speaking, are you in favor of the death penalty for persons convicted of murder, or are you opposed to that—or haven't you heard enough about that to say?

12 Do you support or oppose: The death penalty for people who are convicted of murder?

13 I'd like to ask you about some public policy issues. For each issue I read, please tell me if you strongly favor, somewhat favor, somewhat oppose, or strongly oppose it. . . . The death penalty.

14 In general, do you favor or oppose the death penalty?

15 Do you favor or oppose the death penalty for persons convicted of premeditated murder?

16 Should the death penalty be allowed in America today?

17 I'm going to read you a list of programs and proposals that are being discussed in this country today. For each one, please tell me whether you strongly favor, favor, oppose or strongly oppose it. . . . The death penalty for persons convicted of murder.

18 Are you personally in favor or against the use of the death penalty?

19 I'm going to read you some proposals that are now being discussed nationally. As I read each one, please select the number that best expresses how much you favor or oppose it. . . . If you do not really care about one issue, please say so. . . . The death penalty for persons convicted of murder.

2 : CAPITAL PUNISHMENT, FEDERAL COURTS, AND THE WRIT OF HABEAS CORPUS

Larry W. Yackle

The controversy over capital punishment in the United States is entangled with a related debate regarding the role the federal courts should play in the adjudication of death penalty cases. That related quarrel turns on the federal courts' authority to entertain habeas corpus petitions filed by death row prisoners. Historically, the writ of habeas corpus ensured that individuals did not suffer deprivations of liberty without a prompt judicial determination that their incarceration was lawful. In modern times, the writ supplies the principal means by which federal courts consider prisoners' claims that they were convicted and sentenced to death in violation of the United States Constitution.

It is not surprising that the dispute over capital punishment should be accompanied by this important analogue debate. Americans often wrestle with perplexing substantive questions of value by converting them into procedural or structural issues that may be more tractable. Experience shows that the substantive argument between opponents and advocates of the death penalty defies reconciliation. Capital punishment evokes too much symbolism, too many moral, ideological, and religious considerations—and (sadly) too many opportunities for political exploitation. One would have thought, however, that we might find common ground by changing the subject (consciously or unconsciously) and discussing the procedural arrangements for adjudicating capital cases and the involvement of federal authorities in cases in which prisoners were sentenced to death in state court.

Federal habeas corpus is plainly a matter of procedure and political structure. Federal court adjudication of prisoners' claims is itself a procedural safeguard— a second-order procedural means by which to enforce the first-order procedures that are supposed to be observed at the trial and sentencing stages of capital cases in state court. And the procedural safeguard that federal habeas corpus provides touches the structural relationship between the federal government, on the one hand, and the states, on the other. When federal courts entertain habeas petitions from state prisoners on death row, they necessarily exercise federal governmental power with respect to the implementation of local policy—namely, the policy of state-sponsored homicide. The analogue debate over federal habeas corpus thus provides an opportunity to address capital punishment in a different, comparatively dispassionate way.

One might expect that both opponents and advocates of the death penalty would endorse federal habeas corpus. No one would want to execute a person who was convicted or sentenced in violation of the Constitution, far less a person who is ineligible for a death sentence or even innocent but falsely charged, convicted, and condemned. If federal courts can identify errors in capital cases, thoughtful people who agree on little else should recognize that this additional means of avoiding mistakes should be available. Even the most zealous death penalty advocates argue that only a comparative few offenders *deserve* to die. Accordingly, they should embrace federal habeas to see that those offenders, and only those offenders, are put to death. Similarly, both opponents and advocates of the death penalty should acknowledge that this is an instance in which the introduction of federal authority is warranted. The claims that prisoners advance in habeas petitions rest on federal constitutional law—the very law that federal courts should be expected to implement.

As a matter of fact, death penalty advocates typically denounce federal habeas corpus. They are not alarmed that state courts may impose death sentences in violation of federal procedural requirements. Nor are they haunted by the possibility that innocent defendants may be executed by mistake. They insist that state courts provide adequate machinery for processing capital cases and that subsequent adjudication in federal court implies disrespect for the states and their courts. Death penalty advocates suspect that opponents of capital punishment promote federal court consideration of death row prisoners' petitions only to add layers of litigation to capital cases, to postpone lawful executions, and thus to frustrate the death penalty by the back door. Put bluntly, death penalty advocates regard federal habeas corpus as a stratagem of the abolitionist movement.

None of these arguments is telling. It is true that capital cases typically require years of litigation before all questions can be settled and a death sentence, if valid, can be carried out. Yet judicial proceedings in *state* court account for much of the time that death penalty cases consume.[1] If federal court proceedings also require considerable time and effort (and they most certainly do), it is because prisoners' claims are unusually challenging and because the law governing habeas proceedings is needlessly complex. It is also true that state courts frequently identify constitutional errors in their own proceedings and correct those mistakes themselves, obviating any need for prisoners to petition the federal courts. During the period from 1973 to 1995, state courts found serious errors in 47 percent of the cases in which death sentences had been imposed at the trial level. Yet all too often state courts overlook violations of prisoners' federal rights. During the same period, 1973 to 1995, federal courts found serious errors in 40 percent of the *remaining* cases, that is, the cases in which state courts had previously affirmed convictions and death sentences.[2] It may be that in some of those cases federal courts were excessively solicitous of prisoners' rights and resolved doubts in their favor. Yet if federal courts correctly identified violations in a nontrivial number of cases, the costs of federal litigation were more than offset. The empirical evidence is overwhelming. Defendants are convicted and sentenced in violation of their constitutional rights; state courts often take no corrective action; and the only practical means of avoiding erroneous executions is federal habeas corpus.

Nevertheless, support for capital punishment goes hand in hand with resistance to federal habeas corpus. Over the last quarter of the twentieth century, death sentences have become more common in many states and routine in some, particularly in the South. Over the same period, the Supreme Court has tightly circumscribed federal court adjudication of death row prisoners' claims. Congress has not only endorsed and fortified the Court's decisions but also restricted habeas even more by the enactment of the Anti-terrorism and Effective Death Penalty Act of 1996 (AEDPA).[3] Curbs on federal habeas are paradoxical. Federal court authority should have been fortified in order to address the growing body of capital cases. Instead, federal court capacity to do this important work has been compromised.

The restrictions that the Court and Congress have placed on federal habeas

---

1. The estimated average period of time from the imposition of a death sentence to the execution of a condemned prisoner is eleven years. Approximately five of those years are devoted to direct review in state appellate courts, and an indeterminate further period is devoted to subsequent postconviction proceedings in state trial and appellate courts. See James S. Liebman, "The Overproduction of Death," 100 *Colum. L. Rev.* 2030, 2119 n.219 (2000).

2. Id. at 2052.

3. Pub. L. No. 104-132, 110 Stat. 1214 (1996).

corpus are also perverse. They are ostensibly meant either to streamline and expedite federal habeas proceedings or to accommodate state interests. On examination, however, many restrictive doctrines and statutes actually make federal proceedings more complex and protracted. Some frustrate the very state interests they are supposed to celebrate. This is true of a host of AEDPA's provisions. Through superficial analysis, poor drafting, or conscious design, that act introduces mind-numbing complications that would be amusing in any other context but are in fact agonizing where capital punishment is concerned. At this point, we have the worst of all possible worlds: a rising tide of death penalty cases coupled with restrictive rules that frustrate the federal courts' ability to prevent erroneous executions for no rhyme or reason.

This chapter explains how we have come to this pass and describes some of the most important impediments to federal court adjudication in death penalty cases now in place. The first part describes the way that death penalty cases reach the federal courts, explains why the vehicle for federal court adjudication is the writ of habeas corpus, and outlines the way in which federal habeas litigation in death penalty cases has developed over the last twenty-five years. The second part discusses the many ways in which doctrines established by the Supreme Court and statutes enacted by Congress impede the federal courts' ability to adjudicate capital cases, squandering time and effort into the bargain.

Why Habeas Corpus?

In the main, the death penalty in the United States is a matter of state law and policy. Defendants are typically charged with state offenses and are then tried, convicted, and sentenced in state court.[4] In those state proceedings, however, the due process clause of the Fourteenth Amendment to the United States Constitution requires state officials to observe a variety of procedural standards.[5] Defendants in capital cases are entitled to the same federal constitu-

---

4. The federal government also authorizes capital punishment in specified instances. Prisoners who are charged with federal offenses are tried and sentenced in federal court. In 1948 Congress largely eliminated the ability of federal convicts to attack their convictions and sentences by means of habeas corpus, but authorized them to employ a motion procedure that performs the same function. The Supreme Court has held that a motion pursuant to 28 U.S.C. § 2255 provides federal prisoners with an instrument for attacking their convictions and sentences that is "commensurate" with the writ of habeas corpus employed by prisoners convicted and sentenced in state court. See Hill v. United States, 368 U.S. 424, 427 (1962).

5. U.S. Const. amend. XIV: "[N]or shall any State deprive any person of life, liberty, or property, without due process of law."

tional safeguards that defendants in serious noncapital cases enjoy. Familiar illustrations include the right to counsel, recognized by the Supreme Court in *Gideon v. Wainwright*;[6] the right to know of any evidence in the hands of the prosecution that would be helpful to the defense, established in *Brady v. Maryland*;[7] and the right to be free of unreasonable searches and seizures, secured in *Mapp v. Ohio*.[8] The basic procedural safeguards applicable in all cases sometimes take on special meaning when prosecutors seek a death sentence. For example, the Court held in *Witherspoon v. Illinois*[9] that the right to trial by jury is violated in a capital case if potential jurors are excluded because they express moral reservations about the death penalty.

In addition, defendants in capital cases are entitled to special procedural protections established by the Eighth Amendment's prohibition on cruel and unusual punishments. The most important of those safeguards is the principle, first recognized in *Furman v. Georgia*,[10] that states cannot leave the decision whether a defendant lives or dies to the unbridled discretion of a judge or a jury. Next in line is the general expectation, approved in *Gregg v. Georgia*,[11] that capital trials should be bifurcated. In the first phase of the proceedings, the judge or jury determines whether a defendant is guilty as charged; in the second phase, the judge or jury determines, in light of aggravating and mitigating considerations, whether the defendant should be sentenced to death.

Defendants who contend that any of these federal safeguards has been violated may present their objections to the state judges who preside at the trial and sentencing stages of the process in state court. If defendants are convicted and sentenced notwithstanding constitutional objections, they usually can press their federal claims on appeal to state appellate courts, in further state "postconviction" proceedings, and (theoretically) in petitions for review in the United States Supreme Court.[12] The Supreme Court is able to accept only a few of the

6. 372 U.S. 335 (1963).

7. 373 U.S. 83 (1963).

8. 367 U.S. 643 (1961).

9. 391 U.S. 510 (1968).

10. 408 U.S. 238 (1972).

11. 428 U.S. 153 (1976).

12. Postconviction proceedings in state court typically take the form of a petition or motion addressed to the court in which a prisoner was convicted, seeking an order vacating the conviction or sentence on the basis of new grounds that did not come to light at trial or on appeal from the conviction. The Supreme Court has appellate jurisdiction to review state court judgments in criminal cases for errors of federal law. See 28 U.S.C. § 1257.

many cases competing for its attention.[13] In most instances, accordingly, defendants sentenced to death in state court can advance federal claims in federal court only if they are permitted to proceed in a court further down in the federal hierarchy—usually a United States district court.[14] Defendants who claim that their federal rights were violated in state court cannot appeal directly to a federal district court.[15] Yet pursuant to the Habeas Corpus Act of 1867, they can petition a federal district court for a writ of habeas corpus on the theory that state authorities are holding them in custody in violation of the Constitution.[16]

The writ of habeas corpus has a long and rich history in English and American law.[17] A petition for the writ initiates an original civil lawsuit, naming as the

13. Every year, the Supreme Court receives thousands of applications for appellate review in all manner of cases. The Court selects cases that present questions of broad significance, transcending the circumstances of individual litigants. In a real sense, then, the Court accepts cases not to correct lower court mistakes *in those cases*, but rather to use the selected cases as vehicles for elaborating federal law for society at large.

14. There is at least one federal district court in every state. Generally speaking, district court judgments are reviewable in one of twelve circuit courts of appeals. Circuit court judgments, in turn, are (typically) reviewable in the Supreme Court. But, here again, the Supreme Court accepts review only in cases that present questions of broad public interest.

15. See Rooker v. Fidelity Trust Co., 263 U.S. 413, 416 (1923) (explaining that federal district courts have no appellate jurisdiction to review state court judgments for error).

16. See 28 U.S.C. § 2241(3). The Habeas Corpus Act was part of the great body of civil rights laws enacted in the Reconstruction era. Commentators are divided over whether the Suspension Clause, U.S. Const., art. I, § 9, cl.2, provides a constitutional basis for federal court jurisdiction, which would empower federal courts to entertain habeas corpus petitions from death row prisoners even if § 2241(3) did not exist.

17. The origins of habeas corpus can be traced to the early central courts in England. Initially, those courts issued the writ to obtain the presence of individuals so that matters in which they were involved could be adjudicated. Later, the common law courts (King's Bench and Common Pleas) used the writ to draw litigation away from local manorial courts and to bring cases under the king's central authority. Later still, those courts also relied on the writ in their competition with Chancery, which administered the king's equity. In the typical scenario, Chancery issued an injunction forbidding a would-be litigant to sue in the law courts and, if he failed to comply, ordered him imprisoned for contempt. Then, the law courts protected their own turf by issuing the writ of habeas corpus to discharge the prisoner and allow him to sue, after all. Ultimately, English courts used the writ to challenge the king's own prerogatives. In the seventeenth century, John Selden and Lord Coke argued that habeas corpus was a procedural device for enforcing the thirty-ninth chapter of Magna Charta, which, by their (creative) account, barred the king from summarily sending Englishmen to the Tower of London. According to Selden and Coke, imprisonment at the king's command alone violated the "law of the land," which Coke abbrevi-

respondent a state official responsible for the prisoner's incarceration (usually the prison warden).[18] The petition claims that the respondent is holding the prisoner in custody on the basis of a criminal conviction or sentence obtained or imposed in violation of the prisoner's federal constitutional rights. The respondent, in turn, proffers that very conviction or sentence as a lawful explanation for the prisoner's detention. A federal court entertaining a petition is not (typically) concerned about whether the prisoner is guilty or innocent. Nor does the federal court presume (formally) to review a previous state court determination of the prisoner's claims and decide whether the state court's conclusions were correct. Yet when the federal court evaluates the prisoner's claims and compares them to the respondent's explanation for the prisoner's custody, the court necessarily examines federal issues that were or might have been decided previously in state court. In the end, then, federal habeas corpus is a means by which death row inmates can ask federal courts to revisit prior state court determinations of federal constitutional claims.

The explanation for this arrangement is historical and functional. Federal habeas corpus for state prisoners is largely the product of the Supreme Court's efforts (prior to the 1970s) to improve the quality of state criminal justice. The basic story can be found in the Court's handling of three famous cases: *Frank v. Mangum* in 1915,[19] *Moore v. Dempsey* in 1923,[20] and *Brown v. Allen* in 1953.[21]

Early on, the Court took the view that the procedural safeguards for criminal cases listed in the Bill of Rights (including, for example, the right to counsel and the right to trial by jury) were applicable only to prosecutions by the federal government and not to prosecutions by individual states. The Court recognized

---

ated as "due process." The English Habeas Corpus Act of 1679 established procedures for using the writ routinely to prevent the Crown from holding prisoners in jail for lengthy periods awaiting trial. Thereafter, Parliament occasionally denied the writ ad hoc in cases of "high treason." On the whole, however, habeas corpus continued to develop as the Great Writ of Liberty.

18. In classic English practice, the writ of habeas corpus was not itself an order requiring the respondent to release a prisoner. It was a preliminary order requiring the respondent to produce the prisoner in court so that the validity of his or her detention could be determined. If the court concluded that the prisoner was held unlawfully, the court issued another order actually commanding the prisoner's release. In modern practice, federal courts almost never issue the writ as a means of obtaining a prisoner's presence in court. Instead, a prisoner's application for the writ is treated much like the complaint in an ordinary civil lawsuit.

19. 237 U.S. 309 (1915).

20. 261 U.S. 86 (1923).

21. 344 U.S. 443 (1953).

that the due process clause of the Fourteenth Amendment required states to give criminal defendants some kind of process. But the process that was "due" was minimal. Accordingly, defendants who were convicted of state offenses in state court could not petition the federal courts for a writ of habeas corpus claiming that state courts had failed to comply with some particular provision of the Bill of Rights. They could claim only that their trials were fundamentally unfair and that the state appellate courts had refused to consider their claims of unfairness.

The decision in *Frank v. Mangum* is the classic illustration. Leo Frank was sentenced to die for murdering a young girl in his factory in Atlanta. He was almost certainly innocent. His mob-dominated trial forms one of the most notorious episodes of anti-Semitism in American history.[22] Nevertheless, the Supreme Court held that Frank was not entitled to habeas corpus relief. According to the Court, the Georgia Supreme Court had accorded him the process that was due when it had considered his complaints about the trial on appeal from his conviction.[23] Justice Oliver Wendell Holmes dissented. According to Holmes, the proceedings against Frank in state court had been an "empty shell," masking the truth. Holmes insisted that federal habeas was a means of cutting through that shell and addressing the gross mistreatment that Frank had suffered.

In *Moore v. Dempsey*, Justice Holmes persuaded the full Court that he had been right in *Frank*. The *Moore* case grew out of a famous incident at Hoop Spur, Arkansas. A gang of white men hired by local landowners attacked black tenant farmers planning to form a union. Some blacks fought back. After the fighting, local authorities charged five black men with murdering several whites. Blacks were excluded both from the grand jury that indicted the defendants and from the trial jury that convicted them and sentenced them to die. A threatening crowd of whites surrounded the court room. The trial judge appointed a single lawyer to represent all five defendants. That lawyer did not consult with his clients. He filed no motions and called no witnesses. He declined even to put the defendants themselves on the stand to tell their side of the story. The trial lasted forty-five minutes, and the jury took just five minutes more to return guilty verdicts and death sentences.[24]

The Arkansas Supreme Court concluded that the defendants had been treated

22. For a full account of the story, see Leonard Dinnerstein, *The Leo Frank Case* (1968).

23. The relationship the Court saw in *Frank* between the meaning of due process and the availability of federal habeas corpus was actually a bit more subtle. See Larry W. Yackle, "The Habeas Hagioscope," 66 *S. Cal. L. Rev.* 2331, 2339–41 (1993).

24. For a full account, see Richard C. Cortner, *A Mob Intent on Death* (1988).

fairly. But when the five convicts petitioned for federal habeas corpus relief, Justice Holmes wrote the Supreme Court's opinion holding that the writ was available and that the petitioners were entitled to a federal hearing on their claims. According to Holmes, the federal constitutional errors at trial were glaring. The Arkansas Supreme Court had brushed aside the defendants' race-discrimination claims because their court-appointed lawyer had failed to object soon enough and had rejected their claim that the jury had been influenced by the mob because the trial procedures were formally correct. That was insufficient. Holmes abandoned the Court's sterile understanding of habeas corpus in *Frank* and substituted a fundamentally different conception: Federal courts could entertain petitions from state prisoners advancing federal constitutional claims that the state appellate courts had rejected.

The Supreme Court solidified that conception of habeas in *Brown v. Allen*. The petitioners in *Brown* raised a host of constitutional claims about their treatment at trial in state court. The Court ultimately denied relief on the merits of all those claims. Yet in the process the Court elaborated a framework for habeas corpus litigation that would last through the two decades to follow. The Court explained, first, that all federal constitutional claims were cognizable in federal habeas corpus; second, that federal district courts entertaining petitions from state prisoners were empowered to make their own determinations of the facts underlying prisoners' claims; and, third, that district courts were entitled to exercise independent judgment regarding those claims, notwithstanding previous state court decisions finding them without merit. With *Brown*, federal habeas corpus came of age as a general means by which state prisoners could litigate federal claims in federal court.[25]

There followed an extraordinary period in modern American constitutional history. In the 1960s, under the leadership of Chief Justice Earl Warren and Justice William Brennan, the Supreme Court interpreted the due process clause of the Fourteenth Amendment to require state courts to respect most of the Bill of Rights safeguards that previously had been mandatory only in cases in which the federal government prosecuted defendants for violations of federal law. It was in that period that the Court rendered its famous decisions in *Gideon*, *Brady*, and *Mapp*. Building on *Brown*, the Court held that federal district courts had habeas corpus jurisdiction to enforce those and other procedural safeguards. The Warren Court recognized, however, that it could not police fifty

25. See Paul M. Bator, "Finality in Criminal Law and Federal Habeas Corpus for State Prisoners," 76 *Harv. L. Rev.* 441 (1963).

state courts by itself and, accordingly, turned to federal district courts as surrogates. The Court ensured that habeas proceedings in the district courts would provide the practical federal judicial machinery for implementing its innovations in constitutional criminal procedure.

All three of the formative cases (*Frank, Moore,* and *Brown*) involved state prisoners under sentence of death. The stakes in those cases undoubtedly influenced the Court's thinking. Still, the Warren Court did not orchestrate the evolution of federal habeas primarily as a mechanism for federal adjudication of death penalty cases. There were comparatively few prisoners on death row at that time; federal courts received relatively few habeas petitions from those prisoners; and, in the wake of the *Furman* decision in 1972, it appeared that death sentences would soon cease to be imposed in this country.[26] In the 1970s, however, public enthusiasm for capital punishment surged, and capital cases reached federal district courts in increasing numbers. In 1976 the Court held in *Gregg* that capital punishment was not per se a violation of the Eighth Amendment and could be employed so long as certain safeguards were observed—for example, the bifurcation of the proceedings into guilt-determination and sentencing phases. Since then, habeas corpus proceedings in the district courts have been inextricably linked with the death penalty.

The justices who served on the Supreme Court during the Warren era developed constitutional safeguards and habeas corpus in a creative way to ensure that federal courts enforced federal constitutional rights. By contrast, the justices who joined the Court in the 1970s exercised equally active imaginations in an effort to restrict federal court authority. Soon after President Nixon's appointees arrived, the Court's decisions touching both criminal procedure and habeas corpus began to change. William Rehnquist in particular lamented the "costs" of federal habeas litigation, complained that "a single federal judge" could reexamine claims previously rejected by a state appellate court, and insisted that death row prisoners filed federal habeas petitions only to postpone their execution.[27] The Court's assault on habeas corpus accelerated after Rehnquist became chief justice. New members of the court named by Presidents Ronald Reagan and George Bush (the senior) offered the chief justice their enthusiastic support.

During the Warren Court years, Congress embraced the Court's decisions

26. See Austin Sarat, "Recapturing the Spirit of *Furman*: The American Bar Association and the New Abolitionist Politics," *Law & Contemp. Probs.*, Autumn 1998, at 5 (recalling post-*Furman* events).

27. Sumner v. Mata, 449 U.S. 539, 543–44 (1981) (opinion of Rehnquist, J.).

fostering aggressive federal court adjudication of federal constitutional rights. As late as 1977 Congress adopted a special set of procedural rules to be followed by district judges handling habeas petitions from state prisoners in light of the Court's existing precedents. Those rules sometimes restricted federal adjudication, but only to ensure that federal claims were processed efficiently.[28] In time, however, critics of federal habeas corpus introduced bills meant largely to eliminate the federal courts' authority. The Nixon administration promoted a proposal that would have overruled the decisions in *Moore* and *Brown* and revived the conception of habeas corpus stated in *Frank v. Mangum*. The Reagan and Bush administrations sponsored not only that proposal but also a variety of other measures meant to restrict federal habeas in capital cases. The Reagan and Bush bills were hotly debated in many congressional sessions. In the end, Congress enacted AEDPA in 1996.[29] Some provisions in that act essentially incorporate Rehnquist Court decisions limiting the writ; others impose additional restrictions. Some provisions apply to all habeas corpus cases; others address only death penalty cases.[30]

Curbs on the Writ

The Rehnquist Court and Congress have assaulted federal habeas corpus on three general fronts. First, the Court has limited the content of many of the constitutional rights that prisoners seek to vindicate in federal court and, in so doing, has sometimes largely excluded certain claims from the purview of federal habeas. Second, the Court and Congress have restricted federal court authority to address and vindicate constitutional claims that state courts "reasonably" have (or might have) rejected. Third, both the Court and Congress have erected procedural hurdles that petitioners must clear in order to press constitutional claims in federal court.

28. For an account, see Larry W. Yackle, *Postconviction Remedies* 430–32 (1981).

29. See Yackle, supra note 23, at 2350–73 (discussing prior bills).

30. The provisions of AEDPA exclusively addressing capital cases are collected in a special chapter of the United States Code, Chapter 154 of Title 28, United States Code, 28 U.S.C. § 2261–61, which is applicable only to cases arising from states that trigger Chapter 154 by establishing a system for providing indigent death row prisoners with competent and properly compensated counsel in *state* postconviction proceedings. Since states are unwilling to provide properly paid counsel, the provisions in Chapter 154 have yet to come into play in any jurisdiction. See Ashmus v. Woodford, 202 F.3d 1160 (9th Cir. 2000) (finding California's system inadequate); see also notes 39 and 85 and accompanying text.

Limits on Claims

The Rehnquist Court has often curbed death row prisoners' ability to obtain federal habeas corpus relief in the most direct way—by circumscribing the federal constitutional rights to which criminal defendants are entitled in the first instance. The Court's decisions elaborating the right to counsel provide the best and most important illustration. The Court has adhered to the basic principle in *Gideon* that defendants in felony cases are entitled to professional representation at the trial and sentencing stages of state proceedings. Similarly, the Court has held that defendants who are convicted are constitutionally entitled to counsel on direct review in the state appellate courts.[31] Yet the Court has refused to hold lawyers to any serious standard of excellence and thus has rendered the constitutional right to a lawyer little more than a false hope, especially in death penalty cases.

The popular image of defense attorneys is largely a myth. The clever shyster bent on getting his guilty client off on a technicality is a creature of bad novels and television dramas, not authentic police stations and court rooms. To be sure, good defense lawyers are advocates for their clients. Yet the point of the constitutional right to counsel is not to *evade* the truth but rather to *determine* the truth by means of the traditional adversary model of American justice. Professional police investigators and prosecutors develop evidence against the accused, prefer charges, and present the state's case at trial in a manner calculated to achieve a conviction and, in a capital case, a death sentence. The danger is not that unscrupulous police officers and state's attorneys willfully condemn innocent people, though bogus criminal prosecutions do occur.[32] The genuine danger is that honest officers and prosecutors make mistakes. In our adversary system, defense lawyers test the state's evidence, probe for weaknesses, and offer counterevidence that may raise reasonable doubts about a defendant's guilt or eligibility for capital punishment. The idea is to pit professional against professional, each attempting to poke holes in the story told by the other, so that the jury can decide for itself whether a defendant committed the offense of which he or she is charged.

In the real world of death penalty litigation, defense lawyers often fail to provide effective professional representation—or anything like it. None of the

31. See Douglas v. California, 372 U.S. 353 (1963).

32. See, e.g., Lou Cannon, "One Bad Cop," *N.Y. Times Mag.*, Oct. 1, 2000, at 32 (describing instances in which police officers in the Ramparts section of Los Angeles framed innocent people by manufacturing phony "evidence").

states in which capital punishment is routinely employed has a professional public defender system. Typically, trial judges appoint any private lawyers in the vicinity who are willing to work for the grossly inadequate fees the state allows. Those lawyers sometimes perform little better than the attorney in *Moore v. Dempsey*. Through ignorance or neglect, they make serious errors that jeopardize the accuracy and constitutionality of state trials.

The Rehnquist Court has acknowledged that the right to counsel must contemplate professional representation that meets some constitutional test of competence. Yet in *Strickland v. Washington*[33] the Court held that the criteria for constitutionally acceptable legal work are extremely generous to the lawyers concerned. Prisoners can establish ineffective assistance of counsel only by showing, first, that a lawyer's work "fell below an objective standard of reasonableness" and, second, that counsel's deficient performance resulted in "actual prejudice."

In practice, lawyers who display the most shocking ignorance of the law, who commit the most unconscionable acts of negligence, and who offer the most hollow excuses for their shortcomings, nonetheless satisfy the initial "performance" part of the *Strickland* test.[34] When counsel's behavior is bad enough to fail the "performance" component of the test, the Court has rarely been willing to find "actual prejudice." According to the Rehnquist Court, "prejudice" can be established only if there is a "reasonable probability that, but for counsel's unprofessional errors, the result of the proceeding would have been different."[35] This is to say, a prisoner can succeed on a claim of ineffective assistance of counsel only if he or she proves (after the fact) that a defense lawyer's admittedly unprofessional performance probably produced a conviction or a capital sentence when better legal work would have achieved an acquittal or a sentence other than death.

The loose *Strickland* criteria for counsel services not only enfeeble the right to counsel itself but also undermine other constitutional safeguards that defense lawyers are expected to advance. Defense attorneys bear responsibility for monitoring the proceedings and raising constitutional objections at the proper time and in the proper way. For example, defense counsel is expected to object if jurors are excluded in violation of the *Witherspoon* rule, if the prosecution withholds evidence in violation of *Brady v. Maryland*, or if the prosecution attempts to

33. 466 U.S. 668 (1984).

34. For illustrations, see Stephen B. Bright, "Counsel for the Poor: The Death Sentence Not for the Worst Crime but for the Worst Lawyer," 103 *Yale L.J.* 1835 (1994).

35. *Strickland*, 466 U.S. at 694.

introduce illegally seized evidence in violation of *Mapp v. Ohio*. If counsel defaults in those responsibilities, defendants typically forfeit their rights.[36]

The Rehnquist Court has often recognized the connection between effective defense attorneys and other constitutional rights, but has never acknowledged that *Strickland* deprives defendants of any real capacity to demand that lawyers do what is expected of them. Moreover, in some instances the Court has assumed that defense counsel will perform well and, for that (specious) reason, has given defendants' constitutional rights an extremely narrow interpretation. In *Barefoot v. Estelle*,[37] for example, the Court rejected a prisoner's contention that a state trial court had violated the Fourteenth Amendment by allowing a psychologist to testify that the prisoner would present a danger to others if he were not put to death. The Court acknowledged that the testimony had little basis: The psychologist had never so much as interviewed the prisoner; his predictions about the prisoner's future behavior were pure speculation. Nevertheless, the Court insisted that defense counsel could explain all that to the jury and, accordingly, that there was no sufficient reason for finding the testimony inadmissible.

Decisions like *Strickland* and *Barefoot* create an insoluble dilemma. On the one hand, prisoners must rely on defense lawyers to challenge invalid, unfair, and unreliable evidence introduced against them. That is true even to the point that some questionable prosecution tactics are permitted on the assumption that defense lawyers will protect their clients' interests. On the other hand, prisoners are unable to require defense counsel actually to play their part. Prisoners can petition for federal habeas corpus relief on the ground that they have received ineffective assistance of counsel. But *Strickland* sets a woefully low threshold for defense counsel's performance and, even then, requires prisoners to demonstrate that counsel's mistakes were so devastating that they probably made the difference between conviction and acquittal or between a capital sentence and a term of years.

Counsel services are usually no better after the trial, sentencing, and appellate stages are completed. The Rehnquist Court has refused to extend the constitutional right to counsel, such as it is, to subsequent proceedings. When prisoners seek relief in state postconviction proceedings, in federal habeas corpus, or in the Supreme Court itself, they are entitled to counsel only if the relevant state or the federal government decides as a matter of policy that law-

36. See infra text accompanying notes 78–85.
37. 463 U.S. 880 (1983).

yers should be appointed.[38] Some states provide for counsel to assist prisoners under sentence of death in state postconviction proceedings, and a federal statute authorizes counsel for death row prisoners who wish to file federal habeas corpus petitions.[39] Many state courts and all federal courts also have statutory (or inherent) authority to appoint lawyers at their discretion. Nevertheless, in the absence of a general constitutional right to effective counsel at the advanced stages of the process, prisoners under sentence of death often go unrepresented. Young men from the streets are scarcely equipped to marshal sophisticated constitutional claims, advance those claims in court, and contend with aggressive states' attorneys. Accordingly, they may well suffer execution when they would have lived if they had been represented by genuine professionals.[40]

When states choose to supply lawyers at the postconviction stage of the process in state court, the lawyers they provide are not required to meet even the forgiving *Strickland* standards.[41] All too often, those lawyers render incompetent representation, once again defeating the very point of providing counsel to prisoners in the first place. States appoint poor lawyers, invite prisoners to place their trust in those lawyers, and then make prisoners suffer the consequences of whatever misrepresentation the lawyers they get actually deliver. Some prisoners are fortunate enough to obtain effective volunteer counsel from the American Bar Association's Death Penalty Postconviction Representation Project. Yet the demand for pro bono legal services far exceeds the supply.[42]

38. See Murray v. Giarratano, 492 U.S. 1 (1989) (plurality opinion) (stating that there is no constitutional right to counsel in state postconviction proceedings even in death penalty cases); Ross v. Moffitt, 417 U.S. 600 (1974) (holding that there is no constitutional right to counsel for purposes of seeking review in the Supreme Court); see also Norris v. Wainwright, 588 F.2d 130 (5th Cir.), cert. denied, 444 U.S. 846 (1979) (confirming the understanding that there is no constitutional right to counsel in federal habeas corpus proceedings).

39. Some states provide counsel at the postconviction stage in state court in hopes of triggering the special rules for death penalty cases in federal court, established by AEDPA. See supra note 30. No state has been successful in that effort, however, primarily because no state is willing both to supply lawyers and to pay them reasonable fees. For federal court authority to appoint counsel in federal habeas proceedings, see 21 U.S.C. § 848.

40. Some state statutes authorize the appointment of counsel only if prisoners themselves first establish that they have claims that show some merit. Where that is true, prisoners are deprived of the very professional assistance they need to prepare petitions in the first place. The Supreme Court has avoided that anomalous result with respect to 18 U.S.C. § 848. See McFarland v. Scott, 512 U.S. 849 (1994) (holding that district courts have authority to stay executions in order to give counsel appointed under § 848 an opportunity to prepare a petition).

41. See Coleman v. Thompson, 501 U.S. 722 (1991).

42. At one time, Congress financed a variety of organizations that provided competent counsel

Finally, sad to say, prisoners' chances for effective litigation are bleak even when competent lawyers can be recruited to provide effective assistance at the postconviction and habeas corpus stages. Arriving so late in the day, the best of attorneys often can do little for their clients unless they prevail on courts to give them more time. Requests for stays of execution, in turn, evoke charges that lawyers are manipulating legal proceedings simply to put off executions as long as possible. Accordingly, good lawyers must rush to identify and present potentially meritorious claims that were overlooked earlier because prisoners either were not represented at all in prior proceedings or were represented by incompetent lawyers who did them more harm than good. This is largely why death penalty litigation is so maddeningly inefficient. Capital cases are almost always back-loaded because competent lawyers enter the process so late (if they enter the process at all).

The Rehnquist Court has also restricted federal habeas corpus by excluding some claims from the writ's purview. The Warren Court held in *Mapp v. Ohio* that evidence seized in violation of the Fourth Amendment must be excluded from criminal trials in state court. In *Stone v. Powell*,[43] however, the Rehnquist Court held that prisoners ordinarily cannot seek federal habeas corpus relief on the ground that illegally seized evidence was introduced at trial in violation of the *Mapp* "exclusionary rule." According to *Stone*, federal district courts can consider exclusionary rule claims only if prisoners were denied an "opportunity" for "full and fair adjudication" of those claims in state court.

In *Herrera v. Collins*,[44] the Rehnquist Court held that claims of "actual innocence" are also usually barred from federal habeas corpus. The *Herrera* case was startling. The prisoner offered substantial new evidence that he had not committed the offense of which he was charged and that he had been convicted and sentenced to death by mistake. According to sworn affidavits, someone else had actually killed the victim. Yet, by the Court's account, the prisoner's claim was not cognizable because the affidavits did not establish a violation of any of the federal procedural safeguards to which criminal defendants are entitled. The Court assumed, for purposes of argument, that if the state courts flatly refused to consider "truly persuasive" new evidence showing a prisoner's actual inno-

---

to death-sentenced prisoners at the postconviction stage. In 1996, however, Congress terminated funds for those programs. For an account of that story and a state-by-state report on unmet current needs, see Janice Bergmann, "The Crisis in Postconviction Representation in Capital Cases since the Elimination by Congress of Funding for the Postconviction Defender Organizations" (unpublished report, June 1999).

43. 428 U.S. 465 (1976).

44. 506 U.S. 390 (1993).

cence, a federal court might entertain a habeas corpus petition in order to fore-
stall the execution of an entirely innocent person. But it was abundantly clear
that the justices thought it most unlikely that a case fitting that description
would arise.[45]

Limits on Federal Court Authority

Both the Rehnquist Court and Congress have impeded death row prisoners'
ability to obtain habeas relief by restricting federal court authority regarding
claims that were rejected when prisoners were in state court. These developments represent a violent shift from *Brown v. Allen*, which held that federal
courts were not obliged to give effect to previous state court decisions and,
instead, had a duty to exercise their own independent judgment on the merits of
prisoners' claims. The Court has proceeded by indirection. Congress has been
more straightforward.

The Rehnquist court's decisions

The Rehnquist Court has undermined *Brown v. Allen* by manipulating the law
governing the retroactive application of newly established rules of constitutional criminal procedure. The retroactivity issue is real enough. It arises when
the Supreme Court renders a decision establishing a new procedural safeguard
for the conduct of criminal cases. By hypothesis, there will be prisoners who
were denied that safeguard when they were convicted and sentenced prior to the
Court's decision. If the new procedural rule is given retroactive effect, those
prisoners may contend that they are now in custody in violation of federal law
as it currently stands, even if previously their detention was understood to be
lawful. The means by which prisoners seek the benefits of a change in the law is
typically habeas corpus.

The Warren Court recognized that some of its decisions about the meaning of

---

45. Recall that federal courts entertaining habeas petitions are not empowered to second-guess
jury verdicts. Instead, they examine claims that the trials that produced guilty verdicts were
conducted in violation of federal criminal procedure rules. The object of the Bill of Rights, and of
federal habeas corpus as a device for enforcing the Bill of Rights, is to guard against erroneous
convictions and sentences indirectly—by enforcing procedural safeguards meant to generate
accurate verdicts. Nevertheless, the Court's form-over-substance discussion in *Herrera* was
chilling. Bluntly stated, *Herrera* left the impression that the Rehnquist Court was so hesitant to
open the federal courts to capital cases that it could countenance the execution of a prisoner
whose actual guilt was in doubt.

the Fourteenth Amendment broke sharply from the past and, if applied retrospectively, would upset numerous previous convictions obtained under criminal procedure rules that had been valid in their day. To avoid that result, the Warren Court sometimes declined to apply "clear break" decisions to cases in which prisoners had been convicted and sentenced earlier. For example, the Court refused to enforce retroactively the exclusionary rule established in *Mapp*.[46] In the main, however, the Warren Court gave its innovations retrospective reach.[47] That approach had important consequences in death penalty cases. When, for example, the Court rendered the decisions in *Witherspoon* and *Gregg*, prisoners who had been convicted and sentenced previously were typically able to win habeas corpus relief on the basis of the new principles established in those cases.[48]

The Rehnquist Court has adopted an entirely different approach to the retroactivity question. In *Teague v. Lane*,[49] the Court held that federal habeas courts ordinarily can enforce only the criminal procedure rules that were in place when prisoners' convictions were affirmed on appellate review. According to this Court, state courts can be faulted only for failing to respect federal procedural rules that were well established at the time they acted on prisoners' claims. Therefore, federal courts entertaining habeas petitions later should not enforce "new" rules of criminal procedure recognized more recently, except in certain rare circumstances.[50]

At first glance, *Teague* might appear to be of no great practical moment. This right-of-center Court rarely announces changes in criminal procedure that benefit criminal defendants. One would think, then, that very few claims will be excluded from habeas corpus on the theory that they depend on "new" rules. In fact, *Teague* has significant practical implications, because the Court's conception of "new" rules has astonishing breadth. Habeas petitioners do not have to ask a federal district court to be very imaginative at all in order to be charged with inviting the court to create a novel rule of criminal procedure. The precedents in place at the time a prisoner's conviction became final must have "dic-

46. See Linkletter v. Walker, 381 U.S. 618 (1965).

47. For a discussion of the Warren Court's reasoning, see Yackle, supra note 23, at 2349.

48. See *Witherspoon*, 391 U.S. at 523 n.22 (explaining that the Court's decision would be applicable retrospectively).

49. 489 U.S. 288 (1989).

50. The Court recognizes only two exceptions to the usual prohibition on "new rule" claims: (1) new rules that place "certain kinds of primary, private individual conduct beyond the power of the criminal law-making authority to proscribe," and (2) rules "without which the likelihood of an accurate conviction is seriously diminished." *Teague*, 489 U.S. at 311, 313.

tated"[51] a judgment that the prisoner was entitled to relief on the basis of a rule of criminal procedure that existed even then. Otherwise, the Court insists that a federal habeas court would have to create a "new" rule in order to find the prisoner's claim meritorious today. Moreover, a federal court's "application" of a settled rule to the facts of an analogous case may also "involve a new rule of law."[52] That is so, according to the Court, because even a settled rule can be "extended" if it is applied in a "novel setting."[53]

Moving on from these premises, the Rehnquist Court has declared that if the precedents did *not* "dictate" a favorable decision for a prisoner when his or her case was in state court, it must follow that there was room for reasonable disagreement about the proper result. A state court, accordingly, could "reasonably" conclude that the prisoner's claim was without merit, even if, in hindsight, it appears that the Supreme Court itself would have sustained the prisoner's argument (if the case had reached the Court on direct review). That being so, a federal habeas court must create a "new" rule of criminal procedure in order to depart from a previous state court judgment that was "reasonable" at the time it was entered—"reasonable," that is, in the special *Teague* sense that then-existing precedents did not plainly foreclose the state court's decision.

The Rehnquist Court's expansive account of "new" rules of criminal procedure threatens to capture *all* claims advanced in federal habeas petitions—both claims seeking incremental developments in the content of constitutional safeguards and claims seeking the application of well-established safeguards to particular cases. On occasion, the Court admits as much. In *O'Dell v. Netherland*,[54] for example, the Court summed things up this way: "[Federal courts] will not disturb a final state court conviction or sentence unless it can be said that a state court, at the time the conviction or sentence became final, would have acted *objectively unreasonably* by not extending the relief later sought in federal court."[55] Taken literally, the formulation in *O'Dell* contemplates that federal courts entertaining habeas petitions from state prisoners can no longer adjudicate constitutional claims in the ordinary manner. The question now is not whether the state courts accurately enforced prisoners' constitutional rights, but whether they rendered "reasonable" (though erroneous) judgments on the merits of those rights.

51. Id. at 301.
52. Sawyer v. Smith, 497 U.S. 227, 234 (1990).
53. Stringer v. Black, 503 U.S. 222, 228 (1992).
54. 521 U.S. 151 (1997).
55. Id. at 156 (emphasis added).

The *Sawyer v. Smith*[56] case is one of many illustrations. The prosecutor in that case deliberately misled the members of the jury to believe that if they sentenced the defendant to death, that sentence would constitute only a recommendation. The trial judge and the appellate courts would actually decide whether the defendant would die. In fact, the trial judge and the appellate courts had little authority to change a jury-imposed death sentence. Years earlier, the Supreme Court had held that the states were constitutionally obligated to ensure that juries approached their responsibilities "with due regard for the consequences of their decision" to take a defendant's life.[57] Nevertheless, the trial judge in *Sawyer* allowed the jury to impose a death sentence after hearing the prosecutor's misleading argument. The Louisiana Supreme Court affirmed that sentence.

The Rehnquist Court conceded that the Louisiana courts might have been wrong to think that the prosecutor's statement to the jury was constitutionally acceptable.[58] The prosecutor plainly hoped to persuade the members of the jury that they could shift the responsibility for a death sentence to judges. Nevertheless, the Court held that the rule established by prior cases (that is, the rule that states must ensure that juries act "with due regard for the consequences of their decision") did not "dictate" the conclusion that the prosecutor's argument was improper. Accordingly, the Louisiana courts could "reasonably" have thought that the statement was acceptable, and a federal court would have to create an entirely "new" rule in order to decide that the prosecutor's argument made the defendant's death sentence unconstitutional. Given *Teague*, that course was foreclosed. The defendant in *Sawyer* was executed—not because the Rehnquist Court actually held that his death sentence *was* constitutionally valid but rather because the Court held that the state court that approved it could "reasonably" have *believed* that it was valid.[59]

The *Teague* doctrine has been criticized in academic circles. It is implausible to propose that federal courts create entirely "new" rules of constitutional criminal procedure whenever they apply settled procedural rules to the circumstances of particular cases. Certainly, it is implausible to conceive that federal courts forge "new" rules of procedure whenever they reach a judgment regarding

---

56. 497 U.S. 227 (1990).

57. Lockett v. Ohio, 438 U.S. 586, 598 (1978) (plurality opinion).

58. Because the Court concluded in the end that the prisoner's claim relied on a "new" rule, the Court did not formally decide that the prosecutor's argument was unconstitutional.

59. If a prosecutor were to do today what the prosecutor in *Sawyer* did, any resulting death sentence would be unconstitutional. See Caldwell v. Mississippi, 472 U.S. 320 (1985).

a constitutional claim that differs from a previous state court judgment that may have been erroneous but still was "reasonable."[60]

Congress and AEDPA

Congress has established limits on federal court authority that approximate the limits established by *Teague*, albeit by a more forthright means—namely, a new federal statute. A key provision in AEDPA, 28 U.S.C. § 2254(d)(1), reads as follows:

> An application [for a writ of habeas corpus] shall not be granted with respect to any claim that was adjudicated on the merits in State court proceedings unless the adjudication of the claim . . . resulted in a decision that was contrary to, or involved an unreasonable application of, clearly established Federal law, as determined by the Supreme Court of the United States.

In *Terry Williams v. Taylor*,[61] the Rehnquist Court construed § 2254(d)(1) to bar a federal court from awarding habeas relief, unless a previous state court decision regarding a prisoner's constitutional claim fails one of the tests established by its two clauses: the "contrary to" clause and the "unreasonable application" clause. A state court decision fails the test established by the "contrary to" clause either by applying a rule that is "substantially different" from the rule reflected in contemporaneous Supreme Court precedents or by arriving at a result that is different from the result the Court itself reached in a prior case in which the facts were "materially indistinguishable." A state court decision fails the test established by the "unreasonable application" clause if it "correctly identifies the governing legal rule" but "unreasonably" applies that rule to the facts of a particular case.

According to the Court, the "unreasonable application" clause contemplates that a state court application of a federal criminal procedure rule to a particular case can be "incorrect" but still not "unreasonable." It follows, then, that this provision in AEDPA prevents a federal court from awarding habeas relief on the ground that a prior state court determination of a prisoner's claim was errone-

---

60. In *Wright v. West*, 505 U.S. 277 (1992), Justice Thomas indicated that, in his view, the critics are right: *Teague* invites the understanding that federal habeas courts should routinely "defer" to reasonable state court decisions regarding prisoners' claims—including state court applications of settled criminal procedure rules to the facts of particular cases. See id. at 291.

61. 529 U.S. 362 (2000). Justice Stevens wrote the principal opinion for the Court in *Terry Williams*, but Justice O'Connor wrote a separate opinion which spoke for the Court on the meaning of § 2254(d)(1).

ous. Instead, a federal court can grant habeas relief only if the state court decision was "also unreasonable."

There plainly is an overlap between § 2254(d)(1) and the *Teague* doctrine. The Court acknowledged as much in *Terry Williams*, but declined to explain precisely how the statute and the Court's own cases match up. It may be that the difference between the two is simply this. The "unreasonable application" clause in § 2254(d)(1) does not pretend that a federal court must invoke a "new" rule of criminal procedure in order to find a prisoner's claim meritorious in any case in which a state court could reasonably have come out the other way. The statute simply bars federal courts from awarding habeas relief in light of a "reasonable" state court decision.

In any event, *Teague* and § 2254(d)(1) deny federal courts authority to address and vindicate federal constitutional claims that a state court rejected "reasonably"—even if the state court's determination was incorrect.[62] Today, federal courts often cannot grant habeas corpus relief to state prisoners if the state courts were wrong when they found that state proceedings comported with the Fourteenth Amendment; typically they can do so only if the state courts were *unreasonably wrong*.[63]

Procedural Barriers

The Rehnquist Court and Congress have placed a series of procedural obstacles in the path of state prisoners who wish to petition the federal courts for a writ

62. For a more detailed examination of *Terry Williams* and the relationship between *Teague* and § 2254(d)(1), see Larry W. Yackle, "The Figure in the Carpet," 78 *Tex. L. Rev.* 1731, 1749–55 (2000).

63. The Rehnquist Court has also relaxed the standard for "harmless" error in federal habeas corpus. If a district court determines that a prisoner's claim is meritorious, the court nonetheless must deny relief if the error was harmless. Some "structural defects" so undermine the integrity of the process that they can never be harmless. In most instances, however, federal courts identify errors at trial that can be overlooked if they had no significant impact on the proceedings. When the Supreme Court considers cases on direct review of state court judgments, it employs a demanding test: The state must demonstrate that error was harmless "beyond a reasonable doubt." Chapman v. California, 386 U.S. 18, 24 (1967). In *Brecht v. Abrahamson*, 507 U.S. 619 (1993), the Court concluded that a "less onerous" standard is applicable to cases reaching federal court via petitions for federal habeas corpus relief. In habeas cases, a trial error was harmless if it had no "substantial and injurious effect or influence" on the outcome of a prisoner's trial. Id. at 637. The Court has not explained how the *Brecht* test for harmless constitutional error meshes with the *Teague* doctrine or § 2254(d)(1).

of habeas corpus. Procedural arrangements are necessary, of course, if habeas corpus cases are to be handled in a timely and efficient manner. And the procedures for conducting habeas litigation in federal court can sensibly recognize and respect the states' interests in the orderly operation of their own justice systems. Even as the Warren Court promoted federal habeas as a means of enforcing federal rights, that court established procedural doctrines that brought discipline to habeas without hindering the federal courts' ability to perform their function. There was a time, too, when Congress fortified the Warren Court's efforts.

Over the last twenty-five years, however, the Rehnquist Court and Congress have created rigid procedural rules that frustrate federal habeas litigation at every turn—rules that stop prisoners at the federal courthouse door, rules that keep prisoners who manage to get through that door from obtaining an adjudication of the merits of their claims, and (sadly) rules that consume time and resources without any compensating gain for the states and their genuine concerns. The most vivid illustrations can be found in the doctrines and statutes governing the timing of federal petitions, the consequences of failing to raise federal claims in state court, the conditions for obtaining evidentiary hearings in federal court, and the possibility of multiple federal petitions from a single prisoner.

Timing rules

The doctrines and statutes prescribing *when* prisoners can (or must) file federal habeas corpus petitions are notoriously frustrating, particularly in death penalty cases. The "exhaustion doctrine," originally established by the Supreme Court in *Ex parte Royall*,[64] requires prisoners to exhaust state judicial opportunities for litigating federal claims before presenting those claims to a federal court in a petition for habeas corpus relief. The rationale is sound. Postponing federal habeas until after state proceedings are complete both avoids interfering with those proceedings and also gives state courts the chance to correct their own violations of federal law. In *Royall*, for example, the prisoner filed a petition in federal court, claiming that he was charged under an unconstitutional state statute. At the time, he was in jail awaiting trial in state court. It obviously would have disrupted the proceedings in state court if a federal court had presumed to take up the prisoner's claim at that point. The Supreme Court held, accordingly, that the prisoner should present his claim against the state statute

64. 117 U.S. 241 (1886).

to the state courts and then, if necessary, seek federal habeas corpus relief after state court proceedings came to a close. In 1948 Congress codified *Royall* in 28 U.S.C. § 2254(b), which requires prisoners to seek relief in state court first, unless the state court opportunities that appear to be "available" are actually "ineffective" to protect federal rights.

The Warren Court expected prisoners to pursue state court avenues for vindicating their federal claims before they sought habeas corpus relief in federal court. Yet the Warren Court expected district courts, in turn, to be flexible and to demand that prisoners go to state court only when there was a serious chance that the state courts would consider their claims.[65] The point was to minimize friction with state courts. In Chief Justice Warren's description, it was meaningful state court remedies that were to be exhausted, not state prisoners themselves.[66]

The Rehnquist Court has transformed the exhaustion doctrine into a rigid prerequisite that routinely short-circuits federal habeas. In some instances, this Court's version of the doctrine prevents federal court adjudication of federal claims even when state remedies have been exhausted with respect to the claims in question. In *Rose v. Lundy*,[67] the Court recognized that prisoners sometimes file "mixed" federal habeas corpus petitions containing both claims that have been rejected in state court and claims the state courts have not yet considered but may yet address in state court proceedings that remain open.

For example, a prisoner may claim both that the jury that condemned him to death was selected in violation of the *Witherspoon* rule and that his defense attorney performed ineffectively under the *Strickland* test. The prisoner may have exhausted state remedies with respect to the *Witherspoon* claim by advancing that claim at trial and on appeal to the state appellate courts. Yet the prisoner probably did not exhaust state remedies with respect to the *Strickland* claim in the same way. The prisoner obviously was represented at trial by the very attorney who performed so poorly. That attorney was scarcely likely to complain to the trial judge that he himself was providing ineffective assistance. Then, the same attorney probably represented the prisoner on appeal and, again, was unlikely to draw his own behavior into question. Claims about defense counsel performance are typically litigated in state postconviction proceedings after prisoners' convictions are affirmed on appeal. So a prisoner may well have,

65. See Frisbie v. Collins, 342 U.S. 519 (1952).
66. See Parker v. Ellis, 362 U.S. 574, 582 (1960) (Warren, C.J., dissenting).
67. 455 U.S. 509 (1982).

on the one hand, a *Witherspoon* claim that is ripe for consideration in federal court and, on the other, a *Strickland* claim that is not.

One would have thought that in a case of that kind, a federal district court should proceed with the claim that is ready for federal adjudication and should postpone consideration of the claim regarding which state remedies have not yet been exhausted. The Rehnquist Court held in *Lundy*, however, that a district court should dismiss *all* the claims in a "mixed" petition. The Court explained its result in the name of efficiency: If prisoners understand that they will suffer dismissal of all their claims if even a single claim is premature, they will avoid that result by carefully exhausting state remedies with respect to every claim in a multiple-claim petition, thus presenting all their claims together for efficient disposition in one federal habeas proceeding.

The reality is that prison inmates often do *not* understand either the exhaustion doctrine or the *Lundy* rule. Nor do they necessarily have counsel to explain what is expected of them or to act on their behalf in state court. Instead, prisoners invariably think that they should include in their federal petitions all the claims of which they are aware, in hopes that some claim will prove fruitful. Commonly, prisoners advance at least one claim that is not yet ready for federal consideration, and that single claim condemns the lot. The Court itself acknowledges that this is what often happens.[68] Nevertheless, the Court stubbornly holds to *Lundy*.

Once a prisoner files a "mixed" petition, one of two things can happen, neither of which is good. First, the prisoner can accept dismissal of all the claims in the petition, pursue available state court litigation opportunities regarding the claims for which such opportunities still exist, and then return to federal court when the exhaustion doctrine is satisfied with respect to all claims. This first option necessarily defers federal adjudication of claims that are currently ready for consideration. If, then, a prisoner's *Witherspoon* claim is valid, the prisoner cannot obtain relief in federal court unless and until he exhausts state remedies with respect to his *Strickland* claim, which may or may not prove to be equally meritorious. Second, the prisoner can abandon any claims that are not yet cognizable and proceed with claims the state courts have already considered and rejected.[69] This second option entails relinquishing any opportunity, in either state or federal court, to obtain a determination of claims that the prisoner

68. See *Slack v. McDaniel*, 529 U.S. 473, 487 (2000).

69. The Court warned that prisoners who strip premature claims out of their petitions run the "risk" that those claims will be foreclosed, if and when they are renewed in a subsequent habeas application. See *Lundy*, 455 U.S. at 520–21.

discards. If a prisoner drops his *Strickland* claim in order to pursue his *Witherspoon* claim immediately and the *Witherspoon* claim turns out to be invalid, he will be denied relief in federal court both on that claim and on his (abandoned) *Strickland* claim, even if the *Strickland* claim is meritorious.

In other instances, the Rehnquist Court has employed the exhaustion doctrine to postpone federal habeas corpus without any pretense of doing so out of respect for state court sensibilities and interests. In *O'Sullivan v. Boerckel*,[70] the Court held that prisoners must press all their federal claims in a petition for discretionary review in a state supreme court, even if state law instructs them to advance only especially creative claims of broad significance to the public.[71] The Court acknowledged that state supreme courts may not welcome a federal rule that requires prisoners to litigate more familiar claims at the state supreme court level in the teeth of state law. But the Court insisted nonetheless that if discretionary review is an "available" feature of a state's appellate review scheme, the federal exhaustion doctrine requires prisoners to seek review of all their claims in order to preserve them for federal habeas. So, far from mitigating friction with state courts, *Boerckel* deliberately *creates* friction by forcing prisoners to press claims on state supreme courts that those courts do not wish to consider.[72]

AEDPA has also complicated the picture by introducing statutory filing deadlines for federal habeas petitions. Pursuant to 28 U.S.C. § 2244(d), prisoners in both capital and noncapital cases typically must file federal petitions within a year after the date on which the state court judgment under attack becomes "final" by the "conclusion of direct review."[73] Pursuant to § 2263, prisoners under sentence of death must file even sooner—within 180 days after their

---

70. 526 U.S. 838 (1999).

71. The Illinois rule in *Boerckel* expressly encouraged prisoners to search their list of claims for any that warranted discretionary review in the state's highest court: e.g., claims of "general importance" to the public. Ill. Sup. Ct. Rule 315.

72. State authorities may waive the exhaustion doctrine and thus submit claims to federal adjudication before the state courts have had an opportunity to pass on them. Yet they cannot forfeit the state's interests through inattention. Under another provision in AEDPA, 28 U.S.C. § 2254(b)(3), states' attorneys can forgo exhaustion only if they do so "expressly." A state will not otherwise be "deemed to have waived the exhaustion requirement or be estopped from reliance" on it. Pursuant to still another provision in the Act, 28 U.S.C. § 2254(b)(2), a federal district court may ignore a prisoner's failure to exhaust, provided the court denies relief "on the merits." That provision plainly stacks the deck against the prisoner.

73. 28 U.S.C. § 2244(d).

sentences are affirmed.[74] Recall that the chief justice himself has complained that prisoners under death sentences have an incentive to withhold their claims as long as possible in order to perpetuate litigation against the possibility that, in the end, they will be executed. That is the sentiment behind AEDPA's filing deadlines. Yet filing periods do not inexorably expedite federal habeas corpus litigation, but often make it even more time-consuming.[75]

Prisoners who are represented at all at this stage are typically represented by new lawyers who are unfamiliar with what has gone before. If those lawyers are the qualified professionals they should be, they have thriving practices that already demand most of their time and effort. In any case, they need an opportunity to interview their new clients, review files, identify potentially meritorious claims, develop evidence and arguments supporting those claims, and, finally, marshal their work product for presentation in court. Those essential labors cannot be performed in a year, and certainly not in six months. Effective legal representation is not conducted that fast in other contexts, and there is no reason to think that it can and should be conducted so rapidly in capital litigation. Accordingly, counsel must either seek an exemption from filing deadlines or file habeas petitions before they are properly prepared. Litigation over the availability of exemptions from filing deadlines is itself complex and protracted. And litigation over counsel's attempt to fortify claims after a petition has been filed can be even more difficult and prolonged. Either way, valuable resources are wasted on legal battles that would not have to be fought at all but for Congress's insistence on rushing death penalty cases to judgment.[76]

It requires no great insight to see that a fixed filing deadline is in tension with the exhaustion doctrine (which, by the way, AEDPA purports to endorse). Simply

74. This provision appears in the optional Chapter 154, which no state has yet triggered. See supra note 30.

75. Previously, under the rules established in 1977, prisoners did not face rigid filing deadlines, but they suffered dismissal if they unnecessarily delayed filing until the respondent would have difficulty responding to their claims. That system encouraged prisoners to move quickly, but it was still flexible enough to avoid the problems that accompany the deadlines established by AEDPA.

76. E.g., Bowen v. Roe, 188 F.3d 1157 (9th Cir. 1999) (wrestling with the question whether a state conviction is "final" before the time for seeking Supreme Court review has elapsed); Nino v. Galaza, 183 F.3d 1003 (9th Cir. 1999) (struggling with the question whether filing periods are tolled while prisoners are seeking appellate review of state trial court decisions denying post-conviction relief); Kiser v. Johnson, 163 F.3d 326 (5th Cir. 1999) (fielding the question whether a prisoner's compliance with a filing deadline can be raised by the district court without a motion from the state); Flanagan v. Johnson, 154 F.3d 196 (5th Cir. 1998) (grappling with the question whether ordinary computation rules apply to the filing periods for habeas petitions).

put, a filing deadline requires prisoners to seek federal habeas relief early, while the exhaustion doctrine demands that they deliberately forgo federal petitions until state court opportunities to litigate their federal claims have been tried. The contradictions between filing deadlines and the exhaustion requirement have generated yet another layer of thorny questions on which courts must spend time and effort.[77]

Litigation over filing deadlines and the exhaustion requirement is vexing for prisoners' attorneys, most of whom are volunteers at this stage. All too often, lawyers agree to help death row prisoners in a genuine desire to see that constitutional claims are properly adjudicated, but then find themselves mired in distracting procedural complications. Here again, the system is penny-wise and pound-foolish. It withholds legal capital from the enforcement of constitutional rights until the eleventh hour; then it squanders that very capital on tangential procedural matters. Small wonder that competent lawyers who accept one capital habeas case often become exasperated and decline to accept another. In consequence, the cycle of frustration that besets death penalty litigation continues.

Procedural default in state court
Petitioners satisfy the exhaustion requirement if, at the time they file federal habeas corpus petitions, there is no "available" and "effective" state court opportunity to litigate their federal claims. It often happens that no state court opportunities are *currently* open, but only because petitioners failed to advance their claims in previous proceedings in the manner prescribed by state law, and,

77. Consider, for example, the problem presented when a prisoner files a timely federal petition, but it is dismissed (some considerable time later) on the ground that it contains at least one claim for which a state opportunity for litigation remains open. According to the exhaustion doctrine, the prisoner should be entitled to exhaust state remedies with respect to that claim and return to federal court. Yet by the time the prisoner gets back, the filing period may have run. The lower federal courts wrestled for years over the best solution, finally dividing over whether the time during which such a prisoner's first petition was pending might be excepted from the filing period. That disagreement forced the Supreme Court itself to resolve the question. In *Duncan v. Walker*, 533 U.S. 167 (2001), the Court held that AEDPA makes no exception for the time it takes a federal district court to decide whether a prisoner has satisfied the exhaustion doctrine. Accordingly, a prisoner who files a federal petition bears the risk that the district court will require months to determine whether a claim is ready for federal adjudication, that the court will ultimately conclude that the claim cannot be considered (yet) because some state court avenue for litigating it remains viable, that the petition will be dismissed ostensibly to permit the prisoner to pursue relief from the state courts, but that, by then, there will be no time left actually to do so and to return to federal court.

for that reason, the state courts are no longer willing to entertain them. Recall that negligent defense attorneys frequently fail to comply with state procedural rules requiring them to raise federal constitutional objections at a particular time or in a particular way. When defense attorneys "default" by failing to advance claims as they should, their clients usually forfeit any other state court opportunity to litigate those claims thereafter. Over the years, the Supreme Court has fashioned a body of doctrine for dealing with cases in which prisoners satisfy the exhaustion doctrine only because they (or, more often, their lawyers) committed procedural default in state court. That doctrine has shifted with the ebb and flow of the Court's enthusiasm for habeas corpus.

The Warren Court was suspicious of state procedural schemes that denied federal claims any judicial forum at all and thus threatened to frustrate implementation of constitutional safeguards. That Court insisted, accordingly, that if state courts refused to consider federal claims because of procedural default, federal district courts ordinarily should nonetheless adjudicate those same claims on the merits. The Warren Court conceded that a federal court should not reach the merits of a claim if a prisoner or his lawyer deliberately bypassed state court opportunities to vindicate the claim in hopes of gaining some strategic advantage. But that Court held that defaults ascribable to defense counsel's ignorance or neglect should not preclude federal court adjudication of the merits of claims that counsel overlooked.[78]

Beginning with *Wainwright v. Sykes*,[79] the Rehnquist Court has taken virtually the opposite view of default cases. Today, defense counsel's procedural default *does* typically foreclose federal court adjudication of a claim, even if the default was due to ignorance or neglect rather than deliberate strategy. The Court's doctrine is complex. In the main, the Court insists that a federal court entertaining a habeas corpus petition must refuse to consider a claim that counsel failed to raise in state court, unless the prisoner either shows "cause" for the default and "actual prejudice" resulting from it[80] or demonstrates that he or she probably would have been acquitted if counsel had raised the claim properly and thus averted a violation of the prisoner's federal rights.[81]

The Court recognizes that the most common reason for default in state court is that a prisoner's lawyer simply goofed. But the Court insists that defense

78. See Fay v. Noia, 372 U.S. 391 (1963).
79. 433 U.S. 72 (1977).
80. *Sykes*, 433 U.S. at 84–85.
81. See Murray v. Carrier, 477 U.S. 478, 496 (1986).

counsel's mistakes do not ordinarily establish "cause."[82] It is not enough to show that a lawyer was unaware of a federal claim or the need to raise it at a particular time or in a particular way. Nor is it enough to show that counsel inadvertently overlooked a claim or the chance to advance it. The very point of *Sykes* is that petitioners now routinely forfeit the opportunity to litigate claims in both state and federal court for the sole reason that the lawyers they had in state proceedings made tragic procedural mistakes.

Counsel error can count as "cause" only if a lawyer's failure to raise a claim in state court was so incompetent and prejudicial as to constitute ineffective assistance of counsel in violation of the *Strickland* constitutional standards. That possibility is cold comfort. Recall that the *Strickland* standards are extremely weak. Moreover, it is circular to insist that "cause" is established only by ineffective assistance of counsel in the constitutional sense. A prisoner who proves that his or her constitutional right to effective assistance was violated in state court is entitled to federal habeas corpus relief on that independent basis alone. There is no need to advance the claim that counsel failed to raise. Under the Rehnquist Court's doctrine, the only prisoners who can show "cause" on the basis of counsel's error are prisoners who have no need to show "cause" at all.[83]

More's the pity, the Rehnquist Court now seems bent on twisting its doctrine even more. Initially in *Sykes*, the Court disclaimed any purpose to punish prisoners for failing to present federal claims in state court according to the Court's own sense of the way in which state litigation should be conducted. Instead, the Court explained that federal default doctrine reinforces *state* procedural rules and, to that end, gives effect to forfeitures that the state courts imposed (or would impose) for prisoners' failure to comply with state procedural rules for advancing federal claims.[84] In the *Boerckel* case, however, the Court held that the prisoner had committed procedural default even though it was perfectly clear that he had not violated a state procedural rule. Recall that the Illinois rule

82. Id. at 488.

83. The Rehnquist Court has yet to explain what must be shown to establish "actual prejudice." In some instances, however, prisoners must demonstrate that the errors of which they complain "so infected the entire trial that the resulting conviction" violated due process. United States v. Frady, 456 U.S. 152, 169 (1982). Prisoners who hope to satisfy the "probable innocence" standard must offer "new evidence" that, had it been available earlier, would have made it "more likely than not that no reasonable juror would have convicted" them in the first place. See Schlup v. Delo, 513 U.S. 298, 327 (1995).

84. See Rezin v. Wolff, 439 U.S. 1103 (1979) (White, J., dissenting) (explaining that the default doctrine does not "impose its own contemporaneous objection rule independent of state rules").

in that case discouraged prisoners from advancing conventional claims in a petition for discretionary review in the Illinois Supreme Court. The prisoner thus *complied* with that rule when he omitted claims of that character from his petition to the state supreme court.

Before *Boerckel*, the Court's convoluted doctrine for default cases had buried the federal habeas courts under a mountain of procedural issues having little or nothing to do with the efficient adjudication of federal claims or any sensible accommodation of state interests. Now, in *Boerckel's* wake, that doctrine has broken loose from its own (questionable) raison d'être and operates as a free-standing *federal* standard for litigants to follow in *state* court proceedings. To-day, default doctrine both frustrates federal adjudication of federal claims and interferes with state processes.

A provision in AEDPA largely endorses the Court's procedural default doctrine, but tightens it in death penalty cases. Pursuant to 28 U.S.C. § 2264(a), a federal district court ordinarily can consider only a claim that was previously "raised" and "decided on the merits" in state court.[85] There are exceptions, and those exceptions roughly track the Court's definition of "cause." But none of the exceptions explicitly captures the Court's "probable innocence" safety valve. Inexplicably, Congress has contrived to foreclose federal court consideration of constitutional claims even when the Rehnquist Court would open the federal courts to those claims in the interests of saving innocent people from execution.

Here again, the Rehnquist Court and Congress have constructed procedural obstacles that frustrate federal habeas corpus at every turn. None of this has anything to do with enforcing federal rights, far less a sensible and efficient use of scarce resources.

Hearings in federal court

Prisoners seeking federal habeas corpus relief typically advance claims that turn on underlying facts. For example, a prisoner may claim that the prosecutor withheld evidence in violation of the *Brady* rule. The merits of a *Brady* claim often can be assessed only by first determining what actually happened during the period leading up to the prisoner's trial in state court. For example, it is necessary to know whether the prosecutor actually had material evidence that would have been useful to the defense and whether the prisoner asked the prosecutor to disclose it.

The Warren Court thought that federal courts ordinarily should hold their

---

85. Since § 2264(a) forms part of the optional Chapter 154, it applies only in death penalty cases arising from states that activate that chapter. See supra note 30.

own hearings and, on the basis of the evidence adduced in those hearings, should arrive at their own findings of fact. That Court recognized that in some instances the state courts had already found many of the relevant facts and that hearings in federal court might be unnecessary. Accordingly, the Warren Court tempered the basic rule that federal hearings should be held with a series of standards by which federal courts could determine whether to rely, instead, on the facts found in state court. If, however, the facts were not fully developed in state court, the Warren Court insisted that federal habeas courts should make their own findings—unless a prisoner had "deliberately bypassed" state court opportunities to complete the record.[86]

Congress has now made it much more difficult for prisoners to obtain federal hearings. Another key provision in AEDPA, 28 U.S.C. § 2254(e)(2), provides as follows:

> If the applicant has failed to develop the factual basis of a claim in State court proceedings, the court shall not hold an evidentiary hearing on the claim unless the applicant shows that—
> (A) the claim relies on—
> (i) a new rule of constitutional law, made retroactive to cases on collateral review by the Supreme Court, that was previously unavailable; or
> (ii) a factual predicate that could not have been previously discovered through the exercise of due diligence; and
> (B) the facts underlying the claim would be sufficient to establish by clear and convincing evidence that but for constitutional error, no reasonable factfinder would have found the applicant guilty of the underlying offense.[87]

It is a commentary on the ferocity with which some states pursue death penalty cases that state's attorneys in Virginia asked the Court to hold that this provision bars a federal hearing even if a prisoner did his best to develop the facts in state court but the state courts refused to cooperate. Not even the Rehnquist Court could abide that interpretation. Instead, the Court recognized in *Michael*

---

86. Townsend v. Sain, 372 U.S. 293 (1963).

87. True to form, the Rehnquist Court rejected the Warren Court's approach and substituted its own forfeiture rule. In *Keeney v. Tamayo-Reyes*, 504 U.S. 1 (1992), the Court held that if prisoners negligently failed to take advantage of state court opportunities to develop the facts, they must satisfy the now-familiar "cause and prejudice" or "probable innocence" standards. This provision in AEDPA, § 2254(e)(2), partly codifies and displaces the *Tamayo-Reyes* arrangements.

Williams v. Taylor[88] that the opening clause of § 2254(e)(2) specifies that it applies only if the prisoner himself was to blame for having "failed" to develop the facts. Accordingly, the Court held that § 2254(e)(2) does not affect a prisoner's entitlement to a federal hearing if the prisoner exercised "diligence" in an attempt to bring the facts to light in state court. This is scarcely to say that § 2254(e)(2) is especially prisoner-friendly. Prisoners must undertake a "diligent search for evidence" supporting their claims when their cases are before the state courts. If they don't, they will be blamed for the flawed state fact-finding that ensues. Often, of course, it is not prisoners themselves, but rather their lawyers, who overlook opportunities to develop facts in state court. The *Michael Williams* case itself provides an illustration. The Court concluded that the prisoner in that case had not exercised "diligence" in the necessary sense because his attorney had only asked the state for psychological reports regarding prosecution witnesses. According to the Court, that attorney should have "done more" to lay hands on the particular report that would have fortified a claim that the prosecutor had withheld material evidence from the defense in violation of *Brady*.

Prisoners who fail the threshold "diligence" test can obtain a federal hearing only if they satisfy the standards in subsections (A) and (B) of § 2254(e)(2). Few prisoners will be able to squeeze their cases into either of the categories prescribed in subsection (A). Some may argue that they satisfy subsection (A)(i) by advancing claims resting on "new" rules of law within the Court's capacious definition of what counts as "new." But those very rules usually provide no basis for relief because they are not "retroactive" for habeas purposes.[89]

Others may contend that they satisfy subsection (A)(ii) because they would not have discovered evidence even if they had exercised "diligence." But the Court suggested in *Michael Williams* that prisoners can be successful on that score only if the evidence in question "did not exist" at the time to *be* discovered.[90] Those few prisoners who manage to satisfy subsection (A) will almost certainly fail to satisfy subsection (B), which (taken literally) requires an extraordinarily strong showing of actual innocence.

The implications are disturbing, to say the least. In cases in which § 2254 governs, federal courts are poised to consider the substance of claims, and the only question is whether they can do so on the basis of a complete factual

88. 529 U.S. 420 (2000).
89. See supra note 50 and accompanying text.
90. 529 U.S. at 436.

record. If it appears that prisoners' lawyers might have "done more" to discover the underlying facts in state court, federal courts must proceed to the merits in willful ignorance of what happened. Here again, AEDPA establishes demanding standards for prisoners to meet, holds them to account for the blunders of their attorneys, and undermines the federal courts' ability to enforce federal constitutional safeguards meant to ensure that only guilty defendants are convicted and sentenced to die.

Multiple federal petitions

State prisoners who fail to win relief on one petition for a federal writ of habeas corpus sometimes try again with another petition raising the same or different claims. On the surface, second or successive petitions appear troubling. In most minds, one opportunity to litigate federal claims in federal court should be sufficient, and prisoners should not be allowed to return to the well. In death penalty cases, however, there often are very good reasons why more than one petition should be permitted.

Recall that death row inmates often go without legal counsel until their names reach the top of the ABA's waiting list. While on their own, they may try to help themselves by filing their own federal petitions. Petitions prepared by semiliterate prisoners are poor substitutes for what professionals might produce. They often omit potentially meritorious claims, misstate the claims they do advance, and offer little supporting evidence and argument. And they are almost always dismissed summarily. Then, when competent lawyers enter the picture, the only course available is to file additional petitions that properly present prisoners' genuine claims. Even when prisoners themselves have not filed prior petitions, lawyers who face strict filing deadlines may be forced to file petitions before they are ready. If lawyers try to buttress those petitions, federal district courts may treat any new materials they introduce as, in effect, new habeas corpus petitions. It turns out, then, that second or successive federal petitions are commonplace in death penalty cases, not because death row prisoners and their lawyers deliberately litigate claims piecemeal, but because the lamentable system for providing lawyers at the habeas stage leaves counsel with no other option.

The Warren Court was not especially hostile to multiple petitions. That Court employed the "deliberate bypass" rule both to cases in which prisoners failed to raise claims at the proper time in state court and to cases in which prisoners failed to include claims in an initial federal petition.[91] Congress, however, has

91. See Sanders v. United States, 373 U.S. 1 (1963).

established a much less generous regime. Still another provision in AEDPA, § 2244(b), states that a claim that was presented in a previous federal habeas petition "shall be dismissed."[92] Then:

> A claim presented in a second or successive [petition] . . . that was not presented in a prior application shall be dismissed unless—
>
> (A) the applicant shows that the claim relies on a new rule of constitutional law, made retroactive to cases on collateral review by the Supreme Court, that was previously unavailable; or
>
> (B)(i) the factual predicate for the claim could not have been discovered previously through the exercise of due diligence; and
>
> (ii) the facts underlying the claim, if proven and viewed in light of the evidence as a whole, would be sufficient to establish by clear and convincing evidence that, but for constitutional error, no reasonable factfinder would have found the applicant guilty of the underlying offense.[93]

These standards roughly track the exacting requirements for obtaining federal hearings established by § 2254(e)(2).[94] They are obviously difficult to digest and, once digested, extremely difficult to satisfy. Moreover, the standards themselves are only the beginning of the attempt to discourage second or successive petitions. Further subsections of § 2244(b) establish a cumbersome "gate-keeping" mechanism for implementing the standards. A prisoner who wishes to file more than one federal petition must move a circuit court of appeals for an order permitting him or her to file again in a district court.[95] The "gate-keeping"

92. 28 U.S.C. § 2244(b)(1). The Rehnquist Court has construed this provision in a way that avoids especially silly results. In *Stewart v. Martinez-Villareal*, 523 U.S. 637 (1998), the Court explained that dismissals for "technical procedural reasons" do not trigger the prohibition on petitions raising the same claim a second time. Id. at 645.

93. In this context, too, the Rehnquist Court jettisoned the Warren Court's "deliberate bypass" rule in favor of its own forfeiture formulation. In *McCleskey v. Zant*, 499 U.S. 467 (1991), the Court announced that prisoners seeking to file more than one federal petition must either show "cause" and "prejudice" or demonstrate probable innocence. This provision in AEDPA supersedes the *McCleskey* approach.

94. See supra text accompanying note 87.

95. A three-member panel of circuit judges can authorize another petition only if the petition "makes a prima facie showing" that it meets the standards established by § 2244(b)(2). A panel must act within thirty days. Its decision is not subject to a petition for rehearing or to review in the Supreme Court. Circuit courts have found ways to eliminate some unfairness and, certainly, to take the time they need with prisoners' motions. E.g., Triestman v. United States, 124 F.3d

mechanism is presumably meant to promote efficiency by screening unjustified petitions at the door. In the main, however, it simply lays a trap for unsuspecting prisoners. Moreover, it generates a welter of procedural problems. Prisoners who have no lawyers often do not understand that they must go first to the circuit level before they can proceed at the district level. Accordingly, they file second or successive petitions in a district court and suffer dismissal for want of permission from a circuit panel.

To be sure, these last provisions in AEDPA hold out the hope that a few death row inmates may be able to file more than one federal petition. That hope encourages a great many desperate prisoners to try. The consequence is a considerable flow of cases requiring federal court litigation over the threshold question whether prisoners are entitled to file again. At the same time, AEDPA's standards are so demanding that almost all prisoners who make the attempt will fail. That, of course, means that in this context, too, current procedural arrangements for habeas corpus sacrifice time and effort to no serious purpose.

Conclusion

This chapter's message is simple enough. If Americans cannot agree that capital punishment is an unworthy social policy in itself, we should at least agree that judicial proceedings in death penalty cases must be rigorous and scrupulously fair. Otherwise, defendants may be convicted and sentenced to die in violation of their constitutional rights. And, in some instances, defendants who are innocent may nonetheless be executed. Sadly, we have not committed ourselves to exacting procedural arrangements in capital cases. Instead, the Supreme Court and Congress have compromised the one procedural mechanism that might catch mistakes before it is too late: the federal courts' authority to examine prisoners' constitutional claims in federal habeas corpus proceedings.

---

361 (2d Cir. 1997). The Supreme Court held in *Felker v. Turpin*, 518 U.S. 651 (1996), that § 2244(b)(3) eliminates the ordinary certiorari avenue to the Court itself but preserves the Court's independent jurisdiction to entertain habeas applications as an "original" matter.

3 : "UNTIL I CAN BE SURE": HOW THE THREAT OF EXECUTING THE INNOCENT HAS TRANSFORMED THE DEATH PENALTY DEBATE

Ken Armstrong & Steve Mills

Tack twenty more points onto Anthony Porter's IQ and you put him in his grave, forgotten, one more name added to the more than 700 people executed in the United States in the past quarter century.[1]

Porter did not commit the crime for which he was sentenced to die, but we wouldn't know that. His execution would have excited little notice or protest, and afterward his case would have failed to tease the various investigators now searching for the innocent man executed. Once the poison shot through the needle's point and into Porter's blood, his claims of innocence would have died along with him.

Convicted of two Chicago murders on evidence that the Illinois Supreme Court called "overwhelming,"[2] Porter was ultimately saved by journalism students, not the justice system. In September 1998 Porter came within two days of execution before receiving a reprieve that was based on concerns about his intelligence, not his innocence. The Illinois Supreme Court worried that Porter, with an IQ of fifty-one, might not be able to understand his punishment, a requirement before any person can be executed in the United States.

After Porter's execution was put on hold, a group of Northwestern University journalism students under Professor David Protess took up the case. Working

1. As of June 27, 2001, 722 people had been executed in the United States since 1977.
2. See People v. Porter, 489 N.E.2d 1329, 1337 (Ill. 1986) (dismissing Porter's claim that a juror's statement made on entering the jury room demonstrated bias against Porter, the Illinois Supreme Court says, "[A]n equally reasonable explanation for her statement is that after attentively and conscientiously listening to all the evidence presented at trial, she concluded that the evidence against the defendant was overwhelming, which it was").

with a private investigator, they tracked down and obtained a videotaped confession from the real killer. Porter, exonerated, was freed on February 5, 1999.

Instead of adding one more name to the country's list of executed inmates, Porter joined a different list. This one names the men and women who have been convicted of capital crimes and sentenced to die, only to be exonerated. As of June 2001, that list had ninety-six names. Porter is simply number seventy-nine.[3]

Porter's narrow escape from the execution chamber jolted Illinois governor George Ryan, a Republican who supports the death penalty and had even voted for it while in the state legislature. Ryan's faith was again violently shaken nine months later, when the *Chicago Tribune* published a five-part series, "The Failure of the Death Penalty in Illinois."[4] The series exposed a host of fault lines that have radiated through the state's system of capital punishment, heightening the possibility of innocent men and women being sentenced to death.

On January 31, 2000, Ryan took the historic step of declaring a moratorium on executions, making Illinois the first state since capital punishment's reinstatement to suspend the march of inmates from death row to the death chamber. Ryan cited the *Tribune* series and the state's shameful record of condemning the innocent, including Anthony Porter.[5] "Until I can be sure that everyone sentenced to death in Illinois is truly guilty, until I can be sure with moral certainty that no innocent man or woman is facing a lethal injection, no one will meet that fate," Ryan said.

Ryan's announcement resounded throughout the nation and the world. At the Colosseum in Rome, golden lights flickered on and burned through the night in celebration. In Washington, President Clinton praised Ryan's courage, while members of Congress proposed a moratorium on federal executions. The New Hampshire legislature voted to abolish the death penalty, although that mea-

3. These numbers come from a running tally kept by the Death Penalty Information Center, and are current as of July 5, 2001. The ninety-six exonerations reflect the number of men and women who have been freed from death row since 1973. It therefore includes some convictions that predate capital punishment's reinstatement in the United States in 1976. All but one of the ninety-six death row inmates either were acquitted at retrial or had charges against them dropped; the one exception was exonerated after dying on death row. At least ten were exonerated with the help of DNA testing conducted after their trials.

4. See Ken Armstrong and Steve Mills, "The Failure of the Death Penalty in Illinois," *Chi. Trib.*, Nov. 14–18, 1999.

5. When Ryan declared the moratorium, Illinois had, since the state reinstated capital punishment in 1977, exonerated thirteen men who were on death row and executed twelve.

sure was vetoed. As of June 2001, seven states and the federal government have ordered studies of their own systems of capital punishment. In Virginia, Christian Coalition founder Pat Robertson expressed doubts about the death penalty. So did conservative columnist George Will and a variety of other unexpected voices. New polls showed significant declines in capital punishment's public support.

Ryan's decision transformed the national debate over capital punishment. The threat of executing an innocent person—a scenario Ryan called "the ultimate nightmare"—now dominates arguments waged over the death penalty, and the issue has proved far more potent than previous criticisms focusing on such factors as racial bias or capital punishment's arbitrary application. The fear of putting an innocent man or woman to death has refueled efforts to suspend executions or abolish capital punishment outright, and it has eroded support for the death penalty among certain justices, legislators, executive officials, and a significant segment of the public.

This chapter will examine the crucial role that innocence has come to play in capital punishment. It will begin by looking at wrongful convictions historically—first in the United States, then in England. The next section will describe more recent events, with particular emphasis on the country's growing list of exoneration cases and the impact they have had on calls for reform or abolition. This chapter will then examine why so many mistakes happen in capital cases and what, if anything, can be done to prevent them. We'll close with a look at media efforts to prove that an innocent defendant has, indeed, been executed.

Two Very Different Histories

As a federal judge for more than fifty years, Learned Hand helped shape our nation's laws, writing influential opinions celebrated for their clarity and force. Using language that bridged the worlds of law and literature, Hand stripped legal fallacies bare. Other judges would read Hand's writing with a reverence normally reserved for Shakespeare. Nearly forty years after Hand's death, they still do.

In 1923, while serving as a U.S. district court judge in New York, Hand wrote a lyrical line that has been quoted many times since. In typical fashion, it was clear and forceful. It was also utterly, spectacularly wrong. Written, as it was, by a man born into a distinguished legal family, educated at Harvard Law School and destined to become one of the most idolized judges in American history, that line may capture the American legal system's ingrained arrogance better than any words written before or since.

Hand wrote that in criminal cases the accused has "every advantage," and he proceeded to list the various safeguards enjoyed by defendants along with restrictions placed on the prosecution. "Our procedure has always been haunted by the ghost of the innocent man convicted," Hand wrote. "It is an unreal dream."[6]

Eight decades later, as DNA tests unravel one wrongful conviction after another, Hand's belief in the criminal justice system's infallibility seems laughable. But in truth, Hand's conclusion was grossly unfounded even in its own time.

In 1918, five years before Hand wrote of the "unreal dream," convicted murderer Bill Wilson was granted a full pardon by Alabama's governor. That's because the person Wilson was convicted of murdering—his wife, Jenny—had turned out to be alive. Wilson's appellate lawyer found her in Vincennes, Indiana. He convinced her to return to Alabama in order to verify, in person, that she had become a Hoosier and not a corpse.[7]

Six years before Wilson's pardon, convicted murderer Ernest Lyons was exonerated in Virginia because the person he supposedly killed—a local pastor, James Smith—had also turned up hale and hearty. It seems the Reverend Smith absconded with $45 of the church's money. When he departed Alabama, he went to North Carolina, not heaven.

Threatening to become a cliché, the scenario of the murder victim turning up alive repeated itself in 1927, when Condy Dabney was pardoned in Kentucky, and in 1928, when Louise Butler and George Yelder were pardoned in Alabama.

If there is one kind of evidence that eclipses DNA in its power to exonerate a convicted murderer, it is having the supposed murder victim walk back into town after trial. Yet that happened no fewer than four times in a relatively short period before and after Hand's unqualified pronouncement concerning the criminal justice system's infallibility.

To be sure, many of Hand's contemporaries shared his unyielding confidence. His was not a lone and bold voice, but rather an eloquent one that spoke for many in the nation's courts and law enforcement. What is more surprising, though, is how strongly Hand's words have echoed through the years—and how they can still be heard to this day.

In 1986 U.S. Attorney General Edwin Meese, the nation's top law enforcement official, all but obliterated the presumption of innocence on which our

6. See United States v. Garsson, 291 F.646, 649 (S.D.N.Y. 1923).

7. For a more detailed description of the Wilson case, above, and the Lyons, Dabney, Butler, and Yelder cases, below, see Edwin Borchard, *Convicting the Innocent* (1932).

system of justice is founded. "The thing is, you don't have many suspects who are innocent of a crime," Meese said. "That's contradictory. If a person is innocent of crime, then he is not a suspect."

More recently, pronouncements of infallibility have retreated to a new line of defense. Rather than downplaying the possibility of wrongful arrest or conviction, many of today's public officials dismiss the possibility of an innocent person being executed. In doing so, they emphasize capital punishment's layers of appeal and various other safeguards. During his successful campaign for the White House, President George W. Bush expressed unwavering confidence in his belief that no innocent person was ever executed during his stint as governor of Texas. Bush held tightly to that position even as national and state media organizations scrutinized individual cases and exposed systematic weaknesses in Texas's handling of capital cases.

In Illinois, the state with the second highest number of exonerations in capital cases,[8] the chief prosecutor of one of Chicago's largest suburban counties has gone even further than Bush. DuPage County state's attorney Joseph Birkett has told the *Chicago Tribune*, "No innocent person has been executed in this country in the last 100 years, and with safeguards already in place, that will never happen."

Birkett and others maintain such confidence despite the mounting number of near misses in Illinois and nationally. Innocent men have been saved from the death chamber through the work of journalists, through the help of DNA tests conducted over the objection of prosecutors, through confessions from real killers stricken by conscience. The obvious truth is that we simply don't know how many, if any, death row inmates were similarly innocent but were executed before science or outside investigators could save them.

The More Things Change . . .

The advent of DNA technology, with its enormous power to incriminate or exonerate, has helped convince many people that our criminal justice system is highly fallible. But there was abundant evidence of that fallibility long before DNA testing came along, and the debate being waged now was also waged way back when. An odd circularity emerges from the historical record; parallels abound, providing a sense of déjà vu.

In February 2000, Barry Scheck, Peter Neufeld, and Jim Dwyer published *Actual Innocence*, a book focusing on sixty-five wrongful conviction cases in

8. Florida has the highest number, with twenty-one death row inmates exonerated since 1973.

which people were exonerated thanks to DNA testing. With gripping accounts of coerced confessions, mistaken eyewitnesses, misleading scientific evidence, inept defense attorneys, corrupt police officers, and cheating prosecutors, the book has proved influential in eroding confidence that our criminal justice system is foolproof.

But long before *Actual Innocence*, there was *Convicting the Innocent*, a classic work published by Yale University law professor Edwin Borchard in 1932. Borchard, too, examined sixty-five cases of wrongful conviction, all but three of them in the United States. Borchard, too, provided gripping accounts of coerced confessions, mistaken eyewitnesses, misleading scientific evidence, inept defense attorneys, corrupt police officers, and cheating prosecutors. And, like those reported in *Actual Innocence*, Borchard's cases included some in which innocent men had been sentenced to die.

"Only by rare good fortune were some of the sentences of hanging and electrocution commuted to life imprisonment or indictments for first-degree murder modified by verdicts of second-degree murder, so that the error could still be corrected," Borchard wrote. "How many wrongfully convicted persons have actually been executed, it is impossible to say. But that these cases offer a convincing argument for the abolition of the death penalty, certainly in cases of convictions on circumstantial evidence, can hardly be gainsaid."

Long before Anthony Porter, there was Will Purvis—a Mississippi man who came even closer than Porter to being executed for a crime he did not commit. Convicted of murder, Purvis was led to the gallows in 1894. The noose was tied round his neck and the trapdoor opened. Purvis fell, but the knot untwisted, allowing him to hit the ground unhurt. Horror gripped the crowd. Some members ascribed the event to divine intervention. After much back and forth, Purvis was spared a second hanging. Four years later, the prosecution's star witness recanted, and Purvis was pardoned. Years after that, another man confessed to the killing.

In 1901 convicted murderer J. B. Brown was led to the gallows in Florida and, like Purvis, had the noose tied round his neck. Brown would have hanged but for a clerical error: the death warrant mistakenly listed his jury's foreman as the man to be executed. His sentence wound up being commuted to life, and twelve years later he was exonerated after the real killer confessed.

For whatever reason, books like Borchard's and cases like Purvis's and Brown's failed to arouse the public's fear of executing the innocent. Certainly, they did not receive the amount of widespread attention that is paid to contemporary cases and studies. In addition, they came along at a time when supreme arrogance dominated the country's courts, when almost any suggestion that the criminal justice system might make a mistake was blithely dismissed.

While echoes of those arrogant dismissals can still be heard, they are usually restricted to the threat of wrongful execution—and, even at that, such rigid denial is hardly universal. Numerous judges and public officials now express fear that we have already executed innocent people or will do so in the future. That view, shared by a majority of the American public, represents a significant turnaround in the country's death penalty debate. Even so, the shift in attitude pales in comparison to what has happened in England, where arrogance has been replaced by humility.

Reopening Cases and Coffins

Calling the possible execution of an innocent person "a matter of very great public concern," an appeals court in England ruled in 2000 that the body of James Hanratty, a man hanged in 1962, should be exhumed so that DNA tests could be conducted on his corpse. Demonstrating just how much it desired to know whether justice had miscarried, the court called for such dramatic measures even though DNA tests had already been conducted on Hanratty's relatives and suggested, strongly, that he was indeed guilty.

In the annals of crime and punishment, the reopening of a case and a coffin that were closed thirty-eight years ago would seem an extraordinary development. But in England, the country from which the United States inherited its legal tradition, the case is wholly in keeping with a dramatic shift in how the criminal justice system is viewed.

Although English courts and commentators once considered their justice system to be infallible, the country now recognizes the system's proclivity for error. England has even created an investigative agency whose mission includes rooting through old cases and confronting the criminal justice system's greatest nightmare—the execution of an innocent person. That agency, the Criminal Cases Review Commission, began its work in 1996. Two years later, in one of the first cases the commission investigated, a Somali seaman hanged in 1952 was exonerated. Three appellate justices quashed Mahmoud Hussein Mattan's conviction after his case was referred to their court by the Criminal Cases Review Commission as a probable miscarriage of justice.

Charged with slashing a female shopkeeper's throat, Mattan had been convicted almost exclusively on the word of a man who testified that he saw Mattan leaving the shop around the time of the murder. But while reinvestigating the case, the commission turned up stunning evidence that had not previously been disclosed to Mattan's lawyers or the public. Not only had the prosecution's star witness provided police with an earlier statement that was inconsistent with his trial testimony, but according to one police inspector's notes the witness had specifically identified the man leaving the shop as Tahir Gass, not Mattan. Gass, who was allegedly prone to violence against women and obsessed with knives, was tried for a different murder two years after Mattan's execution only to be acquitted by reason of insanity. The witness even told police that the man leaving the shop had a gold tooth—a description that matched Gass but not Mattan.

In quashing Mattan's conviction, the Court of Appeal's Lord Justice Rose said, "The court can only hope that its decision today will provide some crumb of comfort for his surviving relatives." Rose also said that the case demonstrated that capital punishment was "not perhaps a prudent culmination for a criminal justice system which is human and therefore fallible."

Rose's comment illustrated just how dramatically the prevailing position of English courts and public officials has shifted in the debate over the death penalty. Addressing parliament in the 1860s, John Stuart Mill, one of history's great moral philosophers, adamantly opposed the abolition of capital punishment. Mill conceded that the execution of an innocent person would constitute an "invincible" objection to the death penalty, but he firmly discounted that possibility. "[W]e all know that the defects of our procedure are the very opposite," Mill said. "Our rules of evidence are even too favorable to the prisoner."

A century later, England renewed its debate over capital punishment. An official who later became home secretary—a position that corresponds roughly to the U.S. attorney general—echoed Mill's words. Maxwell Fyfe said any suggestion that an innocent man had been hanged in England was "moving in a realm of fantasy."

Soon enough, that fantasy became all too real. In 1950 England hanged a man whose innocence would be officially recognized some sixteen years later. That man was Timothy John Evans, and his case played a crucial role in the abolition of the death penalty in England.

In 1949 Evans's wife and fourteen-month-old daughter were found strangled in an outhouse at 10 Rillington Place, the West London residence where Evans and his family lived on the top floor. Evans, who had an IQ of sixty-eight and could neither read nor write, confessed to the murders but then recanted. He blamed the slayings on John Reginald Halliday Christie, who lived in a ground-floor flat below Evans. Christie denied being the strangler and became the prosecution's main witness against Evans, who was convicted and then hanged a mere three months after the two bodies were found.

But in 1953, three years after Evans's execution, four more bodies were found at 10 Rillington Place, the house shared by Evans and Christie. All four victims were women; all four had been strangled; and one of them was Christie's wife. This time, Christie confessed. At trial, Christie testified that he had killed seven women in all. That total, he said, included Evans's wife. Christie, however, continued to deny killing Evans's daughter.

The shocking similarity between the crimes, along with Christie's confession to killing Evans's wife, fueled cries for a reinvestigation of the case. Ultimately, Queen Elizabeth II issued an unconditional, posthumous pardon to Evans in 1966, declaring him innocent of the crime. From 1953 onward, the Evans and Christie case figured prominently in arguments mounted in England by capital punishment's opponents. In 1965 Parliament agreed to suspend the death penalty for five years. Then, in 1969, Parliament abolished capital punishment permanently.

Creeping Doubts in the United States

In the United States, the threat of executing an innocent person has yet to generate the amount of opposition to capital punishment that can be found among lawmakers and judges in England. But, that said, the litany of wrongful convictions in the United States has clearly unsettled a growing number of public officials, including some judges charged with reviewing the appeals of death row inmates.

Even before the Illinois moratorium and Anthony Porter's much publicized exoneration, the state's mounting number of wrongful convictions had persuaded one Illinois Supreme Court justice that he could no longer vote to uphold any death sentence. "[T]he system is not working," Moses Harrison II wrote while dissenting in a 1998 capital case. "Innocent people are being sentenced to death. . . . If these men dodged the executioner, it was only because of luck and the dedication of the attorneys, reporters, family members and volunteers who labored to win their release. They survived despite the criminal justice system, not because of it. The truth is that left to the devices of the court system, they would probably have all ended up dead at the hands of the state for crimes they did not commit. One must wonder how many others have not been so fortunate."[9]

Gerald Kogan, a former chief justice of the Florida Supreme Court, now says he believes that innocent defendants have been executed in his state. Charles Baird, a former member of the Texas Court of Criminal Appeals, publicly criti-

9. People v. Bull, 705 N.E.2d 824, 847 (1998) (Harrison, J. concurring in part and dissenting in part).

cizes his former court for slipshod work and a desire to grease the way for executions, even when defendants may be innocent. And Sandra Day O'Connor, a U.S. Supreme Court justice who has written several opinions placing substantial obstacles before death row inmates, has also added her voice to those concerned about the threat of wrongful executions. "Unfortunately, as the rate of executions has increased, problems in the way which the death penalty has been administered have become more apparent," O'Connor told a group of Minnesota lawyers in July 2001. "Perhaps most alarming among these is the fact that if statistics are any indication, the system may well be allowing some innocent defendants to be executed."

Most Americans, according to public opinion polls, share these judges' fears. In a national poll released by CNN, *USA Today*, and Gallup in June 2000, 80 percent of the respondents said they believe an innocent person has been executed in the United States in the past five years.

One month after that poll was released, Texas executed an inmate whose claims of innocence attracted widespread attention and controversy. What had become a routine occurrence in Texas—the lethal injection of a death row inmate—became, in Gary Graham's case, a national media event.

Graham was seventeen years old when he was arrested for the murder of Bobby Lambert outside a Houston supermarket—a shooting that occurred during a week-long crime spree in which Graham robbed more than a half-dozen people, shot one, and raped another. Graham, like many death row prisoners, presented a rather unsympathetic figure. But while he admitted his role in the crime spree, he long denied that he had anything to do with Lambert's murder. No physical evidence tied Graham to the shooting, and the police never found a weapon. Instead, the prosecution's case rested on the testimony of one woman—a single eyewitness—who said she caught a glimpse of Graham as he committed the murder.

Graham's appellate attorneys, including veteran death-penalty lawyer Richard Burr, found witnesses who said that they, too, saw the murder and claimed that Graham was not the killer. Graham's attorneys also suggested the murder might have been a drug-related "hit." Lambert, according to federal law-enforcement officials, had been scheduled to testify in an Oklahoma drug case before he was shot dead. Nothing tied Graham to that narcotics investigation or to the victim.

As Graham's execution neared, the controversy surrounding the case grew. Not only was Graham's guilt at issue, but the quality of his defense at trial was questioned. Graham was defended by Ronald Mock, an attorney who has become an emblem of the troubles with capital defense in Texas. Mock has been disciplined by the state bar at least five times, according to state records. Before Graham's execution, three of Mock's other clients had been executed under Bush, and many more were on death row.

The testimony of the single eyewitness also was questioned. How could she be so sure? And is the testimony of a single eyewitness enough to execute a man, especially given what we know about the fallibility of eyewitness testimony? In their efforts to win Graham a new trial, his supporters held a news conference with a North Carolina rape victim named Jennifer Thompson, who recounted how her mistaken identification of her assailant had sent an innocent man to prison. If she could make a mistake, Thompson said, perhaps the eyewitness in the Graham case could make one, too. After years of maintaining her silence about the case, the eyewitness against Graham came forward to quiet her critics. At a news conference, she declared that she was certain she had seen Graham commit the murder outside the supermarket. She scoffed at all those who doubted her.

Furthering the battle of press conferences, the Reverend Jesse Jackson, Amnesty International activist Bianca Jagger, and others opposed to the death penalty rallied to Graham's side, saying the evidence against him simply was not strong enough. They unsuccessfully sought a court hearing, saying that new evidence supporting Graham's claims of innocence had never been heard by a judge.

Graham appealed to the pardons and paroles board but failed to receive enough votes to spare his life. Bush allowed the execution to go forward. The scene outside the prison was surreal. New Black Panther Party members clad in black fatigues and armed with rifles faced off against Texas Rangers in their jeans, boots, and cowboy hats. Ku Klux Klan members in full regalia exchanged shouts with death penalty opponents.

Inside the prison, meanwhile, Graham struggled with the guards who came to escort him to Texas's death chamber, refusing to go to his death quietly. After delays, he was executed—but not before he proclaimed his innocence one last time and accused prison officials of state-sanctioned murder.

There is no way to know if Graham was innocent. But as his case demonstrated, innocence has become the fulcrum on which the death penalty debate tilts.

Perhaps not surprisingly, hyperbole dominates the far reaches of each side of that debate. Some prosecutors and victims' rights groups refuse to acknowledge innocence even in cases where death row inmates have been exonerated based on overwhelming evidence that they did not commit the crime. On the other side stands the American Civil Liberties Union, which took out full-page advertisements in 2000 seeking support for a national moratorium on executions. In large, bold type that ran atop a picture of a man hooded and strapped into an electric chair, the advertisement said, "Thanks to Modern Politics 23 Innocent People Have Been Removed from the Living."

Although the research was not cited in the advertisement, the ACLU based its claim on the work of Hugo Adam Bedau and Michael Radelet, two scholars who have cataloged hundreds of cases they believe to be miscarriages of justice, including twenty-three that ended in execution. But in not one of those twenty-three cases has a government body or official acknowledged that the executed person was innocent. That conclusion was simply the authors' subjective determination based on their review of the evidence—and their conclusions about those cases have been vigorously contested. In addition, the advertisement's use of the word "modern" seems misleading. Only one of the twenty-three cases was tried after capital punishment's reinstatement in 1976.

But while the question of whether an innocent person has been executed remains largely unanswerable, there is no doubt that innocent people have been condemned. The next section explores why such miscarriages of justice occur.

Why Mistakes Happen and How to Prevent Them

In the criminal justice system, mistakes happen for many reasons—and those reasons are not always easy to identify and measure. But in two investigative projects at the *Chicago Tribune*, we isolated certain key elements that pop up regularly in miscarriages of justice and, by working with a finite universe of capital cases, determined how frequently they surfaced.

Disbarred Attorneys, Jailhouse Informants, and Hair Comparisons

Shortly after Anthony Porter's exoneration, the *Tribune* began an investigation of Illinois's death penalty system in hopes of learning why so many innocent people were being convicted in cases where mistakes can be irreversible and safeguards supposedly abound. We adopted a comprehensive approach that examined the system as a whole rather than relying on anecdotal evidence and individual miscarriages of justice. In a project that took eight months to complete, we investigated all 285 cases in which a person had been sentenced to die since Illinois reinstated the death penalty in 1977. Ultimately, we were able to isolate systematic flaws that heightened the possibility of an innocent person being convicted and condemned.

For the adversarial system to work, defense attorneys must be competent and able to put the prosecution's case to a vigorous test. A high level of skill is particularly important in capital cases, which tend to be extraordinarily complicated and stressful. But in Illinois the defense attorneys in death penalty cases have too often represented the legal profession's worst, not its best.

At least thirty-three defendants who were sentenced to die in Illinois were represented at trial by an attorney who has been disbarred or suspended—disciplinary sanctions reserved for conduct so incompetent, unethical, or even criminal that the state believes an attorney's license should be taken away. Robert McDonnell, a convicted felon and the only attorney in Illinois history to be disbarred twice, represented four men who landed on death row. He handled those cases after being disbarred once and then reinstated despite concerns about his emotional stability and drinking, according to state records. Another attorney, Herbert Hill, was appointed to represent a defendant in a capital case just ten days after getting his law license back. The Illinois Supreme Court had suspended Hill for nine months, citing a half-dozen cases in which he took advantage of vulnerable clients or failed them through incompetence or dishonesty.

Sometimes, even attorneys with clean disciplinary records have otherwise dubious credentials for trying a capital case. In Illinois, defense attorneys appointed by the courts to represent indigent defendants in capital cases have included a tax lawyer who had never before tried a case, civil or criminal, and an attorney just two years out of law school.

While analyzing each of the state's 285 capital cases, we also tried to determine what kinds of evidence the prosecution was built on. We were looking for different types of evidence that have proved highly unreliable and wound up focusing on two in particular.

In at least forty-six cases in which a defendant was sentenced to die in Illinois, the prosecution's evidence included a jailhouse informant—or "snitch," in the parlance more commonly used in courthouse hallways. Such witnesses have proved so untrustworthy that some states instruct jurors to treat their testimony with special skepticism. Even prosecutors concede that informants deserve special scrutiny. "When we deal with snitches," said Bob Benjamin, a spokesman for Dick Devine, the state's attorney of Cook County, Illinois, "we deal from this point: Most likely they're lying, so you have to double-prove and triple-prove everything they say."

When jailhouse informants testify, the scenario typically goes along these lines: One inmate, the informant, says another inmate, the defendant, made incriminating statements or confessed outright during a conversation the two inmates held while sharing a cell. For his testimony, the jailhouse informant can, and often does, receive a variety of benefits—for example, having pending charges dropped or getting years shaved off a sentence. The state is supposed to disclose such benefits because they provide jailhouse informants with ample motive to lie, but prosecutors have repeatedly failed to do so, according to appellate rulings nationally. In Illinois, five of the state's thirteen exonerated death row inmates were convicted or condemned with the help of jailhouse-informant testimony.

Another kind of evidence that has been linked to wrongful convictions at an alarmingly high rate is the visual comparison of hairs. In Illinois that kind of forensic evidence has been used in at least twenty cases in which a defendant has been sentenced to death. Prosecutors have been presenting such evidence for more than 100 years in the United States. But over the last decade or so visual comparisons of hair have been exposed as notoriously untrustworthy. Some courts have even begun restricting the use of such evidence, saying it is scientifically suspect and has little value as proof.

When testifying about hair comparisons, forensic scientists often dress up their work so that it sounds for all the world like hard science. But the practice consists of nothing more than placing two strands under a microscope and determining whether they look alike. The examinations are highly subjective, and even if a lab employee determines that two hairs do look alike, the most he can say is that they are similar and could have come from the same person. The visual comparison of hairs has far less value than fingerprints because hair lacks unique qualities that allow for a match or positive identification.

The dangers of hair evidence have become increasingly apparent thanks largely to the advent of DNA testing, which offers the very precision that visual hair comparison lacks. Barry Scheck examined the first sixty-five cases in the nation in which DNA evidence exonerated someone convicted of a crime. In eighteen of those cases, prosecutors used hair comparison to help win conviction.

Another fault line that radiates through wrongful conviction cases concerns the racial makeup of the jury. At least thirty-five times, we found, a defendant sentenced to death in Illinois was black and the jury that determined guilt or sentence was all white. Prosecutors consider that racial composition so advantageous that they have removed as many as twenty African Americans from a single trial's jury pool in order to achieve it. In another Illinois capital case, prosecutors secured an all-white jury by using their discretionary strikes to remove sixteen blacks from the jury pool. Of sixty-five death penalty cases in Illinois with a black defendant and a white victim, twenty-one of them, or nearly a third, involved all-white juries.

In postmortems of cases in which justice has gone awry, each of the elements discussed above surfaces regularly. And sometimes, rather remarkably, they all intersect in one case. Dennis Williams, who is black, was sentenced to die by an all-white jury; prosecuted with evidence that included a jailhouse informant and hair comparison; and defended, none too well, by an attorney who was later disbarred.

Williams is a victim of one of Illinois's most notorious miscarriages of justice. His is a case study in how a capital case can go so horribly wrong. Williams and three of his friends, all black, were convicted of the 1978 murders of a white couple in East Chicago Heights, an infamously poor and predominantly black suburb of Chicago. East Chicago Heights has since changed its name to Ford Heights, and, typical of the place-and-number shorthand used to describe numerous miscarriages of justice, Williams and his friends are now known as the Ford Heights 4.[10]

When Williams first stood trial in Cook County Circuit Court, he was represented by Archie Weston. While defending Williams against criminal charges that might cost Williams his life, Weston was simultaneously defending himself against disciplinary charges that might cost him his law license. Weston lost on both counts. Williams was convicted and sentenced to death, and Weston was subsequently disbarred for mishandling a probate matter.[11]

While representing Williams, Weston failed to file crucial motions and raise obvious objections. Even so, the Illinois Supreme Court initially upheld Williams's conviction, turning aside his contention that he had received ineffective assistance of counsel. That changed after Weston was disbarred—and after a member of the Illinois Supreme Court, rather fortuitously, became aware of that disbarment. The Illinois Supreme Court changed its mind and vacated Williams's conviction, saying it could no longer assume that Weston had been competent.

Williams was retried. This time, he was represented by an attorney who was later suspended. Williams was again convicted and sentenced to death.

10. For a dramatic and detailed account of the Ford Heights 4 case, see David Protess and Rob Warden, *A Promise of Justice* (1998). Protess and Warden spent years investigating the case and figured prominently in its unraveling.

11. Of the thirteen Illinois death row inmates who have been exonerated since the death penalty's reinstatement, four were represented at trial by an attorney who has been disbarred or suspended.

When Williams first stood trial, the prosecution's evidence included the testimony of Michael Podlecki, an Illinois State Police forensic scientist who said he had examined three hairs found in Williams's car. Based on a microscopic examination, Podlecki said two of the hairs were "similar" to victim Carol Schmal's and the third was "similar" to victim Larry Lionberg's. As often happens, the prosecutors then stretched Podlecki's findings, substituting the word "matched" for "similar" in their questions and arguments. One prosecutor went further, stating flat-out that the hairs came from the victims—a powerful piece of evidence, if true.

It was not true. Eight years after Williams's first trial, a different examiner for the police studied the three hairs and reached a conclusion dramatically different from Podlecki's. He not only disagreed that the hairs were "similar" to samples from the victims' scalps; he concluded that one of the hairs did not even come from a person's head. It was "a body hair of some sort," the examiner wrote in his report.[12]

In securing Williams's initial conviction and death sentence, the prosecution also offered another kind of evidence that, if anything, is even more dubious than the visual comparison of hairs. The state presented the testimony of David Jackson, a jailhouse informant. Jackson testified that shortly after Williams and codefendant Willie Raines were arrested, he overheard them talking in the Cook County jail about how they had killed a man and "taken" sex from a woman. This squared with the crime for which both men were charged. Schmal, one of the murder victims, had also been raped.

Years later, Jackson recanted. He said his testimony was a lie. He also said, in an affidavit, that a burglary charge had been dropped against him in exchange for his testimony. That contradicted what Jackson told jurors. On the witness stand, Jackson said he had received nothing for his testimony, suggesting he had no motive whatsoever to lie.[13]

In all, three trials were held for Williams and his three codefendants. And in all three trials defense attorneys complained that prosecutors had used their peremptory strikes in a manner that minimized the number of African Americans on the jury. In Williams's first trial, that charge was even made by a black member of the jury pool. When Leroy Posey's name was called, seven people sat on the jury, and all were white. Posey answered the standard questions typically

12. Of course, the clincher came when DNA evidence exonerated Williams and his codefendants, and the true killers were subsequently convicted.

13. One of the prosecutors told the *Tribune* that he does not recall making any deal with Jackson.

posed to voir dire members and then asked the judge if he could speak. "It's obvious the state's attorneys want an all-white jury," Posey said. "They don't want me here." The courtroom broke out in applause. Ultimately, the jury that convicted Williams consisted of eleven whites and one black woman. Afterward, another jury was selected for sentencing. It was all white.

Of the four men convicted for the murders of Schmal and Lionberg, two received death sentences—Williams and Verneal Jimerson. Although Jimerson stood trial separately, his prosecution shared much in common with Williams's odyssey through the criminal courts. For one thing, Jimerson's jury had only one African American on it—that, despite a relatively large number of blacks in the jury pool.

On two separate days of jury selection, the jury pool started with nearly three dozen people, thirteen of them African American. At the end of each day, eight people had not been called up for possible duty. Each day, all eight were black. The court clerk said she shuffled the juror cards, and that was just the way it turned out. The odds of that happening are approximately one in 250 million, according to a mathematics professor asked to calculate the odds by the *Tribune*.

In the end, Jimerson's prosecution fell into another category of cases that provides additional explanation for the growing number of innocent people who have been sentenced to death. In 1995 the Illinois Supreme Court vacated Jimerson's conviction, ruling that prosecutors had allowed their star witness to lie while testifying against Jimerson. That makes Jimerson one of at least 381 people nationally who have had a homicide conviction reversed because prosecutors failed to disclose evidence favorable to the defendant or presented evidence they knew to be false, according to a *Tribune* investigation of prosecutorial misconduct that was published in January 1999.

In sixty-seven of those 381 cases, the defendant had been sentenced to death. And of those sixty-seven defendants, at least twenty-four were subsequently freed: their charges were dropped, or they were acquitted at retrial, or they received full pardons.

The Ford Heights 4 were ultimately freed in 1996, thanks to DNA testing that Cook County prosecutors initially opposed and thanks to confessions from the real killers that were obtained as part of an investigation by Northwestern University journalism students. When it falls to journalism students, working with their professor and private investigators, to unravel the convictions of innocent men on death row—as happened with Anthony Porter, Dennis Williams, and Verneal Jimerson—the criminal justice system is not working. Errors are being caught by people outside the system, not within it.

Collectively, the Ford Heights 4 spent sixty-five years in prison for crimes they did not commit. Williams alone lost eighteen years of his life. The case also cost Cook County taxpayers. The Ford Heights 4 filed suit alleging, in effect, that Cook County sheriff's officers had framed them for the murders. In 1999 the county settled the suit for $36 million.

Texas and "Super Due Process"

Perhaps nowhere has the issue of innocence been as hotly debated as in Texas. In the election year of 2000, journalists flocked to Texas—the nation's leader in executions and the home state of future president George W. Bush—to find an innocent man who had been executed, as well as to investigate the state's death penalty system and Bush's oversight of it.

As a follow-up to our investigation of the death penalty in Illinois, the *Chicago Tribune* conducted a four-month investigation of capital punishment in Texas. The problems that precipitated the Illinois moratorium, we found, were equally pronounced in Texas. In addition, Texas suffered from a variety of other flaws, including several that undermined the fairness of its sentencing proceedings.[14]

We examined 131 executions that took place while Bush was governor.[15] Since these were convictions and death sentences that had made their way through the courts and the governor's office, they theoretically represented the best, or fairest, of the state's capital cases. But what we found indicated serious problems.

In forty-three cases, or one-third of the 131, a defendant was represented at trial or on initial appeal by an attorney who had been, or was later, disbarred, suspended, or otherwise sanctioned. In at least twenty-three cases, the prosecution's case included a jailhouse informant. In another twenty-three cases, the prosecution's case included the visual comparison of hairs. Sometimes, these elements overlapped in the same case.

The prevalence of sanctioned attorneys and jailhouse-informant testimony in capital cases figured prominently in Governor Ryan's decision to suspend executions in Illinois. But in Texas, those factors failed to unsettle then-governor Bush. After our series was published, he continued to express confidence in his state's system of capital punishment. "If you're asking me whether or not as to

14. Steve Mills, Ken Armstrong, and Douglas Holt, "State of Execution: The Death Penalty in Texas," *Chi. Trib.*, June 11–12, 2000.
15. That was the number of executions under Bush as of June 11, 2000, the first day of our two-part series.

the innocence or guilt or if people have had adequate access to the courts in Texas, I believe they have," Bush told reporters, when asked to respond to the *Tribune*'s findings. "They've had full access to the courts. They've had full access to a fair trial."

Our investigation also focused on the fairness of the state's sentencing hearings. With their client's life at stake, defense attorneys in forty cases presented no evidence whatsoever or only one witness during the trial's sentencing phase. And in at least twenty-nine cases the prosecution presented damaging testimony from a psychiatrist who, based on a hypothetical question describing the defendant's past, predicted the defendant would commit future violence. In most of these cases, the psychiatrist offered this opinion without ever examining the defendant. Although this kind of testimony is sometimes used in other states, the American Psychiatric Association has condemned it as unethical and untrustworthy.

In Texas, the state's court of criminal appeals has also cast a long shadow over the fairness of capital cases. The state's court of last resort, the panel of nine judges has frequently proved tolerant of flawed convictions and reluctant to acknowledge holes in the prosecution's case. The court of criminal appeals refused relief to death row inmates represented by an attorney who slept at trial. The court refused relief to a convicted rapist, Roy Criner, even though DNA testing conducted after trial showed the semen found in the victim was not his. The court refused relief to Cesar Fierro, even though nearly everyone involved in the case, including the prosecutor who sent Fierro to death row, had come to agree that a confession police obtained from Fierro had been coerced and was unworthy of trust. The court refused relief in a case in which a psychologist testified that a defendant was more likely to commit violence in the future simply because he was Hispanic—a conclusion that the Texas attorney general's office later acknowledged was erroneous. Even the court's conduct in administrative matters has proved controversial. To handle death row appeals, for example, the court has appointed attorneys with previous disciplinary records or little experience.

Since capital punishment's reinstatement, seven men sentenced to death in Texas were later exonerated. They include Randall Dale Adams, whose conviction was unraveled by filmmaker Errol Morris in the documentary "The Thin Blue Line." But neither the exoneration of a convicted person nor the prevalence of sanctioned defense attorneys and unreliable evidence has punctured the aura of confidence projected by many of the state's top judges and law enforcement officials.

During Bush's presidential campaign, the state's attorney general, John Cornyn, consistently defended Texas's criminal justice system. Texas, Cornyn said, afforded defendants "super due process"—although when he spelled out such due process in a newspaper opinion piece, there was nothing particularly super about it. "While there may have been wrongful convictions in Illinois," Cornyn wrote, "this is Texas . . . not Illinois. . . . The defendant receives his or her *Miranda* warning upon arrest. An indictment, based on probable cause, by a grand jury follows. The defendant has a right to counsel, a trial by a jury of one's peers under the supervision of a judge and . . . unanimous verdicts beyond a reasonable doubt."

Such safeguards are purely routine. The next section will examine some proposed reforms that go beyond *Miranda* warnings and a trial by jury.

Proposals to Shore Up the System

The publicity surrounding the Anthony Porter case and other high-profile miscarriages of justice has prompted the creation of numerous panels to study flaws in how capital punishment is administered and to propose reforms. Those committees have ranged from the one appointed by Illinois Governor George Ryan when he announced a moratorium on executions to the Constitution Project, a diverse panel that included former judges, state attorneys general, federal prosecutors, defense attorneys, and governors. The balance of the Constitution Project's membership, which included people both for and against the death penalty, likely enhanced the credibility of its proposed reforms.

Lawmakers at both the federal and state level have also issued a variety of legislative proposals, including many that have already been acted upon. In addition, some courts, most notably the Illinois Supreme Court, have taken it upon themselves to enact rules changing the way in which capital cases are tried.

This section of the chapter will quickly review some of the measures that have been bandied about, including some that enjoy widespread support and others that have received relatively little attention.

Following a year-long study, the Constitution Project proposed eighteen reforms in June 2001. Many of the proposals applied to issues of fairness more than innocence—for example, recommendations to ban the execution of mentally retarded persons and defendants who were under eighteen when the crime was committed. But several of the recommended safeguards focused squarely on protecting the innocent from being marched into the execution chamber:

—Every jurisdiction with the death penalty should impose minimum standards for defense attorneys in capital cases. These jurisdictions should create bodies that would screen, appoint, train, and supervise lawyers who try death penalty cases. This proposal also calls for adequate compensation for defense attorneys trying such cases.

—DNA evidence should be preserved and made available for testing in cases where it could help exonerate a defendant awaiting execution. At the same time, jurisdictions with the death penalty should ensure that powerful, exculpatory evidence discovered after trial can be introduced on the defendant's behalf rather than being barred by procedural rules.

—Prosecutors should adopt an "open-file" policy in capital cases, ensuring that the defense has access to all materials that may benefit it while preparing for trial. This proposal calls for prosecutors to establish internal guidelines on seeking the death penalty in cases that are built exclusively on certain types of suspect evidence—for example, the testimony of an accomplice.

The above proposals are, for the most part, hardly novel. They have appeared repeatedly in the reform packages issued by other groups studying the death penalty. In January 2001, the Illinois Supreme Court passed rules along the lines of the first proposal, although the capital litigation bar that Illinois established went even further than the Constitution Project's proposal. The Illinois Supreme Court also applied minimum standards in capital cases to prosecutors, a highly unusual step that separates Illinois from other states. As for the preservation and testing of DNA evidence, that issue is a centerpiece of the proposed Innocence Protection Act, federal legislation sponsored in the Senate by Democrat Patrick Leahy of Vermont and Republicans Gordon Smith of Oregon and Susan Collins of Maine.

Some proposals that have been issued nationally concentrate on the manner in which police gather evidence and put together a case. Probably the most prominent of these measures has been the call for police to videotape confessions. Such video would allow jurors to see the context in which a statement was made and to better judge the confession's credibility. This proposal would reduce the possibility of confessions being coerced, and it would protect police from such allegations as the often-heard claim that officers failed to apprise a suspect of his *Miranda* rights.

Lawrence Marshall, a Northwestern University law professor who has helped represent several innocent men freed from Illinois's death row, has come up with his own list of proposed reforms geared toward minimizing the risk of executing innocent defendants, including the following:

—Prohibiting the pursuit of the death penalty in cases that rest primarily on the testimony of one eyewitness. This proposal recognizes the fallibility of eyewitness testimony and even finds support in the Bible, which declares that "on the testimony of two or three witnesses a man shall be put to death, but no one shall be put to death on the testimony of only one witness."

—Prohibiting the use of jailhouse-snitch testimony in a capital case unless the trial judge first holds a pretrial reliability hearing to determine that the evidence can be trusted. Oklahoma already holds hearings of this kind, during which the judge considers such crucial elements as whether the witness will receive anything for testifying and the degree to which his testimony can be independently corroborated.

—Allowing jurors and appellate judges to consider "residual doubt" in deciding whether to impose or uphold a death sentence. This proposal recognizes that in measures of proof, considerable room lies between "a reasonable doubt" and unequivocal certainty.

Regarding the last proposal, Missouri, for one, already has a law that requires its state supreme court to consider "the strength of the evidence" when reviewing a death sentence and determining whether it is proportionate to other capital cases. In 1998 the court used that law to vacate a death sentence in a case that rested largely on forensic evidence of questionable value, including analysis of hairs, fibers, and metal shavings. The prosecution also presented DNA evidence indicating that the victim's genetic profile was consistent with hairs found in the defendant's van. Less than one-half of 1 percent of the population shares that profile, the evidence showed.[16] Ruling that the evidence was sufficient to convict but not to execute, the Missouri Supreme Court reduced the defendant's sentence to life imprisonment.[17]

The Search for the Innocent Man Executed

For the media, investigating possible miscarriages of justice has been a time-honored tradition. American reporters have unraveled dozens of convictions

16. See State v. Chaney, 967 s.w.2d 47 (Mo. 1998).

17. By no means do the above proposals represent a comprehensive accounting of all the reform measures under consideration in jurisdictions having the death penalty. For that matter, our description of problems plaguing the system of capital punishment is hardly comprehensive either. For an excellent, more detailed accounting of elements that undermine the criminal justice system, we recommend *Actual Innocence* (2000) by Barry Scheck, Peter Neufeld, and Jim Dwyer. The authors include a roundup of reform measures addressing the systematic weaknesses described in their book.

over the decades, helping free innocent inmates serving long prison sentences or even awaiting execution. In the 1940s such work by two Chicago reporters became the basis for the movie *Call Northside 777*. In the 1960s and 1970s Gene Miller of the *Miami Herald* exposed a series of wrongful convictions, including cases in which innocent men had been sentenced to death. Newspapers like the *Philadelphia Inquirer* and *Detroit Free Press* also have proud histories punctuated with such investigations. So the remarkable work conducted by Northwestern University journalism students, who helped free three innocent men from Illinois's death row during the 1990s, has long roots in American journalism.

In recent years, though, a new type of investigation has emerged among newspapers and television news shows probing the country's criminal justice system. As the amount of attention devoted to the death penalty has increased, so have media efforts to find an innocent person who has been executed. Rather than working to spring innocent people from prison or death sentences, many reporters now dig through closed cases that ended with the defendant's execution. Akin to the quest for the holy grail—Does there even exist a case of an innocent man having been executed? And, if so, how do we find him?—the media's search tests the new line of defense presented by many of capital punishment's strongest backers, who insist that the death penalty's safeguards would prevent an innocent man from ever being ushered into the execution chamber.

The search presents extraordinary obstacles. Witnesses may have died or their memories faded. Physical evidence may have been discarded or lost. Even if such evidence is preserved, authorities might refuse to make it available for testing. In addition, many of the investigative techniques typically used to poke holes in a prosecution's case can be easily dismissed. Witness recantations are often met with skepticism. So are confessions from other suspects. In some recent cases, authorities have even explained away DNA tests excluding convicted rapists or murderers. (None involved a defendant who had already been executed.) In these cases prosecutors came up with a new theory of the crime—usually one involving multiple rapists or killers—that attempted to square the defendant's guilt with the absence of a DNA link.

But, despite those difficulties, the search for the innocent man executed has captured the imagination of a growing number of reporters and editors. During President Bush's campaign for the White House, several media powerhouses turned their sights on Texas and began scrutinizing executions held while Bush was the state's governor. Television's most esteemed investigative program, "60 Minutes," profiled the case of Jerry Lee Hogue and suggested that he might have been innocent. The *New York Times* published a lengthy piece that included sketches of a half-dozen executions resulting from the prosecution's seemingly suspect evidence. And while the *Chicago Tribune* employed a systematic approach that quantified various fault lines in Texas, we also examined the innocence claims of David Wayne Stoker, a carpenter and handyman who had been executed in 1997.

Stoker was convicted of killing a convenience store clerk in a 1986 robbery that, according to prosecutors, netted $96. The case featured a variety of elements that surface repeatedly in wrongful-conviction cases. The state's star witness received reward money from a crime-stopper program and had drug charges against him dismissed. Two other prosecution witnesses—an investigator from the district attorney's office and a top police official—gave false testimony relating to that witness and any incentive he may have had to lie. Yet another prosecution witness recanted after trial.

As for Stoker's defense, his lead attorney was forced to surrender his law license less than two years after Stoker's trial; he eventually pleaded guilty to criminal charges. Stoker's other court-appointed lawyer had been an attorney less than a year when the case went to trial. A member of the Texas Board of Pardons and Paroles said that he was so bothered by the possibility that Stoker might have been innocent that he cast a vote for clemency. It was, the board member said, one of only two times that he had voted to spare the life of a condemned man.

The *Tribune* went to Hale Center, the small community north of Lubbock where the crime occurred, and tried to reconstruct the case. We reviewed court records and police files, looking for leads that perhaps had been neglected years ago. We tracked down and interviewed witnesses. We spoke with prosecutors and police, hoping to get their perspective on Stoker's case and to confront them with inconsistencies. We also spoke with the jurors. In interviews, several of them said that had they known of some of the troubles with the case, they might have cast their votes for a different verdict. Stoker, they suggested, might still be alive.

But proving innocence in a case like this—one where there is no DNA, as is true in the majority of capital cases—becomes a Herculean task. By the time the *Tribune* arrived in Hale Center, Stoker had been dead for nearly three years. His final statement, directed at the family of the victim—"I am truly sorry for your loss . . . but I didn't kill anyone"—had grown faint in the growing discussion about capital punishment. Our work had the feel of an archaeological dig. We were dusting off artifacts that had been buried along with Stoker. In the end, we were able to identify a host of weaknesses in the prosecution's case, but we did not unearth irrefutable proof of innocence.

Recognizing the limitations of traditional investigation, some newspapers have concentrated on cases that offer the potential of DNA testing. The *Boston Globe* has been the most aggressive, sifting through execution cases in search of claims of innocence coupled with biological evidence that was never tested or that was examined using older, less powerful methods. Only once, though, has DNA testing been ordered in the United States in an effort to determine whether an executed man was innocent. At the *Globe*'s request, a Georgia judge issued that order in July 2000 in the case of Ellis Wayne Felker, who was executed in 1996 for the rape and murder of a college woman. But the laboratory subsequently reported that it could not find the assailant's DNA when examining slides prepared at the time of the victim's autopsy, meaning no conclusion could be reached from the evidence.

With the sole exception of the Felker case, authorities in the United States have rejected appeals for DNA testing in cases where a person has already been executed. In one case Virginia officials even incinerated the DNA evidence rather than let it be tested. That stands in marked contrast to England, where the government has already acknowledged executing innocent men. In England, they dig up graves to make evidence available for testing. In Virginia, they take evidence that is already available and burn it.

Conclusion: Questions That Are Destined to Linger

Most crime scenes do not offer biological evidence that can conclusively implicate or exonerate a suspect. For example, when a robber shoots and kills a convenience store clerk, he typically does not leave behind blood, semen, or other tissue that can implicate him and no one else.

In December 2000, the *Chicago Tribune* published a series examining four cases that fit the more common profile—cases that cannot be unlocked with genetic testing but in which questions of innocence and guilt linger after a defendant's execution. The cases we wrote about were not necessarily those with the most compelling claims of innocence. Instead, the cases illustrated themes that we thought illuminated the innocence question.

Wilburn Henderson's was a case nobody knew, a man who went to his execution even though a federal appeals court once said there was "significant doubt" about his guilt and substantial evidence that another man was the real killer. A career criminal, Henderson was executed in July 1998 in Arkansas for the murder of a shop owner in Fort Smith. But considerable evidence pointed to other suspects, including the victim's husband. In one opinion, the U.S. Court of Appeals for the Eighth Circuit named five suspects other than Henderson.

Alvin Moore's was a case that had never been tested, one in which the defense did no investigation before trial or on appeal. The case against Moore appeared open and shut, yet our own investigation showed that it was anything but. Moore was executed in Louisiana's electric chair in 1987.

Bennie Demps's was a case built on sand, a case that relied on unreliable witnesses—convicted murderers, mostly. The murder that placed Demps on death row occurred in prison. He was executed in Florida in 2000.

Leo Jones, executed in 1998, presented a powerful claim of innocence, but the evidence in his favor accumulated gradually. During the sixteen years his conviction remained on appeal, Jones struggled mightily to get judges to examine the evidence anew. His was a story of legal roadblocks and the difficulty in overcoming them.

A drug dealer in Jacksonville, Florida, Jones was convicted of the 1981 murder of a Jacksonville police officer killed by a sniper's bullet. The evidence against him was a vague two-sentence statement police claimed he made, in which Jones said he shot the officer with a "gun or rifle," plus testimony from Jones's cousin.

But Jones's cousin recanted, and there was considerable evidence to call into question how the statement was obtained. Jones claimed he was beaten by police—the kind of claim many defendants make. But the lead detective in the case told the *Tribune* that he, in fact, had to pull officer Lynwood Mundy off Jones when Jones was arrested. "He hit him, but he didn't bust him up," the detective said of Mundy. "But he hit him pretty good." Another officer said Mundy boasted of beating Jones. Mundy later resigned under pressure because of misconduct allegations. He has denied hitting Jones.

More important, perhaps, was evidence that pointed to someone else. Close to a dozen people claimed that another man—a man with an extensive record that included trying to shoot and run over a police officer—had confessed to the murder for which Jones was convicted. Interestingly, some of them were jailhouse informants—just the sort of witnesses that prosecutors use to win convictions. In the Jones case, prosecutors argued that jailhouse informants could not be trusted. Other witnesses said they saw the alternative suspect at the scene of the crime—with a weapon. Still others said they helped him to escape just after the murder.

In the end, it was not enough. Although two Florida Supreme Court justices said that the state risked executing an innocent man—and even detailed all the evidence that pointed away from Jones in one lengthy opinion—Jones was executed, still proclaiming his innocence.

In each of these cases, we investigated the crime anew. We began with the appellate opinions, trial transcripts, and police reports. Then we went to towns where these cases played out and interviewed witnesses. In some cases, we discovered important witnesses who had never been interviewed by police, prosecutors or defense attorneys. In others, we talked to witnesses who had been interviewed, but now told us they had lied.

In several of these cases we broke new ground. We punched holes in the prosecution's case. Did we prove innocence? No. But had Anthony Porter been executed, it's highly unlikely that his innocence would ever have been proved either. Consider the background of his case.

The crime that was pinned on Porter received nominal publicity. In 1982, 670 people were murdered in Chicago. Marilyn Green and Jerry Hillard were but two of them. They were shot to death in a park on the city's South Side. Police said the crime appeared to be drug-related. The victims were black and poor. So was Porter, who had robbed and shot a man before. The media paid little attention.

Porter claimed to be innocent, but many guilty people claim innocence. (More than 100 people executed in the United States since capital punishment's reinstatement proclaimed their innocence until the end, including some defendants who were guilty beyond any doubt.) Two eyewitnesses had identified Porter as the killer, and a police officer said he had stopped Porter in the park minutes after the shootings. The Illinois Supreme Court called the evidence against Porter "overwhelming." The crime offered no old, untested DNA evidence that might exonerate Porter, so his case would have generated little enthusiasm among investigators seeking definitive proof that an innocent person has been executed in the United States.

Had Anthony Porter been executed, he would simply be another Wilburn Henderson. Or Alvin Moore. Or Bennie Demps. Or Leo Jones. He would belong to a long line of condemned men who claimed innocence to the end—but never could prove it.

4 : RACE AND CAPITAL PUNISHMENT

Sheri Lynn Johnson

In the last year of the twentieth century, two big race and death penalty stories hit the news. Both of these stories are complicated, but they are worth detailing—both for the light they shed on how race influences capital sentencing and for the light they shed on when the influence of race catches the attention of the media.

The first story, a truly bizarre one, concerned Victor Saldano, a Venezuelan who was convicted of capital murder in Texas. A jury in Texas may only impose the death penalty if it finds that the defendant will be dangerous in the future, a question that places a premium on the testimony of any witness who claims to be able to predict violent behavior. The American Psychological Association has disavowed such testimony, making the professional judgment that such predictions are so unreliable as to be improper for experts to offer them.

Nevertheless, psychologists issue such opinions, and in Saldano's case a Filipino psychologist testified for the government that Saldano would indeed be dangerous in the future. For our purposes, the general unreliability of such testimony is of only incidental interest; what is crucial was the fact that the psychologist based his prediction of future dangerousness in part on the defendant's Latino ancestry. Moreover, he did not do so silently; he openly informed the jury that race was one factor that led to his prediction. Yet defense counsel did not object to this testimony. When an equal protection argument was raised before the Texas Court of Criminal Appeals, that court held that defense counsel's failure to object constituted a procedural default of that claim.[1] This ruling conveniently permitted the court to avoid deciding the merits of the claim.

1. A claim is "procedurally defaulted" if the defendant fails to comply with a state procedural rule governing how and when the claim should have been presented. The doctrine of procedural

Fortunately for Saldano, he was from Venezuela, not Texas, and the Venezuelan government retained a prominent Texas firm to inquire further into the matter. As a consequence—and perhaps in part because George W. Bush was both running for president and somewhat vulnerable on issues related to the death penalty—the firm persuaded the Texas attorney general to both concede error in the United States Supreme Court and waive the procedural default. Saldano therefore had his death sentence reversed. Subsequently, six other capital defendants (mostly black) against whom the same psychologist had testified, claiming their race increased the likelihood of their being a danger in the future, also received new trials on the issue of their sentencing.

The second news story does not really amount to a new story; it is only a new incarnation of a very old story—one not so easily deemed isolated. Juan Garza was sentenced to death in federal court, and nothing overtly racial occurred during his trial. But, as has long been apparent, federal capital defendants and the federal death row are overwhelmingly black and Latino; moreover, capital prosecutions and death sentences are overwhelmingly more likely in cases where the victim is white.[2] This is not news, but it was news when President Clinton halted Garza's execution in order to study the phenomenon. Garza, however, fared less well than Saldano. Before Clinton left office, he granted Garza a stay of six months but left the issue of race discrimination in the administration of the federal death penalty unresolved.

Certainly Clinton did not choose this course of action in anticipation of further study of the issue by George W. Bush. Although one might hypothesize that the death penalty is just too controversial an issue for even an outgoing president to tackle, such a hypothesis would be overly broad. Interestingly enough, at the very end of his term Clinton did issue a commutation of sentence to another federal death row inmate—but not on the basis of racial discrimination. (Similarly, Clinton issued a rash of last-minute pardons in noncapital cases, but Leonard Peltier did not make the list, despite, or perhaps because, his equitable

---

default therefore permits the affirmance of a conviction even in the face of constitutional error, provided that the error was not raised at the proper time or in the proper way. A state may, however, choose to "waive" procedural default and allow the merits of the claim to be adjudicated. Indeed, a state may go even further and concede that it has committed error, obviating the need for a court to decide whether it has done so—as the state of Texas ultimately did in the Saldano case.

2. See Staff of House Subcomm. on Civil and Constitutional Rights, House Comm. on the Judiciary, 103d Cong., 2d Sess., "Racial Disparities in Federal Death Penalty Prosecutions 1988–1994" (Comm. Print 1994).

claim depended on allegations of racial discrimination.)[3] Of course, an executive decision to grant relief to Garza, unlike the executive decision to permit relief for Saldano, could not have dumped all the blame in the lap of a purportedly renegade psychologist, but it would perforce have implicated the fairness of an entire system. Concomitantly, were the executive to acknowledge injustice in Garza's case, relief could not have been confined to a half dozen cases, as it could in Saldano's.

In thinking about race and death penalty issues that have caught the public eye, it is interesting to note one that might have but did not. The biggest death penalty story is surely the innocence story, played out in Illinois through the governor's decision to declare a moratorium on the death penalty in that state because of the large number of cases in which innocent defendants were discovered on Illinois's death row. Another part of the innocence story is the growing number of DNA exonerations, as recounted in *Actual Innocence* by Jim Dwyer, Peter Neufeld, and Barry Scheck.[4] Although this wrongful conviction story has received enormous amounts of press, one part of it has been largely neglected: The exonerated defendants are overwhelmingly African American. Moreover, the largest subset of the innocence cases were based on mistaken cross-racial identifications.

This chapter focuses on three questions that stem from these stories: First, are these race stories just blips on the very large radar screen of the death penalty? Put more formally, have we largely eliminated the long history of race discrimination in the application of the death penalty? Second, if they are not blips, why does racial discrimination persist in this area? And, third, what are the prospects for eliminating race discrimination in the administration of the death penalty in the foreseeable future?

A Brief History

There is no question that the death penalty in this country historically was sought and imposed in a racially discriminatory manner. The "distorting effects of racial discrimination"[5] in the administration of the death penalty are in truth as old as our Republic. The long history of the relation between race and capital

---

3. Leonard Peltier is a Native American activist whose prosecution and conviction are alleged to have been racially motivated.

4. Jim Dwyer, Peter Neufeld, and Barry Scheck, *Actual Innocence: Five Days to Execution and Other Dispatches from the Wrongly Convicted* (2000).

5. See Godfrey v. Georgia, 446 U.S. 420, 439 (1980) (Marshall, J., concurring).

cases has been painstakingly documented elsewhere;[6] a very brief history will suffice for our purposes.

The First Two Centuries: Egregious Discrimination

During the antebellum period, the form of racial discrimination in capital cases varied with the jurisdiction, but it included statutory discrimination based on the race of the defendant and on the race of the victim, as well as blatant discrimination in administration. Moreover, evidentiary rules limiting the admissibility of testimony of African Americans created additional disparities even in cases where the fact finders might have otherwise been more evenhanded.[7]

The Civil War and the Fourteenth Amendment did little to remedy such discrimination, though they did cause the form of that discrimination to change. For nearly a century, extreme procedural deprivations, such as coerced confessions, were common in the capital prosecutions of African American defendants. In part because of these deprivations, and in part because most capital juries were either all white or overwhelmingly white, racial disparities in the application of the death penalty were prevalent across the country; they were particularly stark in capital prosecutions for the crime of rape. It must also be remembered that during much of that period, racially motivated lynching was a common extralegal analogue of the death penalty.

By the late 1960s and early 1970s, many of the worst state procedures had been addressed and at least ameliorated by the Supreme Court, yet major racial disparities remained. In 1972, however, the Court seemed ready to directly confront the many inequities of capital punishment, including racial inequities. Indeed, concern that race influences who lives and who dies was perhaps the most significant factor in the Supreme Court's decision to overturn all then-existing death penalty statutes in *Furman v. Georgia*.[8] Justice William O. Douglas decried the wide discretion given judges and juries in imposing the death penalty because such discretion is often responsible for "feeding prejudices against the accused if he is poor and despised, and lacking political clout, or if he is a member of a suspect or unpopular minority, and saving those who by social

---

6. See, e.g., Stephen B. Bright, "Discrimination, Death and Denial: The Tolerance of Racial Discrimination in the Infliction of the Death Penalty," 35 *Santa Clara L. Rev.* 433 (1995).

7. See Sheri Lynn Johnson, "The Color of Truth: Race and the Assessment of Credibility," 1 *Mich. J. of Race & Law* 261, 267–68 (1996).

8. Furman v. Georgia, 408 U.S. 238 (1972) (per curiam).

position may be in a more protected position."[9] Justice Thurgood Marshall discussed the history of racial discrimination at length in his opinion, noting that "[n]egroes [have been] executed far more often than whites in proportion to their percentage of the population."[10] Even Justice Potter Stewart noted that "if any basis can be discerned for the selection of these few to be sentenced to die, it is the constitutionally impermissible basis of race."[11]

Even when the Court subsequently upheld death penalty statutes in *Gregg v. Georgia*,[12] its reasoning was consistent with *Furman*'s concerns about racial discrimination; in the plurality's view, the new statutes sufficiently channeled the discretion of the sentencer to eliminate the possibility that the death penalty was arbitrarily or capriciously imposed. *Gregg* acknowledged the possibility that race may influence capital punishment, even under the new "guided discretion" statutes; but since discrimination had not yet been proven under those statutes, the Court upheld them.

A year after *Gregg* was decided, the Court struck down the death penalty for rape,[13] which was notorious for the extremity of its racial imbalance.[14] Although not discussed by the Court, observers believed that the likelihood of racial discrimination was the key motivating factor in the Court's decision to invalidate the death penalty for rape. Many litigators and academics therefore viewed *Gregg* as posing the opportunity to demonstrate that race was still an important factor in the administration of capital punishment. Over the next decade, a number of statistical studies were conducted, all of which revealed that race—both the defendant's and the victim's—played a significant role in how the death penalty is meted out.[15] Among these studies was one conducted by Dr. David Baldus of the University of Iowa.

---

9. Id. at 255 (Douglas, J., concurring); see also id. at 364 (Marshall, J., concurring) ("It is usually the poor, the illiterate, the underprivileged, the member of the minority group—the man who, because he is without means, and is defended by a court-appointed attorney—who becomes society's sacrificial lamb") (internal citation omitted).

10. Id. at 331 (Marshall, J., concurring).

11. Id. at 216 (Stewart, J., concurring).

12. 428 U.S. 153 (1976) (plurality opinion).

13. See Coker v. Georgia, 433 U.S. 584 (1977).

14. See, e.g., *Furman*, 408 U.S. at 364 n.149 (Marshall, J., concurring) (noting that of the 455 persons executed for rape after the Justice Department began compiling statistics, 405 were black).

15. U.S. Gen. Acct. Off., "Death Penalty Sentencing: Research Indicates Pattern of Racial Disparities" (1990) (collecting studies).

McCleskey v. Kemp[16]

Baldus's study examined over 2,000 murders that occurred in Georgia during the 1970s. After considering 230 variables that could have explained the data on nonracial grounds, Baldus concluded that defendants charged with killing white victims were 4.3 times more likely to receive the death penalty than defendants charged with killing African Americans and that black defendants were 10 percent more likely to receive the death penalty than other defendants.[17] Thus a black defendant who killed a white victim had the greatest likelihood of receiving a death sentence.[18]

Warren McCleskey was just such a defendant; indeed, as Justice William Brennan stated in dissent, Baldus's statistical analysis showed that "the jury *more likely than not* would have spared McCleskey's life had his victim been black."[19] When the United States Court of Appeals for the Eleventh Circuit sitting en banc rejected McCleskey's challenge, the Supreme Court granted certiorari. McCleskey's case was a particularly appropriate vehicle for the Supreme Court to address racial disparities under post-*Furman* statutes, both because the case arose from Georgia (as had *Furman* and *Gregg*) and because it involved the most comprehensive of the statistical studies conducted by a respected statistician.

A bare majority of the Court, in an opinion authored by Justice Lewis Powell, affirmed the judgment of the court of appeals. The majority held that general statistical evidence showing that a particular state's capital punishment scheme operated in a discriminatory manner did not establish either an Eighth or Fourteenth Amendment violation. Having found that Professor Baldus's study established "at most . . . a discrepancy that appears to correlate with race,"[20] the Court then refused to "assume that which is unexplained is invidious."[21]

In the past, the Court had sometimes found that statistics standing alone were sufficient proof of discriminatory intent, so Justice Powell's opinion had to distinguish these cases. Ordinarily, he said, statistical disparities must be "stark" to be accepted as the sole proof of discrimination, apparently viewing

16. 481 U.S. 279 (1987).

17. The raw data indicated that the death sentencing rate for all white victim cases was eleven times greater than the rate for black victim cases. See id. at 327.

18. Id. at 286–87.

19. Id. at 325 (Brennan, J., dissenting).

20. The majority opinion states that "[e]ven a sophisticated multiple-regression analysis such as the Baldus study can only demonstrate a *risk* that the factor of race entered into some capital sentencing decisions and a necessarily lesser risk that race entered into any particular sentencing decision." Id. at 291 n.7.

21. Id. at 312–13.

McCleskey's showing as less than "stark." The prior cases, which involved discrimination in jury selection, had accepted less extreme statistical disparities as sufficient to shift the burden of proof to the government to show nondiscrimination. But these cases, Powell explained, involved less complicated decisions and fewer decision makers. The larger number of actors and factors in the capital sentencing process would increase the likelihood that other factors were responsible for racial effects—or so said Justice Powell—and therefore rendered the jury selection precedents inapplicable; moreover, this complexity would have intolerably increased the rebuttal burden if the state were required to explain the statewide statistics that McCleskey had proffered.

Because they neither constituted a stark statistical pattern nor warranted departure from the stark pattern standard, the Court dismissed Baldus's statewide statistics as "clearly insufficient to support an inference that any of the decision makers in McCleskey's case acted with discriminatory purpose."[22] The only other evidence of racial discrimination proffered by McCleskey was historical. Although the evidence of past race-consciousness in the Georgia criminal justice system was extensive, the Court found that because it lacked recency, it had little probative value in assessing the likelihood of post-*Furman* discrimination. Thus McCleskey had offered "no evidence specific to his own case that would support an inference that racial considerations played a part in his sentence."[23] He therefore failed to demonstrate a violation of either the Equal Protection Clause or the Eighth Amendment.[24]

For the reader who finds this conclusion unpersuasive, the majority augmented its doctrinal analysis with practical considerations: "McCleskey argues that the Baldus study compels an inference that his sentence rests on purposeful discrimination. McCleskey's claim that these statistics are sufficient proof of discrimination, without regard to the facts of a particular case, would extend to all capital cases in Georgia, at least where the victim was white and the defen-

22. Id. at 297.

23. Id. at 292–93.

24. See id. at 297. The majority opinion is somewhat unclear as to who the relevant decision maker is: the jury that sentences the defendant to death, the prosecutor who makes the decision to seek the death penalty, or both. However, the passage above seems to indicate that if either the jury's or the prosecutor's decision to seek or impose the death sentence was affected by race, the Equal Protection Clause would be violated. As a commonsense matter this must be correct. Imagine, for example, a prosecutor who announces that his policy is that he will only seek the death penalty in cases involving black defendants and white victims. Would the constitutionality of such a death sentence be saved by the fact that the sentence was imposed by a non–racially biased jury? To ask the question is to answer it.

dant is black."[25] Thus, the Court feared that ruling for McCleskey on the basis of the Baldus study would call into question the validity of a large class of capital cases throughout Georgia. And since there was little reason to think that the Baldus study could not be replicated in cases in other states (and likely would have been had McCleskey prevailed), McCleskey endangered at least hundreds of what might be otherwise valid capital convictions and sentences. As the Court stated in its opinion, "McCleskey's claim, taken to its logical conclusion, throws into serious question the principles that underlie our entire criminal justice system."[26]

Nonetheless, inferring from *McCleskey* a broad prohibition against racial discrimination challenges to death sentences would exaggerate the sweep of the decision. Justice Marshall's papers reveal a *McCleskey* case memorandum from Justice Antonin Scalia indicating that the latter would hold that *no* showing of racial discrimination in the death sentencing process—no matter how strong or direct—would violate the Eighth or Fourteenth Amendments. Justice Scalia did not mean to say that he believed race played no role in capital sentencing decisions. Rather, his memorandum states, "Since it is my view that the unconscious operation of irrational sympathies and antipathies, including racial, upon jury decisions and (hence) prosecutorial decisions is real, acknowledged in the decisions of this court and ineradicable, I cannot honestly say that all I need is more proof."[27] Thus Justice Scalia appears to have been prepared to acknowledge the existence of racial discrimination—and then to deem its presence to be of no legal consequence. Clearly the majority eschewed this course. Indeed, only five members of the Court were of the view that McCleskey's evidence itself was insufficient to establish a constitutional violation, and one of them, the author of the majority opinion, later expressed regret for his own vote.

The Prevalence of Race: Discrimination in Capital Cases Today

Much ink has been spilled over the fallacies of *McCleskey*, and more blood has been spilled premised on its correctness. Lest the reader have any doubt, my

25. Id. at 293.

26. Id. at 314–15.

27. See Memorandum of Antonin Scalia, Justice, United States Supreme Court (Jan. 6, 1987) (on file with the author). See generally Dennis D. Dorin, "Far Right of the Mainstream: Racism, Rights, and Remedies from the Perspective of Justice Antonin Scalia's *McCleskey* Memorandum," 45 *Mercer L. Rev.* 1035 (1994).

own view, expressed elsewhere in detail,[28] is that *McCleskey* was wrongly decided. Certainly *McCleskey* was a turning point in Supreme Court death penalty jurisprudence; in effect, the Court washed its hands of the problem of racial discrimination. At this time, however, it is more fruitful to explore how subsequent developments have illuminated the underlying discrimination issue than it would be to rehash the Court's original doctrinal errors. Not surprisingly, at least to *McCleskey*'s critics, the passage of nearly fifteen years has not diminished the so-called unexplained disparities. Instead, the evidence that those disparities indeed stem from invidious discrimination continues to accumulate. Both statistical studies and more conventional legal research document the persistence of discrimination.

The GAO Study

The most comprehensive study to date is really a compendium of studies. The United States General Accounting Office (GAO) was instructed by statute to study capital sentencing procedures to determine whether the race of the defendant or the victim influences the likelihood that a defendant will be sentenced to death. To fulfill this mandate, the GAO performed an evaluation synthesis—a review and critique of existing studies. The GAO Report to the Senate and House Committees on the Judiciary was issued in 1990, and considered twenty-eight post-*Furman* studies based on twenty-three different data sets.[29]

The GAO rated half of the studies of high or medium quality, based on the strength of the design and the rigor of the analysis. Their synthesis of these studies "shows a pattern of evidence indicating racial disparities in charging, sentencing, and imposition of the death penalty."[30] In 82 percent of the studies, the race of the victim was found to influence the decision; that is, defendants who murdered whites were more likely to be sentenced to death than were those who murdered African Americans. This finding was "remarkably consistent" across data sets, states, data collection methods, and analytic techniques. Moreover, in the high-quality studies, these differences remain after controlling

28. See Sheri Lynn Johnson, "Unconscious Racism and the Criminal Law," 73 *Cornell L. Rev.* 1016 (1988). Undoubtedly my view today is influenced by my clients, whose execution *McCleskey* has made possible, but even before I represented death row inmates, and long before any of them were executed, I thought *McCleskey* was indefensible. See id.

29. U.S. Gen. Acct. Off., supra note 15. Many of the relevant studies are referred to in the GAO study.

30. Id. at 5.

statistically for legally relevant variables, such as aggravating circumstances, and other factors thought to influence sentencing, such as region.

The evidence for race of the defendant was more varied. Nevertheless, in more than half of the studies, the race of defendants influenced the likelihood of their being charged with a capital crime; and in three-quarters of those, black defendants were more likely to receive the death penalty. The effects of the defendant's race were often more complex than those of the victim's. For example, in one study researchers found that while in rural areas African Americans were more likely to receive the death penalty, in urban areas whites were more likely to receive it. In several studies, researchers found that black defendant/white victim cases were most likely to receive the death penalty.

The Baldus Philadelphia Study

Since the GAO report, David Baldus, the author of the *McCleskey* study, has collected seven more studies that find race-of-victim effects, race-of-defendant effects, or both.[31] And, as the Juan Garza story implies, significant racial disparity has also been noted in the application of the federal death penalty.[32] Moreover, Baldus himself embarked on a new study. This study finds substantial race-of-defendant effects, a finding that is particularly significant in light of the study's sophisticated design—and the fact that it was conducted in the North.

After identifying the universe of death-eligible cases in Philadelphia, Baldus and his coauthors randomly sampled the death-sentence cases, the life-sentence penalty-trial cases, and the cases that did not proceed to a penalty trial. Using multiple data sources for each case, they coded *all* of the statutory aggravators, *all* of the mitigating circumstances, and the *strength* of the evidence of each, as well as a host of other variables not related to culpability, such as race and socioeconomic status. They then estimated the effects of race using a statistical technique known as logistic multiple regression, and employed three alternative measures of culpability: (1) the number of aggravating and mitigating factors actually found by the jury (as reflected in its verdict form); (2) the "salient factors" used by various state courts in their proportionality reviews, a method of classifying cases in terms of their most prominent aggravating circumstance;

---

31. David C. Baldus et al., "Racial Discrimination and the Death Penalty in the Post-*Furman* Era: A Empirical and Legal Overview, with Recent Findings from Philadelphia," 83 *Cornell L. Rev.* 1638 (1998).

32. Staff of House Subcomm. on Civil and Constitutional Rights, supra note 2.

and (3) the murder severity index, a ranking based on a blind reading of the narrative description of the case in which all references to the race and socioeconomic status of defendant and victim were edited out.

Among the unanimously decided cases, the race-of-defendant effects were substantial, consistent, and statistically significant for *all* of the three measures of defendant culpability. When culpability—measured in these three different ways—was held constant, African American defendants were more likely to receive the death penalty. These race-of-defendant effects were strongest in the middle range of cases, and they were found in two different stages of the jury's deliberations. First, given the same strength of the evidence, jurors were *more* likely to find aggravating factors present in black defendant cases than in white defendant cases; and, second, again given the same strength of the evidence, jurors were *less* likely to give weight to mitigating factors. The net result was that the average black defendant's risk of receiving a death sentence was 1.6 times greater than that of a similarly situated white defendant.

The Baldus Philadelphia study also finds substantial and statistically significant (or nearly so) race-of-victim effects across each of the three culpability measures, though those effects are weaker than the race-of-defendant effects. In particular, again holding constant the strength of the evidence, juries were more likely to find aggravating factors in white victim cases than in black victim cases, and less likely to find mitigating factors in white victim cases.

Studies of Individual Prosecutors' Decisions to Seek the Death Penalty

The Baldus Philadelphia study does not find race-of-defendant effects in the decision to seek the death penalty; the race of the defendant influences the jury, not the prosecutor. Race-of-victim effects, however, flow jointly from the decisions of Philadelphia prosecutors and juries, and studies of individual prosecutor's decisions to seek the death penalty replicate these findings. Studies of five different counties in South Carolina find statistically significant race-of-victim effects in the prosecutor's decision to notice a case for death.[33] Studies of counties in Florida, Missouri, Nevada, California, Illinois, and Alabama have similarly found that the prosecutor is more likely to seek death when the victim is white.[34]

33. John H. Blume, Theodore Eisenberg, and Sheri Lynn Johnson, "Post-*McCleskey* Racial Discrimination Claims in Capital Cases," 83 *Cornell L. Rev.* 1771 (1998).

34. Id. at 1794–98. See also Ruth E. Friedman, "Statistics and Death: The Conspicuous Role of Race Bias in the Administration of the Death Penalty," 11 *La Raza L.J.* 75 (1999).

Nonstatistical Evidence

Nonstatistical evidence is necessarily anecdotal, even when large numbers of anecdotes are collected. Nevertheless, the collection of anecdotes is the way in which legal research ordinarily proceeds, and it is likely to add richer details to the picture painted by statistics alone. Moreover, such case studies sometimes illuminate the causal mechanism by which a statistical result was produced.

Future dangerousness predictions

The story of Victor Saldano is one such example, which, as it turns out, may shed light on more than the half-dozen other cases in which the expert involved testified. Certainly it raises the question of whether experts in other cases have in fact relied on race in coming to their predictions of future dangerousness but have not referred to that fact in their testimony. Might it also be that guards who testify about an inmate's behavior, and predict how much trouble he will or won't be in prison, use race as part of their assessment? Even more broadly, the Saldano case suggests that perhaps *jurors*, even without an expert's race-dependent testimony, may rely on their own racial stereotypes of propensity to commit crime in determining how likely the defendant is to act violently in the future. Do such lay predictions explain some of the racial disparities? At this point, the Saldano case raises these questions, but it cannot answer them.

Cross-racial identification errors

As noted above, little media attention has been directed toward the fact that a disproportionate number of the DNA exoneration cases have involved African Americans and that many of these wrongful convictions have depended on cross-racial identification. Peter Neufeld, one of the authors of *Actual Innocence*,[35] states that the black defendants with white victims are exonerated at *three times* the rate one would expect from the number of prosecutions of such black defendant/white victim crimes. Are these cases a subset of a larger number of wrongful conviction cases based on erroneous cross-racial identifications?

One would imagine so. There is no reason to think that cross-racial identifications would be more likely to be mistaken in those cases in which DNA is available than in those in which it is not. But does this help us explain statistical disparities based on race? Probably not, at least not directly. The statistical disparities described above relate to whether the death penalty is imposed on equally culpable, presumably factually guilty, defendants. In contrast, the exon-

35. See Dwyer et al., supra note 4.

eration cases suggest a *new* racial disparity in the death penalty: the death penalty may be imposed on disproportionately more *innocent* African American defendants.

Jury misconduct claims

Jury deliberations are usually both private in the short run and secret in the long run. Nevertheless, in some noteworthy cases, jurors have come forward to talk about the operation of racial bias in the jury room.

For example, Gail Lewis Daniels, the only African American on a jury in Georgia that sentenced William Henry Nance—also an African American—to death, reported that although she never voted for death during deliberations, the white jurors decided to tell the judge that the jury had reached a verdict in spite of her dissent. A white juror corroborated Ms. Daniels's story and further volunteered that another white juror had described the defendant as "just one more sorry n— that no one would miss."[36] In the Utah capital case of William Andrews, a note was found in the jury room that depicted a man on a gallows, above the inscription: "Hang the n—."[37] Both Nance and Andrews have since been executed, but their cases raise the question of how often death sentences silently reflect open racial animosity.

In a more recent Nevada case, a juror called the African American defendant "a gorilla, a baboon, a native tribesman who is not dangerous to his own people but would club or murder anyone outside his territory, an amoeba, an organism whose only ability is to reproduce, a predator, a non-human."[38] On the one hand, such remarks may be outliers that could hardly account for the large statistical disparities reported in the studies discussed above; on the other hand, such remarks may be more common than we suspect and may reflect underlying attitudes that infect jurors even in cases where such attitudes are not verbalized in the jury room.

The biased conduct of trial participants

Because prosecutor's remarks are made in the courtroom, we have a better sense of how often they invoke race. As it turns out, they do so all too frequently; in numerous reported capital cases, prosecutors have resorted to racial arguments to help obtain death sentences.

36. Bob Herbert, "In America: Mr. Hance's 'Perfect Punishment,' " *N.Y. Times*, Mar. 27, 1994, §4, at 17.
37. Andrews v. Shulsen, 485 U.S. 919 (1988) (Marshall, J., dissenting).
38. White v. State, 926 P.2d 291 (Nev. 1996).

For example, a prosecutor in a Nevada capital case emphasized the African American defendant's sexual "preference" for white women and his ongoing relationship with a white woman.[39] A prosecutor in an Indiana capital case referred to the black defendant as "Superfly" and "boy" and to the defense witness as "shucking and jiving on the stand."[40] A prosecutor in North Carolina, in a black defendant's capital case, referred to the jury as "twelve people good and true, twelve White jurors in Randolph County." Only last year, a prosecutor in South Carolina repeatedly referred to a black defendant as "King Kong" and to his girlfriend as "Blondie."[41] Moreover, in at least five capital cases in Georgia, the accused was referred to with a racial slur *by his own lawyer*.[42] In one Georgia case, the *judge* referred to the defendant as "a colored boy."[43] And in a Florida case the *judge* referred to the defendant's "n— mom and dad."[44]

These cases are of interest for two related reasons. First, such behavior by trial participants may itself account for racial disparities. Thus, to the extent prosecutors use racial arguments, they may sway jurors' sentencing decisions; in addition, these arguments may reflect the underlying racial attitudes that influence a prosecutor's prior decision to seek the death penalty. To the extent defense counsel are racially biased, those biases may first inhibit their preparation of the case and then influence the jurors' perception of the strength of the case for a life sentence. It is not difficult to imagine that my client, Ricky Drayton, would have had a better chance of receiving a life sentence if his trial attorney had investigated and presented evidence of his mental retardation—and refrained from saying, "You want to sentence him to death, okay."[45] Racially biased attitudes on the part of the trial judge may be similarly detrimental: they may indirectly influence the jury's sentencing decision by altering rulings concerning the evidence that is presented to the jury, and they may more directly influence the jury if the jury perceives those attitudes.

The second way in which the conduct of trial participants may be probative is that it prompts us to ask *why* these actors—despite being all professionals, all aware of the high stakes of a capital trial, and all presumably informed of the

39. Dawson v. State, 743 P.2d 221 (Nev. 1987).

40. Smith v. State, 516 N.E.2d 1055 (Ind. 1987).

41. Clif LeBlanc, "Swansea-Area Man Sentenced to Death a Second Time," *The State*, July 17, 2000.

42. See Bright, supra note 6, at 447.

43. Id. at 444.

44. Id. at 447.

45. J.A. at 1558, Drayton v. Moore, 168 F.3d 481 (4th Cir. 1999) (No. 98–18).

constitutional prohibition against racial discrimination—would behave the way they do. The answer to that question is closely related to the answer to the question, to which I now turn, of why racial discrimination in capital sentencing persists.

Explaining the Persistence of Discrimination in Capital Sentencing

Having examined several reliable sources of evidence concerning racial discrimination in the administration of the death penalty, it is impossible to conclude that such discrimination has been eradicated. In theory, the "guided discretion" scheme approved in *Gregg v. Georgia*[46] was supposed to eliminate arbitrariness, and it should have left little room for the operation of racial prejudice. Moreover, most observers believe that racial prejudice has declined substantially during the course of the past century. Why, then, does racial discrimination persist in capital sentencing?

There are three interrelated answers: the aversive, often unconscious nature of modern racial prejudice; the complex and indeterminate nature of the capital sentencing decision; and the limited legal remedies for racial discrimination in this arena.

Changes in the Form and Manifestation of Prejudice

Social science data on prejudice and communication support the hypothesis that racial stereotypes continue to exert a powerful influence on the thoughts and actions of many Americans. Indeed, social science documentation of the persistence of negative attitudes toward African Americans is overwhelming.[47] What has changed concerns the specifics of those attitudes and the common ways in which they are expressed.

"Dominative" racists, persons who express bigotry and hostility openly, often employing physical force, are clearly on the wane.[48] But the diminution in the ranks of the openly racist has been neither steady nor an unmitigated blessing;

46. 428 U.S. 153 (1976) (plurality opinion).
47. For summaries of the primary literature, see, e.g., Howard Schuman et al., *Racial Attitudes in America: Trends and Interpretations* (1985); T. Alexander Aleinikoff, "The Constitution in Context: The Continuing Significance of Racism," 63 *Colo. L. Rev.* 325 (1992); Howard Schuman, "Changing Racial Norms in America," 30 *Mich. Q. Rev.* 460 (1991); Sheri Lynn Johnson, "Black Innocence and the White Jury," 83 *Mich. L. Rev.* 1611 (1985).
48. See Johnson, supra note 28, at 1027–28 (surveying the literature).

the early 1990s brought an upswing in bias-related violence and hate speech, and the long term trend away from dominative racism has been paralleled by a trend toward a more silent form of stereotyping known as "aversive" racism.[49] The phenomenon of the modern aversive racist points to alteration of judgments due to reliance on stereotypes, particularly in close cases where there are no clear rules and particularly when reasons need not be articulated for the decision.

Modern racists do not want to associate with persons of color, largely because of the stereotypes they still hold.[50] Indeed, they do not approve of others closely associating across racial lines either: 25 percent of white Americans still approve of antimiscegenation laws.[51] Because modern racists usually find it possible to avoid the close interracial associations they dislike, their stereotypes are likely to remain intact.

Explaining race-of-defendant effects

Several of these stereotypes have clear relevance for the sentencing of black defendants. Some states allow or require jurors to determine whether the defendant will be dangerous in the future; even in states where future dangerousness is not formally part of the sentencing process, surveys of jurors who have served in capital cases demonstrate that they weigh future dangerousness heavily.[52] What does social psychological research tell us about how race will influence the determination of this issue?

In a 1990 survey by the respected National Opinion Research Center of the University of Chicago, more than half of all whites said that they believe that blacks are more prone to violence than whites.[53] This number almost certainly underestimates the number of respondents who actually believe in racially different propensities toward violent behavior. Such views are socially stigmatized, and they may therefore be embarrassing to report, even to a pollster.[54]

---

49. Id.

50. Teun A. van Dijk, *Communicating Racism* 225 (1987).

51. Aleinikoff, supra note 47, at 332 n.21.

52. See, e.g., William J. Bowers and Benjamin D. Steiner, "Death by Default: An Empirical Demonstration of False and Forced Choices in Capital Sentencing," 77 *Tex. L. Rev.* 605, 655 (1998); Theodore Eisenberg and Martin T. Wells, "Deadly Confusion: Juror Instructions in Capital Cases," 79 *Cornell L. Rev.* 1, 7 (1993).

53. Aleinikoff, supra note 47, at 332.

54. See Harold Sigall and Richard Page, "Current Stereotypes: A Little Fading, a Little Faking," 18 *J. Personality & Soc. Psychol.* 247 (1971) (more negative attitudes toward black people reported when subject thought experimenter had a physiological basis for determining whether

Thus many white jurors walk into the jury room believing that African Americans are more likely to be violent, and it would hardly be surprising if they were more likely to find a black defendant more dangerous than a white defendant, regardless of the crime committed. Moreover, this tendency would be exacerbated by the fact that in considering whether a person's bad behavior is attributable to underlying character traits, as opposed to situational factors, a member of the majority group is more likely to conclude that character determines conduct if the actor is a member of the minority group rather than of the majority.

Another part of the sentencing task, assessing mitigation, is similarly vulnerable to specific stereotypes about African Americans. Some kinds of mitigation findings will be biased on the basis of race for the same reason that findings of aggravation are biased. For example, a white jury will be more likely to treat the defendant's crime as representative of his true character than as a product of his extreme intoxication.

Other kinds of mitigation, such as evidence of good character, are less likely to be credited because jurors attribute fewer positive traits to people of color; the majority group sees African Americans as less intelligent, less hard-working, less patriotic—less *good* (except at sports and music)—than white Americans. The effort to present any form of good-character evidence is therefore a struggle: white jurors walking into the jury room are less likely to believe that a particular black defendant possesses any desirable trait than they would if the defendant were white. Moreover, this tendency is exacerbated by differences in assumptions about the likely origin of *good* behavior; majority jurors are more likely to conclude that circumstances, rather than enduring character traits, determined any reported good conduct of a minority group member.

These inferences from general principles of social psychology explain a general race-of-defendant effect. But they also account for a specific finding in the Baldus study of capital sentencing in Philadelphia: jurors are more likely to perceive the presence of aggravating factors in black defendant cases than they do in white defendant cases with equal evidence of aggravation, and they are less likely to give weight to mitigating factors.

Explaining race-of-victim effects
Race-of-victim effects, like race-of-defendant effects, make sense from the perspective of aversive racism. The typical aversive, or unconscious, racist does not feel openly punitive toward minorities, but her desire to maintain distance

subject was being truthful); see also Deborah A. Byrnes, "Contemporary Measures of Attitudes toward Blacks," 48 *Educational & Psychol. Measurement* 107 (1988) (attempting to devise a scale that measures racial attitudes masked by rationalization).

from persons of color results in less empathy for such persons. It is a small step to then predict that a lower level of empathy will result in viewing any given crime as less serious when the victim is a minority group member and, hence, less deserving of the death penalty.

Another form of modern racism, sometimes called "regressive" racism, is of particular relevance here. The regressive racist claims to accept egalitarian norms and behaves in accordance with those norms in most situations. In situations in which anger is aroused, however, the regressive racist resorts to more traditional patterns of racial discrimination. White victim/black defendant murder cases may frequently arouse such anger. Thus part of the race-of-victim effects that are observed may be attributable to silent failures of empathy: if black victim cases had instead been white victim cases, they would have been perceived as serious enough to warrant the death penalty. And such effects may also be in part attributable to aroused anger, such that white victim cases would not have been perceived as warranting the death penalty if the black defendant/ white victim combination had been absent.

Explaining the adamant denials of racial motivation
Interestingly enough, the phenomenon of aversive racism also explains why the individual perpetrators of discrimination so loudly proclaim their own race neutrality. In ordinary conversation, the aversive racist recognizes a formal antidiscrimination norm that forbids openly racist evaluations and conclusions. Recognition of the antidiscrimination norm does not, however, prevent the telling of racial stories or the conveying of racial imagery. In a fascinating linguistic study of white conversations about minorities, Teun A. van Dijk observed a variety of recurring speech patterns.[55] When people talk about race, they usually try to speak as a group member, who expresses the opinions of the group, rather than as an individual with a particular point of view. Talking about race is most comfortable when the whole group can see itself as a victim and thus entitled to the negative feelings it has about a racial outgroup. The telling and hearing of stories about a racial minority is thus functional for the majority and, despite the antidiscrimination norm, occurs quite frequently.

The formal norm, particularly in settings where the racial views of the audience are unknown, makes direct attribution of negative personality characteristics to a race risky and therefore relatively rare. Instead, prejudiced talk often includes contrasts between the majority group and the disliked minority. Such contrasts may, however, be stated in very vague terms, with nonverbal

55. See van Dijk, supra note 50.

cues such as pitch, intonation and facial expression conveying the opinion of the speaker about the ethnic outgroup. Prejudiced talk often utilizes pronouns of distance. "They," "them," "those people," and similar euphemisms emphasize separation while protecting the speaker from the risk of social disapproval that accompanies overt racial pronouncements.

Consequently, one would expect relatively few "smoking gun" cases, cases in which racial motivation was openly stated. One would further expect decision makers, whether prosecutors or jurors, to deny the influence of race, sometimes out of fear of social stigma and sometimes because of their lack of conscious awareness of that influence. Finally, one would expect that this entire process—the communication of racialized thinking and the resulting biased decision making—to work best (or "worst" in the normative sense) when all or most participants belong to the majority group. Indeed, empirical studies of former capital jurors confirm this prediction: juries with several black jurors are less likely to impose a death sentence on a black defendant whose victim was white than are juries that are overwhelmingly or totally white.[56]

The Nature of the Capital Sentencing Decision

The nature of modern prejudice (including the content of prevalent racial stereotypes) interacts with the issues at stake in capital sentencing to produce a variety of racially disparate effects, ones that the decision makers will generally deny. As explained above, a social scientist would make this prediction regardless of the structure of capital sentencing, relying on the nature and prevalence of modern racial stereotypes. That structure nonetheless possesses at least two features that are likely to increase racial disparities.

The guidance received by jurors

When rules are clear, modern racial prejudice is less likely to play a large role. If, at the one extreme, the death penalty were mandatory for certain crimes, then jurors would have to determine whether the crime was committed, and there would be small opportunity for stereotypes to sway decision making. There would still be some cases in which it might do so, cases, for example, in which the evidence of identity was less than clear, thus allowing jurors to rely on their stereotypes to decide whether the defendant was the kind of person *likely* to be

---

56. William J. Bowers, Benjamin D. Steiner, and Marla Sandys, "Death Sentencing in Black and White: An Empirical Analysis of the Jurors' Race and Jury Racial Composition," 3 *U. Pa. J. Const. L.* 171, 191–94 (2001).

the perpetrator of the crime. But a mandatory death penalty would minimize the number of cases in which race would play a role (though of course it would do so by sacrificing individualized decision making).

In contrast, the sentencing process in every state is multifaceted and indeterminate; the Supreme Court has held that the Constitution requires individualized decision making. That means both that numerous factors must be considered and that there is no ascertainably correct answer, at least in most cases. Social psychology tells us that this is the very kind of decision in which stereotypes have their greatest influence; human beings use stereotypes of every kind when they lack enough specific information to make an individualized judgment. Moreover, this general psychological principle explains why it is in the medium-severity cases—those that are neither clear death cases nor clear life cases—that race effects are strongest; the lack of compelling facts, one way or the other, "liberates" the juror to rely on preconceptions. It is when people are uncertain about what to think that racial bias is most likely to play a role.

The presentation of victim impact testimony

Jurors will know the race of the victim and defendant regardless of whether victim family members testify as to the way in which the victim's death has altered their own lives. Moreover, it is likely that the jury will have seen at least one of those family members testify during the guilt phase, in addition to having seen photographs of the victim. Consequently, the salience of the victim's race will be high regardless of whether family members testify at sentencing.

Nonetheless, it seems likely that victim impact testimony, because it occurs during the sentencing phase, will be perceived by the jury as a request by the victim's family for the imposition of the death penalty. (Indeed, it is; if they did not want the death penalty, they would not testify for the state in the penalty phase.) Perceiving such a request is likely to increase a juror's sense of obligation to—and even identification with—the victim's family. But such increased identification bears the risk of emphasizing, where it exists, commonalities between the juror's and the victim's family, including the commonality of race. If the state alone is asking for death, the request is less racially charged and less likely to prompt differential empathy than if the victim's family were doing the requesting.

Thus both the nature of prejudice and the nature of the process make racial disparity the likely outcome of capital sentencing. Let me offer a third, personal hypothesis for the persistence and prevalence of racial disparities in capital sentencing. To my knowledge no empirical research yet exists to support this hypothesis, but here it is: the capital sentencing decision, in order to result in a death sentence, necessarily requires dehumanizing the defendant. How could it not? And, in this country, the traditional, ingrained way to dehumanize people, to make both their pain and their individuality irrelevant, is to rely on their race. We should not be surprised, I think, if it is easier for white jurors to dehumanize black defendants than it is for them to dehumanize white defendants.

The Limits of the Law

Given the nature of modern prejudice and the nature of the capital sentencing decision, it would take extraordinary vigilance and sensitivity to cabin, let alone eliminate, racial discrimination in capital sentencing. Unfortunately, failures of both will and skill prevail.

Review of charging practices

As the *McCleskey* case itself made clear, statewide statistical showings of racial discrimination are doomed to fail as constitutional claims, and, to date, all lower court challenges based on county data specific to one prosecutor have likewise failed. Attempts to pass a federal statute presuming that evidence such as that proffered in *McCleskey*, if unrebutted, constitutes proof of racial discrimination have also failed;[57] even *investigation* of racial disparities in capital sentencing is mandated by statute in only one state, Kentucky.[58] Elsewhere, there is little incentive for prosecutors to examine their own charging decision making.

Verdict impeachment rules

Although the rule is slowly eroding in a few jurisdictions,[59] jurors have long been prohibited from impeaching their own verdicts. Consequently, jurors have little incentive to refrain from racial generalizations or other racially biased remarks or to report racially charged behavior on the part of fellow jurors. Moreover, even if such remarks come to light, the chances of legal redress are remote; usually, when courts do entertain complaints about racial remarks made by

57. See Don Edwards and John Conyers Jr., "The Racial Justice Act: A Simple Matter of Justice," 20 *U. Dayton L. Rev.* 699, 700–701 (1995) (reviewing legislative history).

58. See Ky. Rev. Stat. Ann. § 17.1531 (Michie 1992).

59. See, e.g., Perez v. United States, 124 F.3d 204 (7th Cir. 1997); State v. Santiago, 715 A.2d 1 (Conn. 1998); State v. Bowles, 530 N.W.2d 521 (Minn. 1995); Commonwealth v. Laguer, 571 N.E.2d 371 (Mass. 1991).

jurors, they tend to dismiss them as isolated or otherwise unimportant. In one especially disheartening capital case, one juror had likened the defendant to "a gorilla, a baboon," and a "native tribesman who is not dangerous to his own people but would club or murder anyone outside his territory"; nonetheless, the reviewing court affirmed the defendant's death sentence on the supposition that it did not affect the jury's decision.[60]

Prohibitions against racial arguments

Although all courts agree that racial arguments are improper, enforcement of that principle is virtually nonexistent.[61] Reviewing courts give a host of reasons to justify affirming even in the face of egregious racial argument, including the fact that a curative instruction was given, the fact that defense counsel failed to object to the remark, the fact that the remark was "isolated," the fact that the prosecutor did not intend to arouse racial animosity, and so on.[62] The bottom line is that fear of reversal, except possibly in the federal courts, is unlikely to deter a prosecutor from making a racially tinged argument.

Jury composition

In theory, voir dire should eliminate jurors who cannot put aside their biases and decide a case based solely on the evidence and the law as given them by the judge. In fact, voir dire on racial prejudice is frequently limited to a single question, and except in interracial capital cases, need not be allowed at all.

The problem with a single question—such as "Will the race of the defendant or victim affect your ability to follow the law?"—is that, given the nature of modern prejudice and the prevailing antidiscrimination norm, few jurors will be *aware* that the race of the defendant and victim may influence their verdict, and even fewer will admit to that fact in open court. Extensive questioning concerning racial attitudes might elicit information from which an inference about prejudice may be drawn, and some courts will allow such questioning, but most will not.

The larger problem is that far too many white jurors are influenced by racial stereotypes and racial distance; it is impractical to *exclude* all of them even if we could discern them. It would probably be more effective to affirmatively *include* minority race jurors,[63] but this is a remedy that has no political support.

---

60. See, e.g., White v. State, 926 P.2d 291 (Nev. 1996).

61. See Sheri Lynn Johnson, "Racial Imagery in Criminal Cases," 67 *Tul. L. Rev.* 1739 (1993).

62. See id. at 1776–85.

63. See Johnson, supra note 47, at 1695–1700.

Indeed, it is clear that many prosecutors attempt to diminish even the small number of minority jurors who appear on the panel through the use of peremptory challenges.[64] Although this practice is forbidden,[65] commentators agree that it is widespread and generally goes unpunished.[66]

Conclusion: The Future of Racial Discrimination in Capital Sentencing

As I write this conclusion, Juan Garza's six-month stay of execution has almost expired; he is scheduled to be executed on June 19, 2001,[67] a fact that has been overshadowed by the looming spectacle of Timothy McVeigh's earlier date. The furor over Victor Saldano has faded; the issue has been transmogrified into the far more mundane question of what role the Texas State Attorney General's Office should play in capital cases in front of the United States Supreme Court.[68] And still no real attention has been paid to the disproportionate number of African Americans who have been exonerated by DNA evidence. In short, we forget what we have learned and we deny what we do not wish to know, in part because we wish not to be interrupted in the pursuit of capital punishment, and in part because this is how we handle racial issues in America.

Race neutrality is the judicially and politically sanctioned approach to race problems, but it is poorly suited to solving racial disparities in capital sentencing. The tool of race neutrality cannot address discrimination that is based on unconscious stereotypes and emotional distance, and it is an especially poor tool in areas, such as capital sentencing, where the decision at issue is multifaceted and indeterminate. Until major societal changes occur, racial stereotypes and attitudes are unlikely to budge. Thus, absent major revamping of the legal controls on the behavior of all of the actors in capital cases, it is sad but safe to predict that racial discrimination in capital sentencing is not going to disappear any time soon.

64. See generally David C. Baldus et al., "The Use of Peremptory Challenges in Capital Murder Trials: A Legal and Empirical Analysis," 3 *U. Pa. J. Const. L.* 3 (2001).

65. See Batson v. Kentucky, 476 U.S. 79 (1986).

66. See Baldus et al., supra note 64, at 34–36 (reviewing literature).

67. Juan Garza has since been executed.

68. Most recently, the Texas Court of Criminal Appeals ruled that the state's confession of error in the Supreme Court was incorrect and upheld Saldano's conviction for a second time.

5 : LESSONS FROM THE CAPITAL JURY PROJECT

John H. Blume, Theodore Eisenberg, & Stephen P. Garvey

Capital sentencing is unique in many ways, not the least of which is the fact that a defendant's sentence usually turns on the judgment of a jury, not that of a judge.[1] Elsewhere in the law juries decide guilt or innocence, but seldom do they impose sentence on anyone; sentencing is typically left to a judge. Yet where the decision is between life and death, the traditional division of labor does not suffice. Capital sentencing calls on the conscience of the community, and the jury, so the theory goes, is best able to express that conscience.

But how do jurors actually reach their decision? Does their choice of sentence really reflect a decision of conscience, or is it a reflection of something less high-minded? Do jurors really behave the way in which the law requires them to, or in which it assumes they will, or do jurors misunderstand, or perhaps ignore, the law? What is it about a crime or a defendant that in the end prompts jurors toward a sentence of death, or conversely, toward a sentence of imprisonment for life?

Our understanding of how capital jurors decide the life-or-death question that the law puts to them has, until only recently, been incomplete. Of course, researchers have studied how people behave when asked to imagine themselves in the role of jurors, and lawyers who argue cases before capital jurors have long had their own ideas and theories about what makes capital jurors tick. But research-

1. According to one recent survey, only four states vested sentencing responsibility in the hands of the trial court; another four required the jury to make an initial nonbinding recommendation to the trial court, with the court then either accepting or rejecting that recommendation. See James R. Acker and Charles S. Lanier, "Matters of Life or Death: The Sentencing Provisions in Capital Punishment Statutes," 31 *Crim. L. Bull.* 19, 20–21 (1995).

ers have rarely talked to folks who actually have served as members of a capital jury. Thankfully, a nationwide research initiative known as the Capital Jury Project (CJP) has begun to fill this void by conducting extensive interviews with over 1,000 capital jurors. This chapter presents some of the results of that research.

The first part briefly introduces the CJP, recounting its genesis, organization, and objectives. The second part uses CJP data to document two important defects in the current process of capital sentencing: one arising from the fact that many jurors not legally qualified to serve on a capital jury end up serving nonetheless; the other arising from the fact that many capital jurors fail to understand some of the most basic legal principles intended to inform their decision making. The third part of the chapter uses CJP data to identify the key variables, legal and extralegal, that appear to exercise the greatest influence on a capital juror's sentencing decision. The fourth part gathers together what we take to be some of the central lessons to be learned from the CJP's research to date.

The Capital Jury Project

The Capital Jury Project is a National Science Foundation–funded, multistate research effort designed to better understand the dynamics of juror decision making in capital cases. The CJP is a loose association of academics from different disciplines (primarily law and criminology) and institutions; in 1990 its members began interviewing jurors from several different states who had served on capital cases, some of which resulted in a sentence of death, and some a sentence of life imprisonment. Analyses of the data collected during these interviews began appearing as early as 1993.[2]

2. Quantitative analyses of CJP data to date can be found in John H. Blume et al., "Future Dangerousness in Capital Cases: Always 'At Issue,' " 86 *Cornell L. Rev.* 397 (2001) (South Carolina data); William J. Bowers, "The Capital Jury Project: Rationale, Design, and Preview of Early Findings," 70 *Ind. L.J.* 1043 (1995) (multistate data); William J. Bowers et al., "Death Sentencing in Black and White: An Empirical Analysis of the Role of Jurors' Race and Jury Racial Composition," 3 *U. Pa. J. Const. L.* 171 (2001) [hereafter Bowers et al., "Death Sentencing in Black and White"] (multistate data); William J. Bowers et al., "Foreclosed Impartiality in Capital Sentencing: Jurors' Predispositions, Guilt-Trial Experience, and Premature Decision Making," 83 *Cornell L. Rev.* 1476 (1998) (multistate data); William J. Bowers and Benjamin D. Steiner, "Death by Default: An Empirical Demonstration of False and Forced Choices in Capital Sentencing," 77 *Tex. L. Rev.* 605 (1998) (multistate data); Theodore Eisenberg et al., "But Was He Sorry? The Role of Remorse in Capital Sentencing," 83 *Cornell L. Rev.* 1599 (1998) (South Carolina data); Theodore Eisenberg et al., "The Deadly Paradox of Capital Jurors," 74 *S. Cal. L. Rev.* 371 (2001)

Prior to the work of the CJP, the study of juror decision making in capital cases—and in particular of the sentencing phase of the trial—was based primarily on mock jury studies and on inferences drawn from observations made in individual cases. Both of these methodologies are valuable, but each has its limitations. Mock studies are open to a variety of criticisms, not the least of which is that the experience of being a mock juror is not true to life: mock jurors are not real jurors.[3] Likewise, inferences based on an individual case may fail to be generalizable across a wider range of cases; worse, they may reflect little more than the preconceptions of the person drawing them. Before the CJP's efforts, information systematically collected from jurors—real jurors—who had actually served on a capital case was simply unavailable.

The CJP and its individual researchers have so far conducted interviews with

---

[hereafter Eisenberg et al., "Deadly Paradox"] (South Carolina data); Theodore Eisenberg et al., "Forecasting Life and Death: Juror Race, Religion, and Attitude toward the Death Penalty," 30 *J. Legal Stud.* 277 (2001) [hereafter Eisenberg et al., "Forecasting"] (South Carolina data); Theodore Eisenberg et al., "Jury Responsibility in Capital Sentencing: An Empirical Study," 44 *Buff. L. Rev.* 339 (1996) (South Carolina data); Theodore Eisenberg and Martin T. Wells, "Deadly Confusion: Juror Instructions in Capital Cases," 79 *Cornell L. Rev.* 1 (1993) (South Carolina data); Stephen P. Garvey, "Aggravation and Mitigation in Capital Cases: What Do Jurors Think?," 98 *Colum. L. Rev.* 1538 (1998) [hereafter Garvey, "Aggravation and Mitigation"] (South Carolina data); Stephen P. Garvey, "The Emotional Economy of Capital Sentencing," 75 *N.Y.U. L. Rev.* 26 (2000) [hereafter Garvey, "Emotional Economy"] (South Carolina data); James Luginbuhl and Julie Howe, "Discretion in Capital Sentencing Instructions: Guided or Misguided?," 70 *Ind. L.J.* 1161 (1995) (North Carolina data); Marla Sandys, "Cross-Overs—Capital Jurors Who Change Their Minds about the Punishment: A Litmus Test for Sentencing Guidelines," 70 *Ind. L.J.* 1183 (1995) (Kentucky data); Benjamin D. Steiner et al., "Folk Knowledge as Legal Action: Death Penalty Judgments and the Tenet of Early Release in a Culture of Mistrust and Punitiveness," 33 *Law & Soc'y Rev.* 461 (1999) (multistate data); Scott E. Sundby, "The Capital Jury and Absolution: The Intersection of Trial Strategy, Remorse, and the Death Penalty," 83 *Cornell L. Rev.* 1557 (1998) (California data); Scott E. Sundby, "The Jury as Critic: An Empirical Look at How Capital Juries Perceive Expert and Lay Testimony," 83 *Va. L. Rev.* 1109 (1997) (California data).

Qualitative analyses of CJP data to date can be found in Ursula Bentale and William J. Bowers, "How Jurors Decide on Death: Guilt is Overwhelming; Aggravation Requires Death; and Mitigation is No Excuse," 66 *Brook. L. Rev.* 1011 (2001) (multistate data); Joseph L. Hoffmann, "Where's the Buck?—Juror Misperception of Sentencing Responsibility in Death Penalty Cases," 70 *Ind. L.J.* 1137 (1995) (Indiana data); Austin Sarat, "Violence, Representation, and Responsibility in Capital Trials: The View from the Jury," 70 *Ind. L.J.* 1103 (1995) (Georgia data).

3. See B. H. Bornstein, "The Ecological Validity of Jury Simulations: Is the Jury Still Out?," 23 *Law & Hum. Behav.* 75 (1999).

1,115 jurors who sat on 340 capital trials in fourteen different states.[4] The capital sentencing systems of each of these states differ in detail from one another, but all conform to the same basic constitutional principles. The CJP's aim was to conduct interviews with at least four jurors randomly selected from a random sample of cases, half of which resulted in a final verdict of death, and half of which resulted in a final verdict of life imprisonment. The number of total interviews to date in each state ranges from fifty-four jurors in Virginia to 187 jurors in South Carolina.

Each juror responded to a set of questions contained in a fifty-one-page survey. Interviewers were trained to administer the survey; each interview generally lasted between three and four hours. The survey asked questions about the guilt phase of the trial as well as the penalty phase; about the evidence presented; about the demeanor of the defendant, the actions of the victim's family, and the performance of the lawyers and the judge; about the legal instructions given; about the process of the jury's deliberations; and about the verdict reached. Demographic information—such as race, sex, age, religion—was also collected, as was information about each juror's attitudes toward the death penalty and the criminal justice system more generally. All told, each survey yielded data on over 750 variables.

Studying jury decisions using data based on interviews with real jurors has the obvious advantage of being true to life. The jurors swear an oath, hear the full range of evidence and argument, observe the defendant, receive instructions, deliberate, and render a verdict they must live with. Still, this interview methodology has its own disadvantages. For example, delay between the time of the trial and the time of the interview opens the door to memory decay and misrecollection; jurors may overestimate the importance of certain facts and underestimate the importance of others; and the answers jurors give may be tailored to meet the expectations of the interviewer. Perhaps the greatest limitation may be the risk of distortion due to the influence of hindsight. The way a juror recalls a trial in retrospect may not be true to the way in which the juror experienced it at the time. For example, a juror may have voted to impose death because he thought the crime was especially serious; alternatively, he might simply have reported at the time of the interview that he believed the crime was especially serious because he voted to impose death. Sorting out the truth is not easy.

Nonetheless, the CJP offers insights into the process of capital juror decision

4. See Bowers et al., "Death Sentencing in Black and White," supra note 2, at 189.

making that can be gained in no other way. Any methodology—mock jury experiments, case studies, post-trial interviews—has limits. Consequently, the most accurate portrait of capital sentencing will emerge only when we combine the insights and results of these different methodologies into a single image. The picture we sketch below is based where possible on data collected from jurors across the eleven states that comprise the CJP; otherwise, we rely on data gathered from jurors in South Carolina, which is the state with the largest share of interviews from among all the CJP states.[5]

Unqualified and Confused

Prospective jurors in all criminal trials are screened through a process known as voir dire, which is intended to weed out those whose ability to be impartial is open to doubt. The details of this process vary from state to state, but typically the lawyers for each side ask prospective jurors a series of questions that are designed to detect any possible bias. In noncapital trials a juror's task is to find the facts and then to apply those facts to the law she receives through the judge's instructions. Applying the law to the facts yields a verdict of guilty or not guilty on the crime or crimes charged. If a prospective juror cannot accomplish this task impartially, one side or the other can move that she not be permitted to serve.

Capital trials add to this standard process an entirely different dimension. In noncapital trials the jury decides the defendant's guilt or innocence; in capital trials the jury must also decide his sentence, either life imprisonment or death. These two decisions—guilt or innocence and the sentence to be imposed—are made separately at the close of two different trials, though the same jury ordinarily makes both decisions in a single case. Because capital trials require a juror to decide not only the defendant's guilt or innocence but also his sentence, each juror must be impartial not only as to her ability to judge fairly the defendant's guilt but also as to her ability to judge the appropriate sentence.

People often hold strong opinions on when the death penalty is appropriate and when it's not. Indeed, for some it may be self-evident that anyone guilty of murder should for that reason and that reason alone be condemned to death. For others it might be equally self-evident that a defendant should never be condemned to death no matter what crime he may have committed. In the law's

5. Published results using data gathered from jurors in some or all eleven of the states comprising the full CJP data set give no indication that South Carolina jurors are in any way unusual or atypical.

eyes, however, a person who holds either of these opinions would be unqualified to serve on a capital jury. The law supposes that death can sometimes be an appropriate punishment for murder, but it also supposes that not all defendants found guilty of murder should for that reason alone be condemned to death. States are free to treat death as being sometimes—depending on all the facts and circumstances—an appropriate punishment for murder, but they cannot treat death—despite all the facts and circumstances—as the only appropriate punishment.

Because the law requires impartiality, it must and does provide a way to identify and to excuse from service on a capital jury prospective jurors whose personal convictions undermine their impartiality. First, prosecutors can excuse any juror who believes death is never an appropriate punishment for murder. This process, called "death-qualification," eliminates jurors who would automatically vote for life.[6] Second, and conversely, defense lawyers can excuse any juror who believes death is the only appropriate punishment for murder. This process, called "life-qualification," removes jurors who would automatically vote for death.[7] If both processes are working as they should, the resulting jury will be composed of members equally prepared to vote for life as they are for death, depending on the particular facts and circumstances of the case before them.

Once qualified to serve, the jury's members first decide on the defendant's guilt. If the jury finds the defendant guilty, the first part of the trial is over, and the second, known as the penalty phase, begins. The penalty phase is a trial over life or death, with the prosecution presenting evidence and arguments to persuade the jury to vote for death and with the defense trying to persuade its members to return a sentence of life imprisonment. Once all the evidence is presented, the trial court instructs the jury on the law its members are dutybound to follow as they deliberate toward a verdict.

In sum, capital jurors are expected to keep an open mind; neither life nor death should for any juror be a foregone conclusion. Moreover, capital jurors are expected to understand and follow the law on which the trial judge duly in-

6. See Witherspoon v. Illinois, 391 U.S. 510, 522 (1968); accord Wainwright v. Witt, 469 U.S. 412, 424 (1985). Empirical studies of the death-qualification process have long and persuasively shown that death-qualified juries are more prone to convict than are juries whose members have not been death-qualified. For a recent review of the literature, see Mike Allen et al., "Impact of Juror Attitudes about the Death Penalty on Juror Evaluations of Guilt and Punishment: A Meta-Analysis," 22 *Law & Hum. Behav.* 715 (1998).

7. See Morgan v. Illinois, 504 U.S. 719, 729 (1992).

structs them before they begin their deliberations. Unfortunately, the CJP's investigations show that many jurors do not keep an open mind, and many more fail to understand some of the most basic and most central rules intended to guide their decision.

Unqualified Jurors

The CJP set out to discover whether the jury selection process in capital cases was measuring up to the law's expectations. Jurors were asked to say how "appropriate" or "acceptable" the death penalty was as a punishment for "convicted murderers." If the life- and death-qualification processes were in good working order, *none* of the jurors interviewed should have said they believed that death was the *only* appropriate punishment for murder or that it was *never* an appropriate punishment. The results for South Carolina jurors are presented in table 1.

Most jurors, it should be said, responded as the law expects them to. Eighty-four percent said they believed the death penalty was the least acceptable punishment, just one of several punishments, or the most appropriate punishment for someone convicted of murder. Any of these responses is consistent, or arguably consistent, with the degree of impartiality expected of capital jurors. Indeed, a majority of jurors chose the most balanced response, saying the death penalty was just one of several appropriate punishments. Nonetheless, 14 percent said death was the *only* acceptable punishment. If we take these responses at face value, then none of the jurors giving this response should have been allowed to serve; all of them should have been disqualified.[8]

In fact, the problem is probably much worse than the results in table 1 suggest. Capital murder is the only ordinary crime that can constitutionally carry a death sentence; no other crimes qualify.[9] What would otherwise be simple

8. Two percent of the jurors responded that death was an unacceptable punishment. Jurors giving this response should also have been excused. However, the number of jurors who say they would always vote for life is noticeably smaller than the number who say they would always vote for death; moreover, on the theory that a wrongful verdict of death is a far more grievous error than a wrongful verdict of life imprisonment, the apparent defects in the existing process of life-qualification present a far greater challenge than do any parallel defects in the death-qualification process.

9. We base this claim on the standard reading of Coker v. Georgia, 433 U.S. 584, 592 (1977), in which the Supreme Court held that the imposition of a death sentence for the rape of an adult woman was unconstitutional under the Eighth Amendment's prohibition on the infliction of "cruel and unusual punishments." U.S. Const. amend. VIII.

Table 1

For convicted murderers, do you now feel that the death penalty is . . .

The only acceptable punishment	14%
The most appropriate of several punishments	31%
Just one of several appropriate punishments	51%
The least acceptable punishment	2%
An unacceptable punishment	2%
	$n = 185$

Note: Results are based on interviews with South Carolina jurors.

murder becomes capital murder, and therefore a "death-eligible" offense, when the state proves the existence not only of murder but also of an "aggravating circumstance." This circumstance is a legal Rubicon; it transforms simple murder into capital murder. Although some aggravating circumstances are common to most states, different states can and do treat different facts and circumstances as aggravating.

Yet no matter how aggravated a defendant's crime may be, the law still insists that death can never be the only legally available option. A state could not, consistent with the Constitution, enact a law imposing the death penalty automatically on a defendant who, for example, killed a corrections officer and who was at the time of the killing serving a life sentence for a prior murder.[10] Nor should any juror hold the view that death, no matter what, is the only appropriate punishment for such a defendant. Once again, however, CJP research suggests that many jurors do indeed hold such views.

Recall that table 1 records jurors' responses to the question of how appropriate or acceptable the death penalty was when the crime was described simply as "murder." In contrast, table 2 records the responses when the crime was described in more detail: for example, "murder by someone previously convicted of murder," which is an aggravating circumstance in many states. The results presented in table 2 are based on responses from jurors in eleven different states.[11]

10. See Sumner v. Shuman, 483 U.S. 66 (1987).

11. The question on which table 2 is based, as well as the question on which table 1 is based, are both phrased in the present tense. Because jurors were interviewed after they completed their service on the jury, the possibility exists that a juror's beliefs about the death penalty may have changed between the time he served and the time he was interviewed. Although we cannot eliminate this possibility, we do discount it. First, although opinions about the death penalty can and sometimes do change, they nonetheless tend to be fairly stable over time. Second, CJP jurors were directly asked, "Have your personal feelings about the death penalty changed as a result of serving on the [defendant's] case?" Seventy-eight percent of the South Carolina jurors

Table 2

Do you feel that the death penalty is the only acceptable punishment, an unacceptable punishment, or sometimes acceptable as punishment for the following specific kinds of murders and other crimes?

	Only acceptable	Sometimes acceptable	Unacceptable	n
Murder by someone previously convicted of murder	70%	27%	2%	892
A planned, premeditated murder	57%	41%	3%	888
Murder in which more than one victim is killed	52%	45%	3%	892
Killing of a police officer or prison guard	48%	49%	4%	888
Murder by a drug dealer	46%	51%	4%	890
When an outsider to the community kills an admired and respected member of the community	22%	73%	5%	883
A killing that occurs during another crime	23%	69%	8%	891
A rape with permanent injury to the victim	24%	55%	21%	886
A planned murder, when the victim survives	16%	53%	32%	888

Note: Results are based on interviews with jurors in Alabama, California, Florida, Georgia, Kentucky, Missouri, North Carolina, Pennsylvania, South Carolina, Texas, and Virginia.
Source: William J. Bowers et al., "Foreclosed Impartiality in Capital Sentencing: Jurors' Predispositions, Guilt-Trial Experience, and Premature Decision Making," 83 *Cornell L. Rev.* 1476, 1505 tbl.6 (1998). An analysis of the responses of South Carolina jurors to the same questions revealed no statistically significant differences between South Carolina jurors and jurors in the national data set.

When the crime was described in more detail, the number of jurors who believed the death penalty was the only appropriate punishment increased, often dramatically so, across all categories. At one extreme, 70 percent believed that death was the only acceptable punishment for murder when the defendant had been previously convicted of murder. Similarly, around half of the jurors

we interviewed said "no" in response to that question; 13 percent said they were "more in favor" of the death penalty; and 9 percent said they were "more opposed" to the death penalty. See Eisenberg et al., "Deadly Paradox," supra note 2, at 388 tbl.4.

believed death was the only appropriate punishment when the murder was planned or premeditated, when more than one person was killed, when the victim was a police officer or prison guard, or when the offender was a drug dealer. A state could make death *an* option for any of these offenses, and many do. In the minds of many jurors, however, death is the *only* option.[12]

Confused Jurors

Capital jurors must not only be impartial, they must also be able to understand and follow the instructions they receive on the law designed to guide their decision. A capital jury enjoys considerable discretion in reaching its decision. The law does not, and indeed cannot, dictate one outcome or the other. But the law does not drop out of the process completely. Jurors are expected to understand a few basic rules, many of which focus on aggravating and mitigating factors.

Many of the legal rules governing mitigating circumstances are grounded in the Constitution, which sets a legal floor of protection for capital defendants in all states. In contrast, the Constitution leaves each state with considerable room to craft its own rules governing aggravating circumstances. Yet whatever the primary source of the relevant legal rule, whether the Constitution or state statute, jurors should understand the rules they are expected to follow.[13]

The CJP asked jurors several questions designed to test how well they understood the rules governing aggravating and mitigating circumstances. In particular jurors were asked (1) if they could consider as aggravating or mitigating *any* factor that made the crime worse (in the case of aggravating circumstances) or not as bad (in the case of mitigating circumstances), or only those factors specifically mentioned by the trial judge in his instructions; (2) if an aggravating or

12. Moreover, no state could make death even an option for two of the crimes listed in table 2. Rape cannot be made a capital offense, even when the victim suffers permanent injury. See Coker v. Georgia, 433 U.S. 584, 592 (1977). Nor can *attempted* murder be made a capital offense, even when the attempt is planned in advance. Cf. id. Nonetheless, 24 percent of the jurors said death was the only acceptable punishment for a rape involving permanent injury, and 16 percent said death was the only acceptable punishment for a planned murder when the victim survives.
13. For helpful surveys of state law governing aggravating and mitigating circumstances, see James R. Acker and C. S. Lanier, " 'Parsing This Lexicon of Death': Aggravating Factors in Capital Sentencing Statutes," 30 *Crim. L. Bull.* 107 (1994) [hereafter Acker and Lanier, "Aggravating Factors"]; James R. Acker and Charles S. Lanier, "In Fairness and Mercy: Statutory Mitigating Factors in Capital Punishment Laws," 30 *Crim. L. Bull.* 299 (1994) [hereafter Acker and Lanier, "Mitigating Factors"].

mitigating circumstance could be considered so long as it was proven to a juror's personal satisfaction, or only if it was proven to some specified standard of proof; and (3) if an aggravating or mitigating factor could be considered only if all jurors agreed on that factor, or even in the absence of such unanimous agreement.

Aggravating circumstances

Consider first the rules governing aggravating circumstances. The Constitution gives states considerable freedom to decide how they will structure the jury's consideration of aggravating factors. Each state is more or less free to decide for itself which facts and circumstances will constitute an aggravating factor, provided that any proposed factor "genuinely narrow[s] the class of persons eligible for the death penalty and . . . reasonably justif[ies] the imposition of a more severe sentence on the defendant compared to others found guilty of murder."[14] In general the Constitution only requires that the state prove the existence of at least one aggravating factor before it can permit the jury to impose a death sentence.

Table 3 explores how well jurors in South Carolina and North Carolina understood the rules in their respective states regarding aggravating circumstances. The relevant rules are different in each state. In South Carolina jurors are instructed that they must first determine if the prosecution has proven beyond a reasonable doubt one of the aggravating factors listed in that state's capital sentencing statute.[15] Such a factor is called a *statutory* aggravating factor. Once the jury has found that the prosecution has proven the existence of one of these factors beyond a reasonable doubt, each juror is then free to consider any other *nonstatutory* aggravating evidence that the prosecution has offered in support of a death sentence.[16] Jurors can assign this nonstatutory evidence as much or as little weight as they see fit.

In contrast, the analogous rules in North Carolina more narrowly circumscribe the jury's discretion to consider evidence in aggravation. In North Carolina, unlike in South Carolina, the jury can only consider aggravating evidence if it falls within the scope of a particular statutory aggravating circumstance. North Carolina does not allow the jury to consider nonstatutory aggravating circumstances.[17] Nor can North Carolina juries consider an aggravating circumstance unless and until the prosecution has proven its existence beyond a rea-

14. Zant v. Stephens, 462 U.S. 862, 877 (1983).
15. See S.C. Code Ann. § 16-3-20 (C) (Law. Co-op. 1985 & Supp. 2001).
16. See id.
17. See N.C. Gen. Stat. § 15A-2000(e) (2000).

Table 3

	South Carolina jurors	North Carolina jurors	p-value
A. Among the factors in favor of a death sentence, could the jury consider . . .			
Any aggravating factor that made the crime worse	48%*	48%	0.015
Only a specific list of aggravating factors mentioned by the judge	23%*	36%*	
Don't know	30%	16%	
	n = 186	n = 83	
B. For a factor in favor of death to be considered, did it have to be . . .			
Proved only to a juror's personal satisfaction	6%*	12%	0.013
Proved by a preponderance of the evidence	5%	14%	
Proved beyond a reasonable doubt	82%*	68%*	
Don't know	7%	6%	
	n = 185	n = 83	
C. For a factor in favor of a death sentence to be considered . . .			
Jurors did not have to agree unanimously on that factor	14%*	22%	0.106
All jurors had to agree on that factor	78%*	76%*	
Don't know	8%	2%	
	n = 185	n = 83	

Note: The reported p-values are based on Fisher's exact test and reflect the statistical significance, if any, of the differences between the responses of South Carolina and North Carolina jurors. An asterisk indicates a legally correct response.

Source: The responses for North Carolina jurors is taken from James Luginbuhl and Julie Howe, "Discretion in Capital Sentencing Instructions: Guided or Misguided?," 70 *Ind. L.J.* 1161, 1165–66 tbl.1 (1995).

sonable doubt,[18] and the jury must unanimously agree that the prosecution has satisfied that burden.[19]

Two features of table 3 warrant additional comment. First, an asterisk marks the legally correct response with respect to each question. In South Carolina the legally correct answer differs depending on whether the factor in question is statutory or nonstatutory. Unfortunately, however, the questions we asked failed to make this distinction. Consequently, in South Carolina, two different answers to each of the three questions could qualify as legally correct, depending again on whether the factor in question is statutory or nonstatutory. Second, the final column in table 3 gives a figure that statisticians refer to as a "*p*-value."

18. See id. at § 15A-2000(c)(1).

19. See, e.g., State v. Kirkley, 302 S.E.2d 144, 157 (N.C. 1983), overruled on other grounds by State v. Shank, 367 S.E. 2d 639 (N.C. 1988).

The *p*-value tells us if the differences observed between the pattern of responses among South Carolina and North Carolina jurors represent genuine differences, or if they could simply be the result of chance. If the *p*-value is equal to or less than 0.05 the differences are referred to as "statistically significant," meaning that the differences between the pattern of responses are most unlikely to be the result of chance alone.

The results from South Carolina are difficult to construe in light of the fact that two different answers could have been legally correct, depending on whether the aggravating circumstance in question is statutory or nonstatutory. The results from North Carolina, however, are less ambiguous—and more troubling. Jurors in North Carolina are required to limit their consideration to statutory aggravating circumstances that the jury has unanimously found proven by the prosecution beyond a reasonable doubt. Nonetheless, panel A shows that 48 percent of the jurors believed they could consider nonstatutory aggravating factors; panel B shows that 26 percent believed they could consider factors the prosecution had not proven beyond a reasonable doubt; and panel C shows that 22 percent believed they could consider an aggravating factor even if the jury had not unanimously agreed on it.

Looking at the general pattern of responses from jurors in both states, two results stand out. First, most jurors believe the prosecution must prove the existence of aggravating factors beyond a reasonable doubt (82 percent in South Carolina and 68 percent in North Carolina). Second, most jurors believe the jury must unanimously agree on the existence of an aggravating factor (78 percent in South Carolina and 76 percent in North Carolina). We suspect that these results have a relatively simple explanation: if popular culture sends any message about the conduct of a criminal trial, it sends the message that the state must prove its case beyond a reasonable doubt to the jury's unanimous satisfaction. Although this popular understanding is usually an accurate reflection of the state's burden when it comes to proving the substantive crime with which the defendant has been charged, it does not necessarily reflect the law governing the jury's consideration of aggravating circumstances at the penalty phase. Jurors tend to rely on this folk wisdom nonetheless.

Mitigating circumstances
When state law imposes limitations on the use of aggravating circumstances, as it does in North Carolina, jurors who fail to understand those limitations may end up voting for death when they might have otherwise voted for life. A similar risk arises when we move from aggravating circumstances to mitigating circumstances. In contrast to the rules governing aggravation, the rules governing

mitigation vary less from one state to the next, primarily because the Constitution prescribes certain critical rules that all states must follow.

No constitutional principle of capital sentencing is more robust or firmly embedded than the so-called *Lockett* doctrine. Derived from the 1978 case *Lockett v. Ohio*,[20] the *Lockett* doctrine broadly stands for the principle that the state cannot erect any barrier to a capital defendant's ability to present, or a capital juror's ability to consider, evidence in mitigation. A capital defendant must be free to present such evidence, and each juror must be free to consider it.

The *Lockett* doctrine is reflected in several more specific rules, three of which are important here. First, a capital juror's consideration of mitigating evidence can never be limited to a specific list of statutorily authorized and enumerated factors; jurors are always free to go beyond any such list.[21] Second, although a state can constitutionally require a defendant to prove the existence of a mitigating factor by a preponderance of the evidence,[22] only a handful do,[23] and none requires the defendant to prove their existence beyond a reasonable doubt.[24] Third, each juror is free to consider a mitigating factor and to assign it whatever weight she sees fit, no matter what her fellow jurors believe about the existence or weight of that circumstance.[25]

Table 4 examines how well jurors from South Carolina and North Carolina understood these fundamental rules. As before, an asterisk marks the legally correct response or responses. In all but one instance, only one answer is legally correct. The exception involves the burden of proof with respect to mitigating circumstances under North Carolina law (see panel B). The ambiguity is due to the fact that North Carolina law treats statutory and nonstatutory mitigating circumstances differently. With respect to statutory mitigating circumstances, North Carolina law requires the defendant to prove their existence by preponderant evidence; but once the jury makes this determination, it must then give that circumstance at least some weight.[26] In contrast, North Carolina law imposes no burden of proof on the defendant with respect to nonstatutory mitigat-

20. 438 U.S. 586 (1978).

21. See id.; see also Hitchcock v. Dugger, 481 U.S. 393 (1987); Eddings v. Oklahoma, 455 U.S. 104 (1982).

22. See Walton v. Arizona, 497 U.S. 639, 649–51 (1990) (plurality opinion).

23. See Acker and Lanier, "Mitigating Factors," supra note 13, at 342.

24. Cf. id.

25. See McKoy v. North Carolina, 494 U.S. 433 (1990); see also Mills v. Maryland, 486 U.S. 367 (1988).

26. See, e.g., State v. Kirkley, 302 S.E.2d 144, 157–58 (N.C. 1983), overruled on other grounds by State v. Shank, 367 S.E.2d 639 (N.C. 1988).

Table 4

	South Carolina jurors	North Carolina jurors	p-value
A. Among the factors in favor of a life or lesser sentence, could the jury consider . . .			
Any mitigating factor that made the crime not as bad	49%*	59%*	0.006
Only a specific list of mitigating factors mentioned by the judge	16%	24%	
Don't know	35%	17%	
	n = 187	n = 83	
B. For a factor in favor of life or a lesser sentence to be considered, did it have to be . . .			
Proved only to a juror's personal satisfaction	26%*	24%*	0.007
Proved by a preponderance of the evidence	7%	23%*	
Proved beyond a reasonable doubt	51%	41%	
Don't know	15%	12%	
	n = 187	n = 83	
C. For a factor in favor of a life or lesser sentence to be considered . . .			
Jurors did not have to agree unanimously on that factor	21%*	47%*	0.000
All jurors had to agree on that factor	66%	42%	
Don't know	13%	11%	
	n = 187	n = 83	

Note: The reported p-values are based on Fisher's exact test and reflect the statistical significance, if any, of the differences between the responses of South Carolina and North Carolina jurors. An asterisk indicates a legally correct response.
Source: The responses for North Carolina jurors are taken from James Luginbuhl and Julie Howe, "Discretion in Capital Sentencing Instructions: Guided or Misguided?," 70 Ind. L.J. 1161, 1165–66 tbl.1 (1995).

ing circumstances, but neither are jurors required to give these circumstances any weight in mitigation.[27]

Overall, the results suggest a fair degree of confusion. Panel B shows that 51 percent of South Carolina jurors and 41 percent of North Carolina jurors wrongly believed that the defendant was required to prove the existence of a mitigating factor beyond a reasonable doubt. Likewise, panel C shows that 66 percent of South Carolina jurors and 42 percent of North Carolina jurors wrongly believed that all jurors had to agree on the existence of a particular factor before they could consider that factor in reaching a decision.

We suspect that these results once again show the power of popular culture at

27. See, e.g., State v. Fullwood, 373 S.E.2d 518, 533–34 (N.C. 1988), vacated on other grounds by 494 U.S. 1022 (1990).

work. Jurors tend to believe that the same rules operate at both the penalty phase of the trial and the guilt-or-innocence phase and that the same rules apply equally to the defense and the prosecution. Consequently, large numbers of jurors in both states tend to believe that mitigating factors must be proven beyond a reasonable doubt and to the satisfaction of each and every juror. Unless the important differences between the guilt-or-innocence and penalty phases of the trial and between aggravating and mitigating factors are emphasized to them in no uncertain terms, far too many jurors will rely instead on the popular and erroneous beliefs they bring with them to court.

Mandatory death sentences

Another basic confusion emerged in the responses to a different set of questions. Among the universe of aggravating circumstances, two used in some states have attracted special attention. According to the first, the defendant becomes eligible for death if the jury finds that the killing was, for example, "especially heinous, atrocious, or cruel."[28] According to the second, the defendant becomes death-eligible if the jury finds that he constitutes a "future danger" or "continuing threat to society." In some states the defendant's future dangerousness is a statutory aggravating circumstance; in many others it functions as a nonstatutory aggravating circumstance, allowing the state to emphasize the defendant's potential for causing future harm once it has proven the existence of at least one statutory aggravating circumstance.[29]

Both of these aggravating circumstances have come in for especially heavy criticism. The core objection has been that both kinds of circumstances are much too vague to serve as a meaningful guide to the jury's decision. The death penalty is meant to be reserved for the worst offenders guilty of the worst murders; its reach should not be broad enough to cover any defendant guilty of any murder. Yet any murder can plausibly be characterized as "heinous," and anyone guilty of murder can plausibly be viewed as a "future danger." Consequently, the heinousness aggravating circumstance and the future dangerousness aggravating circumstance create an undue risk that jurors will impose death on defendants who are not among the worst of the worst.

The CJP asked jurors two questions related to each of these aggravating circumstances. Jurors were first asked if they thought the evidence presented in the case proved the "defendant's conduct was heinous, vile, or depraved," or that

28. See Acker and Lanier, "Aggravating Factors," supra note 13, at 124–30.
29. See id. at 118–21.

Table 5

After hearing all of the evidence [presented during the penalty phase], did you believe it proved that the . . .

	Yes	No	Undecided	n
Defendant's conduct was heinous, vile, or depraved	80%	16%	5%	674
Defendant would be dangerous in the future	76%	18%	6%	672

Note: Results are based on interviews with jurors from Alabama, California, Florida, Georgia, Kentucky, North Carolina, and South Carolina.
Source: William J. Bowers, "The Capital Jury Project: Rationale, Design, and Preview of Early Findings," 70 *Ind. L.J.* 1043, 1091 (1995).

the "defendant would be dangerous in the future." Table 5 shows the results, based on the responses from CJP jurors in several different states.

A significant proportion of the jurors believed that the evidence presented at the penalty phase did indeed prove that the defendant was guilty of a heinous crime and that he himself would be dangerous in the future. Three-quarters said the evidence proved the defendant would be dangerous, and four-fifths said the evidence proved his conduct was heinous, vile, or depraved. While these results alone lend force to the criticism that the heinousness and future dangerousness circumstances fail in any meaningful way to narrow the death penalty's scope, an even more fundamental problem emerges when the results in table 5 are juxtaposed with those in table 6.

Table 6 shows the responses to the second question the CJP asked about the heinousness and future dangerousness aggravating circumstances. Specifically, jurors were asked if they believed the law *required* them to impose death on the defendant *if* they believed the evidence proved the defendant's conduct was heinous or the defendant would be dangerous in the future.

The legally correct response in each case is "no." A state can never require a jury to impose a death sentence, no matter what the evidence proves. Nonetheless, 32 percent believed they were required by law to impose death if they believed the evidence proved the defendant would be dangerous in the future, and 41 percent believed they would be required by law to impose death if they believed the evidence proved the defendant's conduct was heinous, vile, or depraved. The belief that most capital defendants are guilty of a heinous crime and that most capital defendants present a threat in the future, combined with the erroneous belief that the law demands death for defendants so characterized, creates a dynamic whose effect can only be in favor of death.

In sum, the law's reliance on ordinary citizen jurors to make the choice be

Table 6

After hearing the judge's instructions [at the close of the penalty phase], did you believe that the law required you to impose a death sentence if the evidence proved that . . .

	Yes	No	Undecided	n
Defendant's conduct was heinous, vile, or depraved	41%	58%	1%	655
Defendant would be dangerous in the future	32%	67%	2%	652

Note: Results are based on interview with jurors from Alabama, California, Florida, Georgia, Kentucky, North Carolina, and South Carolina.
Source: William J. Bowers, "The Capital Jury Project: Rationale, Design, and Preview of Early Findings," 70 *Ind. L.J.* 1043, 1091 (1995).

tween life and death is premised on at least two assumptions. First, the law assumes that only fair and open-minded jurors will sit in judgment; second, it assumes that jurors will follow the law. The work of the CJP casts serious doubt on both of these assumptions. Many jurors do not understand some of the most basic constitutional rules governing the decision they must make, and a substantial number of them lack the threshold impartiality and open-mindedness they must have in order to be entitled to serve in the first place.

Deciding between Life and Death

How does a capital juror go about deciding between a death sentence or a sentence of life imprisonment? What facts or circumstances are most likely to move a juror to vote for death, and conversely, what ones are most likely to move her to vote for life? Data collected from the CJP provide two different ways to approach these questions.

The first approach is the most direct. It relies on a juror's own self-reports about the factors that influenced his choice. The CJP survey asked each juror about a wide variety of facts and circumstances regarding the crime, the defendant, and the victim that might reasonably have influenced his vote. It then asked how much more or less likely each factor, if present in the case on which the juror sat, led the juror to vote for death; or if the factor was not present, how much more or less likely it would have been to have led him to vote for death assuming it had been present.[30]

As a way of identifying those factors that do in fact exercise the greatest

30. The results of this analysis for jurors from South Carolina can be found in Garvey, "Aggravation and Mitigation," supra note 2, at passim. Here, as elsewhere, South Carolina jurors respond and behave much like jurors from other CJP states. See id. at 1575–76 tbl.10.

influence over a juror's vote, this approach has certain drawbacks. For example, jurors may not be well aware of the actual influences on their vote, or they may try to conceal some influences, especially those they believe the interviewer might consider illegitimate or inappropriate. Moreover, facts about the juror—such as her gender, race, or religion—may help explain how a juror will vote at least as much as, if not more than, facts about the crime, the defendant, or the victim. Consequently, and because the results of the first approach are presented elsewhere,[31] here we follow the second approach, which relies on statistical modeling rather than on juror self-reports. Though less direct, this second approach is less vulnerable to some of the difficulties that hamper the first.[32]

Using data from the South Carolina segment of the CJP, we first identified a number of variables that bore a statistically significant relationship to the juror's first vote at the sentencing stage. We initially focus here on the juror's first vote—and not the final vote—because our aim is to identify the variables that influence an individual juror's decision making, independent of the opinions of her fellow jurors. The juror's first vote reflects her judgment alone; the jury's final vote reflects the judgment of the group. We later examine what, if anything, changes between the first vote and the final one.

This preliminary analysis narrowed the field of potential explanatory variables down to six, which we sorted into two groups of three. The first group involved variables related to the crime and the defendant: the seriousness of the crime, the remorse of the defendant, and the future dangerousness of the defendant. The second group involved variables related to the jurors themselves: their race, their religion, and how strongly they believed death was the appropriate punishment for a defendant convicted of murder.

Before examining the association between each of these variables and the juror's first vote at the penalty phase, we should note that prior research has found that the race of the defendant or the race of the victim—or of both—also helps explain jury decision making in capital cases.[33] Although our analysis of

31. See Garvey, "Aggravation and Mitigation," supra note 2.

32. The analysis and results presented in this section are based on Eisenberg et al., "Forecasting," supra note 2.

33. The principal work in this area is that of David Baldus and his colleagues. Baldus has studied capital sentencing in Georgia, Colorado, New Jersey, and Philadelphia. His most recent work in New Jersey "revealed substantial disparate treatment of black defendants by penalty-phase juries." David Baldus et al., "Racial Discrimination and the Death Penalty in the Post-*Furman* Era: An Empirical and Legal Overview, with Recent Findings from Philadelphia," 83 *Cornell L. Rev.* 1638, 1668 (1998). The results from Philadelphia "strongly support an inference of systemic race-of-defendant discrimination in the jury weighing decisions." Id. at 1688.

the CJP data failed to detect similar associations, the difference may be due in part to differences in the racial makeup of juries in South Carolina and in jurisdictions where such racial effects have been found. For example, in Philadelphia, where these effects have been found, blacks comprise a higher percentage of jurors than in South Carolina.[34]

Facts about the Crime and the Defendant

We begin with the relationship between the first three variables—the seriousness of the crime, the remorse of the defendant, and the future dangerousness of the defendant—and the juror's first vote. For now, we will examine the association between each of these three variables and a juror's first vote in isolation from one another, that is, without controlling for the influence the other variables may have simultaneously exercised on the juror's vote. We will later combine the variables into seven different statistical models that do control for simultaneous influence.

Seriousness of the crime

All capital crimes are serious. Murder—indeed, aggravated murder—is the only crime for which a state can subject a defendant to a capital sanction. Still, not all murders are the same. Some are worse than others, and it stands to reason that the more serious the killing, the more likely a juror will be to vote for death on the first ballot.

In order to gain some measure of the crime's seriousness, we provided jurors with a list of words, such as "vicious" or "depraved," and asked them to tell us how well on a scale of one to four each word described the killing in the case on which they sat. A one indicated that the word described the killing "not at all," and a four indicated that the word described the crime "very well." The results are presented in table 7.

The first column lists each word, and the second shows each word's corresponding mean value. With only two exceptions ("Work of a madman" and "Body maimed or mangled after death"), jurors on average thought that each word described the killing somewhere between fairly well and very well. The third column shows the variance associated with each description, and the fourth gives the *p*-value, which here provides a measure of the statistical significance of the association between the word describing the killing and the juror's

---

34. See Eisenberg et al., "Forecasting," supra note 2, at 296 n.78. The absence of racial effects is likely not a result of relying on juror self-reporting. Jurors have little opportunity to be deceptive about their own race or about the outcome of the case. See id. at 306.

Table 7. Seriousness of the Crime and First Vote

In your mind, how well [on a one to four scale] do the following words describe the killing?

	Mean	Variance	*p*-value	*n*
Bloody	3.34	0.76	0.028	184
Gory	3.14	1.02	0.001	185
Vicious	3.68	0.46	0.000	186
Depraved	3.29	0.83	0.002	185
Calculated	3.15	1.04	0.002	186
Cold-blooded	3.75	0.40	0.000	186
Senseless	3.88	0.13	0.012	187
Repulsive	3.65	0.41	0.040	185
Work of a mad man	2.68	1.24	0.040	185
Made you sick to think about it	3.32	0.85	0.041	186
Victim made to suffer before death	3.11	1.38	0.000	185
Body maimed or mangled after death	1.95	1.49	0.153	182

Note: Results are based on interviews with South Carolina jurors. The *p*-values are based on Kendall's τ. Key: 1 = not at all, 2 = not well, 3 = fairly well, 4 = very well.

first vote on the defendant's sentence. A *p*-value equal to or less than 0.05 signals a statistically significant association, which is to say an association not likely to be observed by chance alone.

Table 7 strongly suggests that the nature or seriousness of the crime—as measured by various descriptions of the killing—does indeed influence a juror's vote. All but one of the words describing the killing bore a statistically significant relationship to the juror's first vote. The more serious a juror thought the crime was, the more likely he was to cast his first vote for death. We will use "vicious" as our proxy or measure for the seriousness of the defendant's crime in the statistical models we construct later on, although most of the other descriptions would have served just as well.

The remorse of the defendant

Both prior research and anecdotal evidence suggest that—in addition to the nature or seriousness of the crime—the defendant's remorse, or lack of it, plays a large role in a juror's capital sentencing decision. The CJP survey asked jurors several different questions designed to measure how remorseful the juror thought the defendant was. One of those questions simply asked how well the juror thought the word "sorry" described the defendant. Responses ranged from "very well" to "not well at all." Table 8 concerns the relationship between a juror's belief that the defendant was sorry or remorseful for what he had done and the juror's first vote on the defendant's sentence.

The results reveal a powerful and highly statistically significant relationship between a defendant's remorse and a juror's first vote: the more a juror thought the defendant was sorry or remorseful, the more likely she was to cast her first vote for life; conversely, the less she thought the defendant was sorry or remorseful, the more likely she was to cast her first vote for death.

The future dangerousness of the defendant

Besides the seriousness of the defendant's crime (which looks to the past) and the defendant's remorse or lack of remorse (which looks to the defendant's present response to the past), prior research and common sense suggest that the future also plays on the minds of jurors as they decide a defendant's punishment. The hypothesis is simple: a juror who believes the defendant presents a substantial risk of future danger is more apt to vote for death than is one who sees him presenting a lesser risk or none at all.

Analytically, the risk a capital defendant presents of future wrongdoing depends on the defendant's *propensity* to violence, and on the *opportunities* available to him to act on that propensity. The CJP asked jurors questions about each of these dimensions. One question—which we interpret as a question about propensity—asked the juror if, after hearing all the evidence, he believed it "proved the defendant would be dangerous in the future." Most jurors (some 80 percent) thought the evidence did indeed prove the defendant would constitute a future danger.

Moreover, further analysis (not reported here) showed that a juror who believed the defendant would be a future danger was more likely to vote for death on the first ballot than was a juror who believed otherwise. Nonetheless, still further analysis (again not reported) revealed that a juror's estimate of a defendant's future dangerousness depended almost wholly on the juror's estimate of the seriousness of the crime and the remorsefulness of the defendant. This measure of future dangerousness therefore adds little explanatory power with

Table 8. Defendant's Remorse and First Vote
How well does "sorry for what he did" describe the defendant?

	Life	Undecided	Death	n
Not at all	16%	8%	76%	74
Not well	28%	13%	59%	54
Fairly well	43%	25%	32%	28
Very well	62%	8%	31%	26

Note: Results are based on interviews with South Carolina jurors. The *p*-value for the association between remorse and first vote (based on Kendall's τ) is highly statistically significant (*p* < 0.0001).

respect to a juror's first vote over and above the two variables—the seriousness of the crime and the defendant's remorse—that we have already considered. Accordingly, we exclude this measure of future dangerousness in the statistical models developed later on.[35]

A second question—which we interpret as a question about opportunity—asked how long the juror thought the defendant would remain in prison if not sentenced to death. The length of time a juror thinks a capital defendant will remain in prison if not sentenced to death no doubt depends in large part on the background beliefs he brings with him into the jury box. But it no doubt also depends on what, if anything, the trial court tells the juror about when, if at all, the defendant will be eligible for release, assuming the juror believes what she's been told.

The law in South Carolina governing parole eligibility for capital defendants, as well as the law governing the manner in which juries are instructed about parole eligibility, changed during the period of time over which the CJP conducted its interviews. At one time, a defendant not sentenced to death would be eligible for parole after twenty or thirty years;[36] at a later time, a defendant not sentenced to death would never be eligible for parole.[37] At one time, trial courts were required to tell jurors about a defendant's parole eligibility, if the defendant asked that they be told;[38] at a later time, trial courts were required to tell jurors nothing about a defendant's parole eligibility, even if the jurors asked.[39] Today, trial courts in South Carolina are required to tell jurors a defendant is ineligible for parole, but only if he in fact is ineligible and only if the prosecution places the defendant's future dangerousness "at issue" during the penalty phase.[40]

---

35. A more complete account of this analysis can be found in Eisenberg et al., "Forecasting," supra note 2, at 290–91.

36. See S.C. Code Ann. § 16-3-20(A) (Law. Co-op. 1985 & Supp. 1993). The defendant would be eligible for parole after thirty years if the jury found the existence of a statutory aggravating factor; otherwise, he would be eligible for parole after twenty years. The one exception involved capital defendants with a prior conviction for a crime of violence, in which case the defendant was ineligible for parole for life. See id. § 24-21-640 (Law. Co-op. 1985 & Supp. 1993).

37. See id. at § 16-3-20(A) (Law. Co-op. 1985 & Supp. 2001).

38. See State v. Atkins, 360 S.E.2d 302, 305–06 (S.C. 1987), overruled by State v. Torrence, 406 S.E.2d 315 (S.C. 1991).

39. See State v. Torrence, 406 S.E.2d 315, 323 (S.C. 1991) (Chandler, J., concurring, joined by majority of the court), overruling State v. Atkins, 360 S.E.2d 302 (S.C. 1987).

40. See Simmons v. South Carolina, 512 U.S. 154, 156 (1994) (plurality opinion); accord Shafer v. South Carolina, 532 U.S. 36, 51 (2001). For an analysis of the relationship between a juror's

Were our aim to identify the factors that influence a juror's estimate of a defendant's release time, we would need to take into account all these changes, since any of them might influence how long a juror believes a capital defendant not sentenced to death will remain imprisoned. Instead, our aim is to assess how, if at all, a juror's estimate of a defendant's release time influences the way she votes, regardless of whatever factors, including changes in the law, influence that estimate to begin with.

Prior studies emphasize three important findings relevant here. First, jurors tend consistently to underestimate the length of time a defendant will remain in prison if not sentenced to death. Second, the less time a juror thinks the defendant will remain in prison, the more likely she is to cast her vote in favor of death.[41] Third, future dangerousness appears to exert its greatest influence on jurors who are undecided at the first vote, prompting them in the end to cast their final vote for death.[42]

Table 9 concerns the relationship between a juror's first vote and her estimate of the length of time a defendant not sentenced to death will remain imprisoned before being released. The results are consistent with prior research. Throughout most of the period under investigation, capital defendants not sentenced to death in South Carolina would be ineligible for parole for at least thirty years. Nonetheless, jurors on average estimated that defendants not sentenced to death would be imprisoned for only nineteen years, eleven years less than the time a defendant would in fact be required to serve before he would become *eligible* for parole, let alone be actually released. South Carolina jurors thus dramatically underestimated the period of time a defendant will actually remain imprisoned if not sentenced to death.

Moreover, jurors who voted for life, both at the first vote and at the final one, estimated on average that the defendant would remain imprisoned for a longer period of time than did jurors who voted for death. The absolute differences between the mean estimates of jurors who voted for life and those who voted for death are not large, ranging from a little under three years on the first vote (21.0 years compared to 18.1 years), to a little over three-and-a-half years on the final

---

estimate of the length of time a capital defendant not sentenced to death will remain imprisoned and the juror's first and final votes on the defendant's sentence both before and after *Simmons*, see Eisenberg et al., "Forecasting," supra note 2, at 291–94.

41. See Bowers and Steiner, supra note 2, at 655; Eisenberg and Wells, supra note 2, at 7.

42. See Bowers and Steiner, supra note 2, at 660; cf. Garvey, "Emotional Economy," supra note 2, at 66–67.

Table 9. Mean Estimated Prison Term (in Years) and First and Final Vote

	Life	Undecided	Death	p-value	Average for all jurors	n
First Vote	21.0	18.6	18.1	0.173	19.0	155
Final Vote	21.0	—	17.4	0.022	19.0	156

Note: Results are based on interviews with South Carolina jurors. The first vote p-value is based on Cuzick's test for nonparametric trends across groups; the final vote p-value is based on a t-test. The p-values reflect the statistical significance, if any, of the differences among the release estimates of the jurors based on their first and final votes. The total number of jurors in the South Carolina data set is 187; however, a number of jurors declined to offer a response to the question of how long they thought the defendant would remain in prison if not sentenced to death.

one (21.0 years compared to 17.4 years). Nonetheless, at least with respect to the final vote, the relationship is statistically significant.

Facts about the Jurors

Facts about the crime and the defendant tell us a good deal about why capital jurors vote as they do. But they don't tell us everything. Left out of the picture are facts about the jurors themselves, facts about who they are and what they believe.

Public opinion polls have long shown that some groups support the death penalty more than others. The two most prominent and enduring group differences are based on race and sex.[43] Whites support the death penalty more than blacks, and men support it more than women. More recent research also suggests that members of white fundamentalist churches, perhaps most notably Southern Baptists, support the death penalty more than members of black fundamentalist churches and members of other faiths more generally.[44]

Because members of different groups support the death penalty to different degrees, they might also vote differently once seated on a capital jury. From among the demographic and attitudinal variables about which the CJP collected information, two demographic variables and one attitudinal variable emerged. First, although a juror's sex had no effect on her first vote, her race and religion did. White jurors were more likely to cast their first vote for death compared to

43. See, e.g., Samuel R. Gross, "Update: American Public Opinion on the Death Penalty—It's Getting Personal," 83 *Cornell L. Rev.* 1448, 1451 (1998).
44. See, e.g., Robert L. Young, "Religious Orientation, Race and Support for the Death Penalty," 31 *J. Sci. Stud. Relig.* 76, 83–84 (1992).

Table 10. Race, Religion, Support for the Death Penalty, and Juror's First Vote

	Juror's first vote				
	Life	Undecided	Death	p-value	n
Race					
White	25%	11%	64%	0.000	151
Black	55%	15%	30%		33
Religion					
Non-Southern Baptist	35%	12%	53%	0.002	151
Southern Baptist	9%	12%	79%		34
Death penalty support					
Unacceptable	50%	25%	25%	0.000	4
Least appropriate	100%	0%	0%		3
One of several acceptable sentences	42%	12%	47%		94
Most appropriate	16%	10%	74%		58
Only appropriate	12%	16%	72%		25

Note: The p-values for race and religion are based on a Mann-Whitney test; the p-value for death penalty support is based on Kendall's τ.

black jurors,[45] and jurors who identified themselves as Southern Baptists were more likely to cast a first vote for death compared to jurors of other faiths and jurors who expressed no religious affiliation.

Second, the more strongly a juror believed death was an acceptable or appropriate punishment for defendants convicted of murder, the more likely she was to cast her first vote for death. These results are based on responses to a question that asked jurors how strongly they supported the death penalty for "convicted murderers." The five available responses ranged from death being the "only appropriate" punishment to death being an "unacceptable" punishment. The question allowed each juror to rank him- or herself along an ordinal scale reflecting the strength of the juror's support for the death penalty. Table 10 gives the details.

Statistical Models

So far we have examined the relationship between each of the six key variables and a juror's first vote separately, on the assumption that they operate independently of each other. But that assumption might be false. It might turn out, for example, that the black jurors we surveyed happened to have served on cases

45. A similar result is reported in Bowers et al., "Death Sentencing in Black and White," supra note 2, at 199.

Table 11. Summary of Key Variables Influencing First and Final Vote

	Mean	Min	Max	*p*-values First vote	*p*-values Final vote (juror-level)	*p*-values Final vote (jury-level)	n
First vote (1 = life, 2 = undecided, 3 = death)	2.276	1	3	—	—	—	185
Death sentence (0 = life, 1 = death)	0.535	0	1	—	—	—	187
Black juror (1 = yes)	0.178	0	1	0.000	0.701	0.573	185
Southern Baptist juror (1 = yes)	0.182	0	1	0.002	0.013	0.020	187
Support for the death penalty (1–5 scale)	3.524	1	5	0.000	0.001	0.001	185
Seriousness of crime (1–4 scale)	3.683	1	4	0.000	0.000	0.001	186
Defendant's remorse (1–4 scale)	2.022	1	4	0.000	0.000	0.000	184
Estimate prison term (all cases) (years)	19.026	4	60	0.249	0.022	0.126	156

Note: The *p*-values are based on a Mann-Whitney test for the association between the first vote and 0–1 variables, on Kendall's τ for ordered categorical variables, and on an analysis of variance for estimated prison time. The *p*-values are based on Fisher's exact test for the association between the final vote (juror-level) and 0–1 variables, on a Mann-Whitney test for ordered categorical variables, and on a *t*-test for estimated prison time. The *p*-values are based on *t*-tests for the association between the final vote (jury-level) and 0–1 variables, ordered categorical variables, and estimated prison time.

involving especially vicious killings, in which case the observed association between a juror's race and his first vote might really be due to the nature of the crime and not the race of the juror. In order to root out any such spurious associations we turn to a statistical technique known as multiple regression.

In simple terms, multiple regression allows us to identify the association, if any, between one variable (called the dependent variable) and another variable (called an independent variable) while holding constant the simultaneous influence of several other independent variables. A set of independent variables produces what is called a "model" of the dependent variable. Accordingly, different groups of independent variables can be combined to produce different models of the dependent variable. Table 11 provides a statistical snapshot of all the variables—dependent and independent alike—that we used in constructing our models.

Table 12. Statistical Models: First Vote and Final Vote

	First vote (1 = life, 2 = undecided, 3 = death)					Final vote (0 = life, 1 = death)	
	Model (1)	Model (2)	Model (3)	Model (4)	Model (5)	Model (6)	Model (7)
Black juror (1 = yes)	-0.527+ (1.85)	-0.604* (2.12)	-0.556* (2.02)	-0.625* (2.30)	-0.691* (2.37)	0.431 (1.56)	0.328 (1.30)
Southern Baptist juror (1 = yes)	0.699* (2.32)	—	0.615* (2.33)	—	0.501+ (1.82)	0.549 (1.59)	0.487+ (1.71)
Support for the death penalty (1–5 scale)	0.390* (2.62)	0.407** (2.86)	0.401** (2.75)	0.421** (3.01)	0.336* (2.35)	0.264* (2.20)	0.278* (2.37)
Seriousness of the crime (1–4 scale)	0.390* (2.20)	0.418* (2.34)	0.415* (2.49)	0.434* (2.61)	0.284 (1.58)	0.567** (3.32)	0.514** (3.08)
Defendant's remorse (1–4 scale)	-0.291** (2.89)	-0.307** (2.94)	-0.318** (3.31)	-0.329** (3.26)	-0.231* (2.31)	-0.291* (2.20)	-0.324** (2.82)
Expected prison term (years)	-0.018+ (1.85)	-0.016 (1.50)	—	—	—	-0.037* (2.64)	—
Constant	—	—	—	—	—	-1.527 (1.61)	-1.984* (2.42)
Death sentence (0 = life, 1 = death)	—	—	—	—	0.777** (3.35)	—	—
Observations	179	179	179	179	179	180	180
Prob. > F	0.0009	0.0027	0.0000	0.0001	0.0000	0.0001	0.0000
Percent correct	77.9%		76.7%				
Error reduction	24.6%		21.2%				

Note: Models one through five use ordered probit regression; the dependent variable in models one through five is the juror's first vote. Models six and seven use probit regression; the dependent variable in models six and seven is the final sentence. + < 0.10, * < 0.05, ** < 0.01. Absolute values of t-statistics are in parentheses. Models that include additional variables (including the age, sex, and socioeconomic status of the juror and the race of the victim and defendant) are presented in Eisenberg et al., "Forecasting," supra note 2, at 300–301 tbl.6.

Next, we enlisted these variables to construct seven different statistical models, five of which used the juror's first vote as the dependent variable and two of which used the jury's final vote. The results are shown in table 12.

Each model produces two figures for each independent variable included in the model. The top figure is called a regression coefficient; the bottom figure (given in parentheses) is called a t-statistic. The regression coefficient tells us how strongly and in what direction the independent and dependent variables relate to each other, holding constant all the other independent variables included in the model. A positive sign on the coefficient of any particular variable means that the variable is positively associated with the dependent variable. In other words, a positive sign on the coefficient indicates a greater tendency to vote for death.

The second figure—the t-statistic—serves the same purpose as the p-values discussed earlier: it tells us whether the relationship between the independent and the dependent variable is statistically significant.[46] A t-statistic greater than 1.96 or less than -1.96 indicates that the relationship between the independent and the dependent variable is statistically significant at or below the 0.05 level ($p \leq 0.05$). We include a symbol beside each coefficient to indicate the level of statistical significance, if any, between each independent variable and the dependent variable ($+ < 0.10, * < 0.05, ** < 0.01$).

For example, the race variable ("Black juror") is coded such that 0 = white juror and 1 = black juror. In other words, if the juror was white, we assigned him a value of 0; if the juror was black, we assigned him a value of 1. The coefficient for the race variable in the first model is -0.527, which indicates that black jurors are less likely to vote for death than are white jurors; that is, as the value on the independent variable increases, the likelihood of a death sentence decreases, holding constant all the other independent variables in the model. The associated t-statistic is 1.85, which means that the relationship between the race variable and the juror's first vote is statistically significant at $p < 0.10$.

Overall, each of the six independent variables with which we began—the seriousness of the crime, the defendant's remorse, the defendant's future dangerousness, and the juror's race, religion, and level of support for the death penalty—continue to influence a juror's first vote even when we control for the simultaneous influence of the other variables. Thus, for example, a white juror is more likely to cast her first vote for death no matter how serious the crime, no matter if she identifies herself as a Southern Baptist or not, no matter how remorseful she thinks the defendant is, no matter how long she thinks the defendant will remain in prison if not sentenced to death, and no matter how appropriate she believes death is for criminal defendants convicted of murder. Holding all these variables constant, we find that a juror's race still influences her first vote.

But now consider what happens when we look to the factors that influence the juror's final vote, not her first one. Four of the variables—the seriousness of the crime, the remorse of the defendant, the defendant's future dangerousness, and how appropriate the juror believes the death penalty is for convicted

46. See supra table 3.

Table 13. Percentage of First Vote for Death and Final Vote for Death

Percentage of jurors voting for death on the first vote	Number of final life sentences	Number of final death sentences	Percentage of final death sentences	Total number of cases within percent range
0–50%	14	0	0%	14
51–66%	7	0	0%	7
67–75%	4	7	63%	11
76–100%	0	21	100%	21

murderers—continue to make a difference, influencing the juror's final vote as well as her first. But two variables—race and religion—both of which exercise a significant influence on the juror's first vote, appear to exercise less, if any, influence on the final one. Why is this so?

The answer lies in the power of majority rule. Consider table 13, which shows the number of final sentences for life and the number of final sentences for death as a function of the percentage of jurors who cast their first vote for death.

The results are striking. If less than two-thirds of the jury's members cast their first vote for death, death is never the final verdict.[47] On the other hand, if more than three-quarters of the jury's members initially vote for death, death is always the final verdict. The final outcome is only uncertain when the percentage of jurors voting for death on the first ballot is more than two-thirds but equal to or less than three-quarters. Put in more dramatic terms, if nine or more members of a twelve-person jury cast their first vote for death, death will almost always be the final verdict; conversely, if seven or fewer jurors cast their first vote for death, life imprisonment will almost always be the final verdict. Juror eight serves therefore as the tipping point. The state can only obtain a death sentence if it can secure the vote of juror eight.

Moreover, table 13 also explains why race and religion, both of which are so powerful at predicting a juror's first vote, lose that power when the final vote is taken. Black jurors who find themselves in the minority after the first vote usually end up voting with the white majority; likewise, Southern Baptist jurors who find themselves in the minority after the first vote usually end up voting with the non–Southern Baptist majority. In either case, the influence of race and

47. When the members of a South Carolina capital jury deadlock and cannot agree unanimously on a sentence of life imprisonment or death, the trial court will automatically impose a sentence of life imprisonment. The results in table 13 assume that all of the juries in our sample were able to reach unanimity on either life or death, and in fact our best estimate is that very few, if any, of the life sentences in our sample were imposed as a consequence of deadlock.

religion fades away, lost to the force of majority rule. Indeed, the single factor that best explains why a juror switches her vote, either from life to death or from death to life, is the size of the first-vote majority. As the number of jurors who make up the first-vote majority increases, jurors who find themselves in the minority on the first vote are likely in the end to conform to the majority's will.

The CJP's Central Lessons

We draw four central lessons from the ongoing work of the Capital Jury Project. Two deal with the processes by which capital jurors are selected and instructed; one deals with the role future dangerousness plays in capital sentencing; the last deals with race.

Selecting Capital Jurors

Capital jurors are required to be fair and impartial. They should not believe either that death is the only appropriate punishment for a defendant convicted of murder or that death is never an appropriate punishment. A juror who holds either of these beliefs is not impartial in the law's eyes and should not be permitted to sit in judgment. The process by which capital jurors are screened and selected is therefore central to the death penalty's legitimacy and fair administration.

The CJP's research has revealed a serious and widespread defect in the way that process works. If the process were working as it should, none of the jurors the CJP interviewed would have believed death was the only appropriate punishment for a defendant convicted of capital murder, but many do. Moreover, it should come as no surprise that jurors who hold this belief, often referred to as "automatic death penalty" or ADP jurors, are routinely among those who do indeed vote for death, and in the marginal case a single vote can mean the difference between a sentence of life imprisonment and a sentence of death.

"Automatic death penalty" jurors may get seated on capital juries for a variety of reasons. First, the scope of voir dire in many states is limited, either by law or practice, such that it fails to provide defense lawyers with an adequate opportunity to identify and weed out unqualified jurors. Second, even when state law and practice do provide opportunities for adequate voir dire, too many defense lawyers don't take full advantage of them, failing to question prospective jurors such that they can successfully detect ADP jurors and remove them from the venire. Third, in some cases ADP jurors themselves are not entirely forthcoming when asked about their beliefs; jurors cannot be removed for bias if they refuse to disclose it. Yet, whatever the cause, the consequences cast serious doubt on the current system's ability to deliver fair and impartial justice.

Instructing Capital Jurors

Capital jurors are solemnly instructed on the law they are bound to follow during the course of their deliberations, and jurors no doubt try to apply the law as best they can based on their understanding of it. While it would of course be unrealistic to expect jurors to understand the law as well as lawyers do, it is not unrealistic to expect capital jurors to understand and follow the basic rules without which the process of capital sentencing loses its claim to constitutional legitimacy.

The CJP has nonetheless shown that even these modest expectations all too often go unrealized. Many capital jurors do not understand or appreciate the basic constitutional rules and principles intended to govern their consideration of the evidence presented to them in mitigation. Moreover, mock jury studies have shown that jurors who do understand these rules are less apt to vote for death compared to jurors who do not.[48] The fact that so many jurors are confused about the law is itself cause for concern; the problem becomes intolerable if this confusion in turn leads some jurors to vote for death when, had they understood the law, they would likely have voted for life.

The culprit here is easy to identify. Capital jurors often receive instructions that no one could reasonably describe as user-friendly. The defects range from undefined concepts to double negatives to sentence structures that would make the keepers of good grammar cringe. Fortunately, the remedy is just as easy to identify. Studies of mock jurors suggest that jury instructions can be reformulated and revised to produce noticeable improvements in the degree to which they truly convey the information they are meant to convey. A state could not, consistent with the constitutional demands of due process, instruct jurors using language that no reasonable juror would understand. Nor should a state be allowed to rely on instructional language that a hypothetical reasonable juror might understand but that many real jurors do not in fact understand.

Moreover, even if state courts and law-review commissions take the initia-

48. See, e.g., Shari Seidman Diamond and Judith N. Levi, "Improving Decisions on Death by Revising and Testing Jury Instructions," 79 *Judicature* 224, 231 (1996); Richard L. Weiner et al., "Comprehensibility of Approved Jury Instructions in Capital Murder Cases," 80 *J. Applied Psychol.* 455, 463 (1995); Marc W. Patry et al., "Instructing Jurors on Death Penalty Decisions: Can It Be Done (Well)?" 22 (July 9, 2002) (unpublished manuscript, on file with authors).

tive needed to formulate comprehensible instructions, defense lawyers need in the interim to appreciate the simple fact that jurors are not lawyers and that jurors often misunderstand legal rules and principles that lawyers and judges treat as self-evident. Consequently, defense lawyers must also appreciate the need to educate the jury, using the occasion of opening statements and closing arguments to elaborate and clarify the legal rules the jury's members must follow during their deliberations. Too many defense lawyers overlook or ignore this critical part of their role.

Future Dangerousness

The CJP has shown that fear looms very large in the minds of most capital jurors. Jurors are afraid that unless the defendant is executed he will be released from the secure confines of prison too soon; moreover, the less time a juror believes a capital defendant who is not sentenced to death will remain in prison before being released, the more likely the juror is to vote for death.

Although predictions of future dangerousness are notoriously unreliable, they remain under existing constitutional doctrine a valid ground on which a capital juror is free to vote for death. Even so, any credible capital sentencing system should present the sentencing jury with the option of imposing life imprisonment without the possibility of parole, often referred to as LWOP. Any state that does not give jurors the option of imposing LWOP instead of death presents them with a false choice. Without the option of LWOP, some jurors will see death as the only real way to guarantee the defendant's incapacitation, while others will see death as the only real way to guarantee that the defendant receives the punishment he deserves. A sentence of life imprisonment with no chance of parole, unlike one with such a chance, presents jurors with a meaningful alternative to death on both grounds.

Moreover, states should do more than simply give jurors the legal option of imposing LWOP as an alternative to death. The CJP has shown that even in states where LWOP is in fact the only alternative to death, many jurors still refuse to believe that LWOP means what it says: that the defendant will never be released from prison. Having presented the jury with the option of imposing LWOP instead of death, states should also take, or allow defense counsel to take, whatever steps are needed to convince jurors that "life without" really means "life *without.*" States should provide capital jurors with a meaningful alternative to death, and they should do everything reasonably possible to convince them that this alternative is real.

Race

History has long taught, and empirical research past and present has long re-vealed, the presence and power of race in capital sentencing. The most sophisti-cated and influential work in this area in recent years has been that of Professor David Baldus and his colleagues, who have studied capital sentencing in Geor-gia, Colorado, New Jersey, and most recently, Philadelphia. Baldus's early re-search, using sophisticated multiple regression techniques, focused on the race of the defendant and the race of the victim, revealing the influence of both, but especially that of the victim, on prosecutorial charging decisions; his more recent research has revealed similar influences at work in the decision making of jurors.[49] Only now, however, has this research begun to examine the effect, if any, of the race of the *juror*.[50]

If our work with the CJP is any harbinger, this research will likely reveal that a juror's race does indeed play a role in the complex racial dynamics of capital sentencing. In particular, we find that black jurors are more likely to vote for life, at least on the first ballot, than white jurors, whose first votes are more likely to be in favor of death. We applaud the efforts of those who are trying to identify and implement reforms designed to reduce the influence of race on capital sentencing. But perhaps the only sure way to eliminate the risk that a capital defendant's fate will turn on the color of his skin, or on that of his victim, or on that of the jurors who sit in judgment of him, is simply not to run it in the first place.

49. See, e.g., Baldus et al., supra note 33, at 1658–66, 1713–15.
50. See David C. Baldus et al., "The Use of Peremptory Challenges in Capital Murder Trials: A Legal and Empirical Analysis," 3 *U. Pa. J. Const. L.* 3, 124 (2001).

6 : INTERNATIONAL LAW AND THE ABOLITION OF THE DEATH PENALTY

William A. Schabas

International human rights law only emerged as a coherent and comprehensive body of norms in the aftermath of the Second World War, a result in no small part of war aims pledged by President Franklin D. Roosevelt in his famous "Four Freedoms" speech and in the Atlantic Charter.[1] Article 1(3) of the Charter of the United Nations, adopted in San Francisco in June 1945, declared that one of the purposes of the United Nations would be "[t]o achieve international cooperation in solving international problems of an economic, social, cultural, or humanitarian character, and in promoting and encouraging respect for human rights and for fundamental freedoms for all without distinction as to race, sex, language, or religion." The most immediate consequence of the human rights perspective within the Charter was the creation of the Commission on Human Rights, chaired initially by Eleanor Roosevelt, the president's dynamic widow. The commission's first important mandate was the drafting of the Universal Declaration of Human Rights, which was adopted on December 10, 1948, by the General Assembly of the United Nations. Article 3 of the Universal Declaration states: "Everyone has the right to life, liberty and security of person." Furthermore, according to article 5, "No one shall be subjected to torture or to cruel, inhuman or degrading treatment or punishment."[2]

Whether the issue of capital punishment was contemplated by the "right to life" was a subject of considerable concern to the drafters of the Universal Dec-

1. See Johannes Morsink, *The Universal Declaration of Human Rights: Origins, Drafting, and Intent* (1999).

2. G.A. Res. 217A, art. 5, at 73, U.N. Doc. A/810 (1948).

laration, including Eleanor Roosevelt. As the Declaration was being prepared, it was suggested that article 3 might be amended so as to correspond more closely to its ancestors in national legislation, such as the Fifth Amendment to the United States Constitution ("nor shall any person be . . . deprived of life, liberty, or property, without due process of law"), by recognizing that the right to life was subject to the important exception of the death penalty. Noting that in some countries there was a movement afoot to abolish the death penalty, Eleanor Roosevelt suggested that it might be better not to make any explicit reference to capital punishment.[3] Ultimately the General Assembly followed Roosevelt's approach, refusing to endorse capital punishment as a limitation on the right to life but also resisting attempts to proclaim that abolition was a necessary and logical consequence of the recognition of every person's right to life.[4] Moreover, because there was nothing in the Declaration to explicitly endorse capital punishment, the prohibition of cruel, inhuman, or degrading punishment might also extend not only to methods of imposing the death penalty but even to the penalty itself.

The Universal Declaration of Human Rights was not intended to be a binding legal instrument. In the preamble, it is described as a "common standard of achievement." This does not mean, however, that it is without legal effect. The Universal Declaration is variously held to be a codification of customary international law, binding on all states, or an authentic interpretation of the very vague human rights provisions in the Charter of the United Nations.[5] Whatever its precise role, the Declaration has provided the initial framework for the development of what is now a sophisticated and complex system of international human rights law. The Declaration does not specifically address capital punishment, and it has been argued occasionally that this is not even a human rights

3. U.N. Comm'n on Human Rights Drafting Comm., 1st Sess., 2d mtg. at 10, U.N. Doc. E/CN.4/AC.1/SR.2 (1947); see also U.N. GAOR 3d Comm., 3d Sess., 102d mtg. at 147, U.N. Doc. A/C.3/SR.102 (1948).

4. William A. Schabas, *The Abolition of the Death Penalty in International Law* 30–40 (2d ed. 1997); Lilly E. Landerer, "Capital Punishment as a Human Rights Issue before the United Nations," 4 *Hum. Rts. J.* 511, 514–18 (1971).

5. See, e.g., Richard B. Bilder, "The Status of International Human Rights Law: An Overview," in *International Human Rights Law and Practice: The Roles of the United Nations, the Private Sector, the Government, and Their Lawyers* 1, 8 (James C. Tuttle ed., rev. ed. 1978); John P. Humphrey, "The Universal Declaration of Human Rights: Its History, Impact and Juridical Character," in *Human Rights: Thirty Years after the Universal Declaration* 21, 28–39 (B. G. Ramcharan ed., 1979).

issue.[6] Countries hostile to the progressive development of international law on the subject of the death penalty take the position that it is sheltered by a provision within the United Nations Charter deeming such matters to be "essentially within the domestic jurisdiction of any state."[7] The debate during adoption of article 3 of the Universal Declaration by the United Nations General Assembly shows that such an argument is unfounded. What specifically the Declaration has to say about capital punishment is something that has evolved since 1948 and that will continue to evolve with the development of the law itself, in much the same way as the interpretation of the broad and general provisions in national constitutions changes with changing times. The position the Declaration takes on the death penalty is explored against the backdrop of article 3—the right to life—as well as the prohibition of cruel, inhuman, and degrading treatment or punishment. The debate about capital punishment has taken its place among the central issues of human rights discourse.

A wide range of international legal instruments—declarations, covenants, treaties, resolutions, bodies of principles—of variable authority and scope now speaks directly to the issue of capital punishment. Many of these texts create binding obligations, applicable to states that have signed, acceded to, or ratified them, or in some other way indicated their recognition that they are subject to them. International tribunals and similar bodies, such as the European Court of Human Rights, the Human Rights Committee and the Inter-American Commission and Court of Human Rights, have contributed invaluable guidance as to the interpretation of some of these norms.

Slightly more than a decade ago, in 1989, Amnesty International published a seminal volume on the issue of capital punishment, titled *When the State Kills*.[8] Amnesty International surveyed the international situation, distinguishing between countries that were abolitionist for all crimes (that is, countries whose laws do not provide for the death penalty for any crime); countries that were abolitionist for ordinary crimes only (that is, countries whose laws provide for the death penalty only for exceptional crimes under military law or crimes committed in exceptional circumstances such as wartime); countries that were abolitionist in practice (that is, countries and territories that retain the death

6. For a recent example, see Ramesh L. Maharaj, Attorney General of Trinidad and Tobago, Remarks in the Working Group on Penalties at the Rome Conference on the International Criminal Court (July 16, 1998) ("We want to make it quite clear that we do not consider the death penalty to be a human rights issue.").

7. U.N. Charter art. 2(7).

8. Amnesty Int'l, *When the State Kills . . .: The Death Penalty, a Human Rights Issue* (1989).

penalty for ordinary crimes but have not executed anyone during the past ten years or more); and retentionist countries (that is, countries and territories that retain and use the death penalty for ordinary crimes).[9] The statistical portrait was as follows:

Abolitionist for all crimes		35
Abolitionist for ordinary crimes only		18
Abolitionist in practice		27
	Subtotal	80
Retentionist		100
	Total	180

Amnesty International also provided the relevant dates of abolition, where applicable. These indicated an unmistakable trend toward abolition, one that was constantly growing in momentum. For example, of the thirty-five countries that were abolitionist for all crimes, twenty-seven had abolished the death penalty since 1948. Moreover, with each decade subsequent to 1948, the number of states that had abolished capital punishment increased. However, the figures also indicated that a majority of states continued to employ capital punishment.

Sometime in the middle of the 1990s, the majority shifted from one favoring capital punishment to one opposing it. According to the report of the secretary-general of the United Nations, issued on March 31, 2000,[10] the numbers are as follows:

Abolitionist for all crimes		74
Abolitionist for ordinary crimes only		11
Abolitionist in practice		38
	Subtotal	123
Retentionist		71
	Total	194

The change throughout the 1990s, subsequent to the Amnesty International study, is most dramatic. Thus, whereas in 1989 some 44 percent of states were abolitionist in one form or another, by the year 2000 the proportion was 64 percent.

Those states that still retain the death penalty find themselves increasingly

9. Id. at 259–62.

10. United Nations, Secretary-General, *Report on Crime Prevention and Criminal Justice: Capital Punishment and Implementation of the Safeguards Guaranteeing Protection of the Rights of Those Facing the Death Penalty* 10, U.N. Doc. E/2000/3 (2000).

subject to international pressure in favor of abolition, sometimes quite direct—for example, in the refusal by certain countries to grant extradition where a fugitive will be exposed to a capital sentence. Most developed countries now refuse to extradite fugitives to the United States without assurances that capital punishment will not be imposed. Abolition of the death penalty is generally considered to be an important element in democratic development for states breaking with a past characterized by terror, injustice, and repression. In some cases, abolition is effected by explicit reference in constitutional instruments to the international treaties prohibiting the death penalty. In others, it has been the contribution of the judiciary, of judges applying constitutions that make no specific mention of the death penalty but that enshrine the right to life and that prohibit cruel, inhuman, and degrading treatment or punishment.

International Law and Abolition of Capital Punishment

It is often said that "international law does not prohibit capital punishment."[11] This is an unfortunate and imprecise statement, however, because several international treaties now outlaw the death penalty. These treaties are, to be sure, still somewhat far from universally accepted. Nevertheless, some sixty-eight states are now bound, as a question of international law and a result of ratified treaties, not to impose the death penalty.[12] As for the suggestion that customary law prohibits capital punishment, such an affirmation is premature. However, the growing trend toward abolition, and its reflection in international norms, would suggest that this is a probable development at some point in the not-too-distant future. The status of the prohibition of capital punishment is not unlike that of issues such as slavery and torture in times gone by, practices that

11. United Nations, Comm'n on Hum. Rts., Special Rapporteur, *Report Submitted Pursuant to Commission on Human Rights Resolution 1999/35*, para. 60, U.N. Doc. E/CN.4/2000/3 (2000).

12. Albania, Andorra, Australia, Austria, Azerbaijan, Belgium, Bolivia, Bosnia and Herzegovina, Brazil, Bulgaria, Cape Verde, Chile, Cyprus, Colombia, Costa Rica, Croatia, Czech Republic, Denmark, Dominican Republic, Ecuador, El Salvador, Estonia, Finland, France, Georgia, Germany, Greece, Haiti, Honduras, Hungary, Iceland, Ireland, Italy, Latvia, Liechtenstein, Lithuania, Luxembourg, Macedonia, Malta, Mexico, Moldova, Monaco, Mozambique, Namibia, Nepal, the Netherlands, Nicaragua, New Zealand, Norway, Panama, Paraguay, Peru, Poland, Portugal, Romania, San Marino, Seychelles, Slovakia, Slovenia, Spain, Sweden, Switzerland, Turkmenistan, Ukraine, United Kingdom, Uruguay, Venezuela, and Yugoslavia. These states are abolitionist both de jure and de facto. Armenia, the Russian Federation, and São Tomé and Principe have signed one or another of the protocols, but the instruments of ratification have not yet been deposited.

were rather widespread despite international condemnation, until a threshold was reached where they were deemed simply beyond the pale of civilized behavior. Lawyers and historians can trace the growth of the abolition of slavery and torture in the parallel evolution of the conduct of states and the development of international legal norms. We are surely now in the midst of the same process, as yet unfinished, with respect to international abolition of capital punishment.

One of the principal international human rights instruments, the International Covenant on Civil and Political Rights, adopted in 1966, transformed the laconic "right to life" provision found in article 3 of the Universal Declaration into a complex text that recognizes capital punishment as an exception or limitation on the right to life.[13] Article 6 of the Covenant affirms the "inherent right to life," adding that it cannot be "arbitrarily deprived." But in a subsequent paragraph, the Covenant states: "In countries which have not abolished the death penalty, sentence of death may be imposed only for the most serious crimes in accordance with the law in force at the time of the commission of the crime and not contrary to the provisions of the present Covenant and to the Convention on the Prevention and Punishment of the Crime of Genocide. This penalty can only be carried out pursuant to a final judgment rendered by a competent court."[14] The provision goes on to state that anyone sentenced to death shall be entitled to seek amnesty, pardon, or commutation of sentence, and it prohibits the death penalty for persons under eighteen at the time of commission of the crime[15] and for pregnant women. A final paragraph, really more programmatic than normative, declares: "Nothing in this article shall be invoked to delay or to prevent the abolition of capital punishment by any State Party to the present Covenant." Currently, the Covenant has been ratified by approximately 150 states, and its principles are therefore approaching near-universal acceptance.

There are at least two other important international treaties within the United Nations system that bear on capital punishment. The Convention on the Rights of the Child, adopted in 1989, states: "Neither capital punishment nor life imprisonment without possibility of release shall be imposed for offences

13. International Covenant on Civil and Political Rights, adopted Dec. 19, 1966, art. 6, S. Treaty Doc. No. 95-2 (1978), 999 U.N.T.S. 171, 174–75.

14. Id. art. 6(2), 999 U.N.T.S. at 174–75.

15. Convention on the Rights of the Child, adopted Nov. 20, 1989, art. 37(a), 1577 U.N.T.S. 3, 55, also prohibits execution for crimes committed under the age of eighteen. It has been ratified by 191 countries, and signed by one other, the United States, without reservation to this provision.

committed by persons below eighteen years of age." The Convention on the Rights of the Child has been ratified by essentially the whole world with the exception of the United States, which signed it without reservation in 1995. Even signatories to international treaties are required "to refrain from acts which would defeat the object and purpose of a treaty."[16] The Convention against Torture and Other Cruel, Inhuman and Degrading Treatment or Punishment may also address issues relating to the death penalty, although there is nothing explicit concerning the subject in its text.[17]

In parallel to the United Nations instruments, regional human rights systems have also emerged in Europe, the Americas, Africa, and the Arab world. In each, there is a general international treaty similar to the International Covenant on Civil and Political Rights. All four instruments recognize the right to life; three of them resemble the Covenant in that they treat the death penalty as a limitation or exception to the right to life, while the fourth is simply silent on the subject. The first of the regional treaties to be adopted, the European Convention on Human Rights, actually predates the International Covenant on Civil and Political Rights by several years. It was drafted in 1950 by a handful of Western European states, members of the Council of Europe at the time, although its reach has now extended to forty-three parties with the dramatic expansion of the organization in the 1990s. Like the International Covenant, the European Convention allows capital punishment as an exception to the right to life.[18] The "right to life" provision in the American Convention on Human Rights, adopted in 1969, rather closely resembles the text of article 6 of the International Covenant on Civil and Political Rights, but with two significant changes, both of them further limiting the scope of capital punishment. Its prohibition is extended to persons over seventy years of age, in addition to pregnant women and juveniles. Furthermore, the Convention specifies explicitly that "The death penalty shall not be reestablished in states that have abolished it," something that is only implicit in the Covenant.[19] The African Charter of Human and Peoples' Rights recognizes the right to life but says nothing about capital punishment. Most commentators conclude that capital punishment must be an implied limitation on the right to life, given the still-

16. Vienna Convention on the Law of Treaties, done May 23, 1969, art. 18(a), 1155 U.N.T.S. 331, 336.

17. Convention against Torture and Other Cruel, Inhuman or Degrading Treatment or Punishment, adopted Dec. 10, 1984, S. Treaty Doc. No. 100-20 (1988), 1465 U.N.T.S. 85.

18. Convention for the Protection of Human Rights and Fundamental Freedoms, Nov. 4, 1950, art. 2(1), 213 U.N.T.S. 221, 224 [hereafter European Convention on Human Rights].

19. American Convention on Human Rights, Nov. 22, 1969, art. 4, 1144 U.N.T.S. 123, 145–46.

widespread use of the death penalty within Africa.[20] However, under a dynamic interpretation informed by jurisprudential developments like the judgment of the South African Constitutional Court abolishing the death penalty,[21] it is now argued that the African Charter also mandates abolition.[22] The Arab Charter of Human Rights, adopted in 1994 by the League of Arab States but not yet in force, allows the death penalty in the case of "serious violations of general law," prohibits its use for political crimes, and excludes it for crimes committed under the age of eighteen and in the case of both pregnant women and nursing mothers for a period of up to two years following childbirth.[23]

Analysis of the capital punishment provisions in the International Covenant and the European and American conventions shows a definite trend toward the limitation of capital punishment. The instrument that is most tolerant of the death penalty, the European Convention, was adopted in 1950. The most recent of the three, the American Convention, seems to flirt with outright abolition. In any event, by the time it was adopted, in 1969, the idea that these instruments should be amended to take into account abolitionist trends was already making the rounds. At the 1969 San José Conference, which adopted the American Convention, the United States delegate spoke of "the general trend, already apparent, for the gradual abolition of the death penalty."[24] Fourteen of the nineteen states present at the negotiation of the Convention adopted a statement calling for preparation of a protocol abolishing the death penalty.[25]

---

20. African [Banjul] Charter on Human and Peoples' Rights, adopted June 27, 1981, Organization of African Unity (O.A.U.) Doc. CAB/LEG/67/3 Rev. 5, 21 I.L.M. 58. It would be wrong to exaggerate the scope of capital punishment within Africa, however. Leaving aside the Arab states north of the Sahara, nearly half of African states have stopped using the death penalty and many have abolished it de jure. On capital punishment in Africa, see generally William A. Schabas, "Abolition of the Death Penalty in Africa," in *The International Sourcebook on the Abolition of the Death Penalty* 30–65 (William A. Schabas ed., 1997).

21. S. v. Makwanyane, 1995 (3) SALR 391 (CC).

22. Manfred Nowak, "Is the Death Penalty an Inhuman Punishment?," in *The Jurisprudence of Human Rights Law: A Comparative Interpretive Approach* 27, 42–43 (Theodore S. Orlin et al. eds., 2000).

23. Arab Charter on Human Rights, approved Sept. 15, 1994, arts. 10–12, League of Arab States Res. 5437, 102d Sess. (unofficial translation in "The Arab Charter on Human Rights," 56 *Rev. Int'l Comm'n Jurists* 57, 61 [1996]); "The Arab Charter on Human Rights," 4 *Int'l Hum. Rts. Rep.* 850, 853 (1997).

24. O.A.S. Doc. OEA/Ser.K/XVI/1.1 doc. 10, p. 9.

25. O.A.S. Doc. OEA/Ser.K/XVI/1.2, p. 467:L. "The undersigned Delegations, participants in the Specialized Inter-American Conference on Human Rights, in response to the majority sentiment expressed in the course of the debates on the prohibition of the death penalty, in agreement

European norms regarding the right to life were the most conservative, although practice on the continent soon began to change. The Council of Europe took the lead in 1983 in adopting a "protocol" to the European Convention abolishing capital punishment.[26] Similar instruments for the other two systems, the Second Optional Protocol to the International Covenant and the Protocol to the American Convention on Human Rights to Abolish the Death Penalty, were adopted at the end of the 1980s and came into force shortly afterward.[27] All three instruments are "optional" and do not amend the original texts as such; rather, they offer states that were parties to the original texts the possibility of enhancing their obligations. But their success is impressive, and more than fifty ratifications have been deposited.

Setting aside the protocols, whose effect seems clear enough, international law may also prohibit capital punishment by implication, through the effect of other norms that do not explicitly call for abolition, and more specifically by the prohibition of cruel, inhuman, and degrading treatment or punishment, a norm found in all major human rights treaties as well as in most domestic constitutions. The concept of what is cruel, inhuman, or degrading ought to change over time to reflect contemporary thinking and values. There is no doctrine of original intent—the bugbear of so much constitutional interpretation within the United States—with respect to international human rights treaties. In fact, it is quite the opposite. It is now well accepted that international human rights norms must receive a dynamic and "evolutive" construction.

---

with the most pure humanistic traditions of our peoples, solemnly declare our firm hope of seeing the application of the death penalty eradicated from the American environment as of the present and our unwavering goal of making all possible efforts so that, in a short time, an additional protocol to the American Convention on Human Rights—Pact of San José, Costa Rica—may consecrate the final abolition of the death penalty and place America once again in the vanguard of the defense of the fundamental rights of man."

26. Protocol No. 6 to the Convention for the Protection of Human Rights and Fundamental Freedoms Concerning the Abolition of the Death Penalty, opened for signature Apr. 28, 1983, Europ. T.S. No. 114.

27. Second Optional Protocol to the International Covenant on Civil and Political Rights Aiming at Abolition of the Death Penalty, G.A. Res. 44/128, U.N. GAOR, 44th Sess., Supp. No. 49, U.N. Doc. A/44/49 (1989); Protocol to the American Convention on Human Rights to Abolish the Death Penalty, adopted June 8, 1990, O.A.S.T.S. No. 73, 29 I.L.M. 1447. The American Convention on Human Rights, supra note 19, is also an abolitionist instrument because it prevents countries that have already abolished the death penalty from reintroducing it. Thus a state that has abolished the death penalty at the time of ratification of the American Convention is abolitionist from the standpoint of international law.

Does the reference to capital punishment in the treaties effectively foreclose any consideration of the death penalty as an intrinsically cruel, inhuman, or degrading punishment? Or is it conceivable that present or future interpreters will consider the capital punishment exception to the right to life to be neutralized or trumped by new conceptions of what is cruel, inhuman, or degrading? In constitutions where there is no allowance for capital punishment as an exception to the right to life, some courts have concluded that it is prohibited by the cruel, inhuman, or degrading clause. But the argument in support of the death penalty's implicit repeal, despite some more explicit recognition, was rejected in 1989 by the European Court of Human Rights (with a lone dissenter),[28] much as it had been dismissed nearly two decades earlier by the majority of the United States Supreme Court in an Eighth Amendment case.[29]

Yet the argument that capital punishment is contrary to the prohibition of cruel, inhuman, and degrading (or "cruel and unusual") punishment is a judicial time bomb, ticking away inexorably as international abolition gains momentum. In 2001 the Supreme Court of Canada, clearly impressed with developments in international human rights law and state practice, reassessed its position on capital punishment, denying extradition to the United States for a capital offense as a violation of the Canadian constitution, whereas a decade earlier it had balked at such a conclusion.[30] The argument has also returned to the European Court of Human Rights in an application filed by convicted Kurdish terrorist Abdullah Öcalan, who was condemned to death by a Turkish court in early 1999. Öcalan's request for provisional measures was granted by the European Court in November of the same year.[31] Much has changed since 1989, and the court may well reverse its earlier judgment, taking into account the dramatic evolution within Europe on the subject of the death penalty and the fact that the prohibition of capital punishment is now a sine qua non for membership in the Council of Europe, something that could not be said a decade earlier. The Öcalan case was argued on admissibility in November 2000 before the European Court of Human Rights, but as these words were written no ruling had yet been issued.

28. Soering v. United Kingdom, 161 Eur. Ct. H.R. (ser. A) (1989).

29. Furman v. Georgia, 408 U.S. 238 (1972) (per curiam).

30. United States v. Burns, 2001 SCC 7, No. 26129 (Can. Feb. 15, 2001) (reassessing Kindler v. Canada [1991] 2 S.C.R. 779).

31. Press Release, Registrar of the European Court of Human Rights, "Interim Measure in the Öcalan Case (Nov. 30, 1999)," available at http://www.echr.coe.int/Eng/Press/1999/Nov/Ocalan interim mesure eng.htm.

There is now a considerable amount of case law on the interpretation of the human rights treaty provisions dealing with capital punishment. The Human Rights Committee, which is the organ established by the International Covenant on Civil and Political Rights to study periodic reports from states parties and to consider petitions from aggrieved individuals and states, has examined capital punishment issues in many of the states parties to the Covenant. Accordingly, it has been implied that the exception allowing capital punishment in countries "which have not abolished the death penalty" may mean that a state that has already eliminated capital punishment cannot reinstate it.[32] The restriction on capital punishment to "the most serious crimes" has led to criticism of countries that impose it for economic crimes and other offenses with nonlethal consequences.[33] The prohibition on executions for juvenile offenders is a norm so fundamental that even a reservation formulated at the time of ratification is ineffective.[34] Methods of execution that inflict superfluous or prolonged suffering on the condemned person—such as the gas chamber—constitute cruel, inhuman, and degrading punishment, in breach of article 7 of the Covenant.[35] An enormous number of cases before the Human Rights Committee have dealt with capital punishment in Jamaica and elsewhere in the English-speaking Caribbean. Most of these have involved procedural flaws at trial or appeal. The committee holds to the view that the strictest respect of

32. *Communication No. 869/1999: Piandong v. Philippines*, U.N. Hum. Rts. Comm., 70th Sess. ¶ 7.4, U.N. Doc. CCPR/C/70/D/869/1999 (2000).

33. See, e.g., U.N. GAOR, Hum. Rts. Comm., 46th Sess., Supp. No. 40, ¶ 509, U.N. Doc. A/46/40 (1991); U.N. GAOR, Hum. Rts. Comm., 45th Sess., Supp. No. 40, ¶ 93, U.N. Doc. A/45/40 (1990); U.N. GAOR, Hum. Rts. Comm., 44th Sess., Supp. No. 40, ¶ 259, U.N. Doc. A/44/40 (1989); U.N. Hum. Rts. Comm., 53d Sess. ¶ 16, U.N. Doc. CCPR/C/79/Add.50 (1995); U.N. Hum. Rts. Comm., 16th Sess., 365th mtg. ¶¶ 7-8, U.N. Doc. CCPR/C/SR.365 (1992); U.N. Hum. Rts. Comm., 5th Sess., 119th mtg. ¶ 14, U.N. Doc. CCPR/C/SR.119 (1978).

34. When the United States ratified the Covenant in 1992, it formulated a controversial reservation to article 6: "The United States reserves the right, subject to its Constitutional constraints, to impose capital punishment on any person (other than a pregnant woman) duly convicted under existing or future laws permitting the imposition of capital punishment, including such punishment for crimes committed by persons below eighteen years of age." The reservation was condemned in objections filed by eleven European states, and it has been declared invalid by the Human Rights Committee. See *Consideration of Reports Submitted by States Parties under Article 40 of the Covenant: United States of America*, U.N. Hum. Rts. Comm., 53d Sess. ¶ 14, U.N. Doc. CCPR/C/79/Add.50 (1995).

35. *Report of the Human Rights Committee, Ng. v. Canada (no. 469/1991)*, U.N. GAOR, Hum. Rts. Comm., 49th Sess., Supp. No. 40, Vol. 2, at 189, U.N. Doc. A/49/40 (1994).

procedural due process guarantees must be ensured if the death penalty is to be imposed.[36] Many death penalty applications are also granted because conditions on death row have been held to breach international standards.[37] Practically, this has meant that in approximately 85 percent of capital punishment cases to be heard by the committee there is a finding of a violation of the Covenant. Some members of the committee will virtually never dismiss a death penalty petition, and there is certainly a constituency among its members for total abolition.

Trinidad and Tobago was so incensed by the Human Rights Committee's findings in death penalty applications that it withdrew from the Optional Protocol to the International Covenant on Civil and Political Rights, the treaty that provides for a right of individual petition. Immediately afterward, Trinidad and Tobago ratified the Protocol for the second time, but on this occasion it appended a reservation excluding all death penalty applications. But, in responding to a subsequent application from Trinidad and Tobago that raised a death penalty issue, the committee held that the subterfuge of denouncing the Protocol and then ratifying it with a reservation was invalid.[38]

States parties to the International Covenant are required to submit periodic reports on their compliance with its provisions. This provides the Human Rights Committee with an opportunity to question states in public session about death penalty issues and to recommend, in its concluding observations, changes to legislation or practice required in order to ensure that there are no violations. The United States ratified the Covenant in 1992 and presented its initial report to the Human Rights Committee in March 1995. The committee made the following comment:

36. See, e.g., *Report of the Human Rights Committee, Yasseen and Thomas v. Guyana (no. 676/1996)*; U.N. GAOR, Hum. Rts. Comm., 53d Sess., Supp. No. 40, Vol. 2, at 151, U.N. Doc. A/53/40 (1998); *Report of the Human Rights Committee, LaVende v. Trinidad and Tobago (no. 554/1993)*, U.N. GAOR, Hum. Rts. Comm., 53d Sess., Supp. No. 40, Vol. 2, at 8, U.N. Doc. A/53/40 (1998).

37. See, e.g., *Report of the Human Rights Committee, Henry v. Trinidad and Tobago (no. 752/1997)*, U.N. GAOR, Hum. Rts. Comm., 54th Sess., Supp. No. 40, Vol. 2, at 238, U.N. Doc. A/54/40 (1999); *Report of the Human Rights Committee, Pinto v. Trinidad and Tobago (no. 512/1992)*, U.N. GAOR, Hum. Rts. Comm., 51st Sess., Supp. No. 40, Vol. 2, at 61, U.N. Doc. A/51/40 (1996); *Report of the Human Rights Committee, Lewis v. Jamaica (no. 527/1993)*, U.N. GAOR, Hum. Rts. Comm., 51st Sess., Supp. No. 40, Vol. 2, at 89, U.N. Doc. A/51/40 (1996).

38. *Report of the Human Rights Committee, Kennedy v. Trinidad and Tobago (no. 845/1999)*, U.N. GAOR, Hum. Rts. Comm., 55th Sess., Supp. No. 40, Vol. 2, at 258, U.N. Doc. A/55/40 (2000).

The Committee is concerned about the excessive number of offences punishable by the death penalty in a number of States, the number of death sentences handed down by courts, and the long stay on death row which, in specific instances, may amount to a breach of article 7 of the Covenant. It deplores the recent expansion of the death penalty under federal law and the re-establishment of the death penalty in certain States. It also deplores provisions in the legislation of a number of States which allow the death penalty to be pronounced for crimes committed by persons under 18 and the actual instances where such sentences have been pronounced and executed. It also regrets that, in some cases, there appears to have been lack of protection from the death penalty of those mentally retarded.[39]

The committee recommended the following: "The Committee urges the State party to revise the federal and state legislation with a view to restricting the number of offences carrying the death penalty strictly to the most serious crimes, in conformity with article 6 of the Covenant and with a view eventually to abolishing it. It exhorts the authorities to take appropriate steps to ensure that persons are not sentenced to death for crimes committed before they were 18."[40]

A relatively limited number of petitions dealing with capital punishment have been addressed to the European Court of Human Rights and, before its disappearance in 1998, to the European Commission of Human Rights. This is explained by the virtual abolition of the death penalty in recent decades within the countries subject to the jurisdiction of these bodies. Turkey remains the exception, as explained above,[41] and there have been a number of applications dealing not with imposition of the death penalty within Europe but with extradition or deportation of individuals from Europe to countries where they might be threatened with execution. European human rights jurisprudence refuses extradition where capital punishment may be imposed, subject of course to obtaining appropriate assurances to the contrary from the requesting nation.[42]

---

39. U.N. Hum. Rts. Comm., 53d Sess. ¶ 16, U.N. Doc. CCPR/C/79/Add.50 (1995).

40. Id. ¶ 31.

41. Turkey continues to pronounce death sentences, although it has not imposed one since the early 1980s and is listed by the secretary-general of the United Nations as being *de facto* abolitionist."

42. Venezia v. Italy, App. No. 29966/96, 87-A Eur. Comm'n H.R. Dec. and Rep. 140 (1996); Meng v. Portugal, App. No. 25862/94, 83-A Eur. Comm'n H.R. Dec. and Rep. 88 (1995); Aylor-Davis v. France, App. No. 22742/93, 76-B Eur. Comm'n H.R. Dec. and Rep. 164 (1994); see also Wá v.

The Inter-American Commission of Human Rights, which is empowered to consider petitions under the American Convention on Human Rights as well as the American Declaration of the Rights and Duties of Man, has considered several death penalty cases, including a number originating in the United States. During the 1980s, the Inter-American Commission ruled that execution of two young men for crimes committed while under the age of eighteen breached the equality rights provision of the American Declaration.[43] The commission has also made provisional-measures requests to the United States, in effect demanding that death sentences be stayed while the issues raised in the petition were examined by the body.[44] The United States has systematically defied these requests.

Imposition of the death penalty has been challenged somewhat indirectly in cases where foreign nationals are threatened with execution. Under article 36(1)(b) of the Vienna Convention on Consular Relations,[45] foreign nationals have a right to be informed of their right to consular assistance in the event of arrest. It has become clear that many if not most foreign nationals condemned to death within the United States have not benefited from this information, which is essentially a due process guarantee akin to the *Miranda* warning given by police as a result of a U.S. constitutional requirement that suspects be informed of their right to counsel. Two cases against the United States have been taken before the International Court of Justice, by Paraguay and by Germany. Provisional-measures requests to suspend at least temporarily the planned executions were issued by the court, but these were once again defied by authorities in the United States.[46] Paraguay dropped its application, but Germany insisted that the matter be fully litigated, despite the executions. In June 2001, the

Portugal, App. No. 25410/94 (Eur. Comm'n H.R. Nov. 27, 1995), available at http://hudoc.echr. coe.int; Leung v. Portugal, App. No. 24464/94 (Eur. Comm'n H.R. Nov. 27, 1995), available at http://hudoc.echr.coe.int.

43. Case 9647, Inter-Am. C.H.R. 147, oea/Ser.l/v/ii.71, doc. 9 rev. 1 (1987); see also Christina M. Cerna, "US Death Penalty Tested before the Inter-American Commission on Human Rights," 10 *Neth. Q. Hum. Rts.* 155 (1992); Donald T. Fox, "Inter-American Commission on Human Rights Finds United States in Violation," 82 *Am. J. Int'l L.* 601 (1988).

44. *Annual Report of the Inter-American Commission on Human Rights 1999*, at ch. 3, ¶¶ 66-68, o.a.s. Doc. oea/Ser.l/v/ii.106, doc. 6 rev. (Apr. 13, 1999).

45. Vienna Convention on Consular Relations, done Apr. 24, 1963, art. 36(1)(b), 21 u.s.t. 77, 101, 596 u.n.t.s. 261, 292.

46. Vienna Convention on Consular Relations (Para. v. U.S.), 1998 I.C.J. 426 (Nov. 10); LaGrand (F.R.G. v. U.S.), 1999 I.C.J. 9 (Mar. 3).

International Court of Justice ruled that by failing to provide the two German nationals, Karl and Walter LaGrand, with the appropriate consular warning, the United States had violated its obligations to Germany and to the two convicts under the Vienna Convention. It also condemned the United States for failing to respect the provisional measures order issued by the Court at the outset of the proceedings and for proceeding with the execution while the case was still pending.[47]

Similar issues were also debated before the Inter-American Court of Human Rights in the context of a request for an advisory opinion filed by Mexico. The Inter-American Court concluded that in a death penalty case the violation of the right to be informed of consular assistance was not only in breach of the Vienna Convention; it also violated the due process provisions of the major human rights treaties as well as the right not to be deprived of life "arbitrarily," which is protected by article 4 of the American Convention on Human Rights and article 6 of the International Covenant on Civil and Political Rights.[48]

The Political Debate in International Organizations

In parallel with the drafting of international legal norms found in the Universal Declaration of Human Rights and the International Covenant on Civil and Political Rights, the political bodies of the United Nations and of other international organizations have been involved in a variety of initiatives aimed at limiting and eventually abolishing the death penalty. Although the issue of the death penalty has been addressed within the specialized bodies of the United Nations that concern themselves with criminal law,[49] the core of the debate has taken place in the Commission on Human Rights. The commission is a special-

47. LaGrand (F.R.G. v. U.S.), I.C.J. Judgment of 27 June 2001, available at http://www.icj-cij. org/icjwww/idocket/igus/igusframe.htm.

48. Advisory Opinion OC-16/99, *The Right to Information on Consular Assistance in the Framework of the Guarantees of the Due Process of Law* (Inter-Am. Ct. H.R. Oct. 1, 1999), available at http://corteidh-oea.nu.or.cr/ci/publicat/series_A/A_16_ING.htm.

49. Notably the United Nations committee and commission on crime prevention and control, which has been considering the subject of capital punishment since the 1950s. See Roger S. Clark, *The United Nations Crime Prevention and Criminal Justice Program: Formulation of Standards and Efforts at Their Implementation* 58–62 (1994); Roger S. Clark, "Human Rights and the U.N. Committee on Crime Prevention and Control," 506 *Annals Am. Acad. Pol. & Soc. Sci.* 68 (1989); Roger S. Clark, "The Eighth United Nations Congress on the Prevention of Crime and the Treatment of Offenders, Havana, Cuba, August 27–September 7, 1990," 1 *Crim. L.F.* 513 (1990).

ized body made up of fifty-three states elected by the Economic and Social Council. Its membership broadly reflects the geographic and political orientations of the entire United Nations membership. Although its interventions may be less robust than those of tribunals and similar bodies like the Human Rights Committee, it has the advantage of being able to address itself to violations of fundamental rights in all United Nations member states, even those that have not fully ratified the relevant treaties. This obviously includes the United States, which has ratified the International Covenant on Civil and Political Rights with reservations to the death penalty provisions and which has not accepted the Optional Protocol to the Covenant that allows for individual complaints.

Much of the monitoring and fact-finding work of the Commission on Human Rights in specific areas is carried out by its special rapporteurs. The special rapporteur on extrajudicial, summary, or arbitrary executions has taken the view that international human rights law seeks the abolition of the death penalty. He has stated that "given that the loss of life is irreparable . . . the abolition of capital punishment is most desirable in order fully to respect the right to life." According to the special rapporteur, "while there is a fundamental right to life, there is no right to capital punishment."[50] In the course of 1996, the special rapporteur sent urgent appeals to the United States concerning death sentences imposed on the mentally retarded, in cases following trial in which the right to an adequate defense had allegedly not been fully ensured, in cases in which individuals had been sentenced to death without resorting to their right to lodge any legal or clemency appeal, and ones in which they had been sentenced to death despite strong indications casting doubt on their guilt.[51] He sent a special appeal to the United States in the case of Joseph Roger O'Dell who, according to his report to the Commission on Human Rights, "has reportedly extraordinary proof of innocence which could not be considered because the law of the State of Virginia does not allow new evidence into court 21 days after conviction."[52] Despite an international campaign, O'Dell was executed in July 1997. The special rapporteur also noted that in response to his urgent appeals the government

50. *Extrajudicial, Summary or Arbitrary Executions, Report of the Special Rapporteur,* U.N.E.S.C., Comm'n on Hum. Rts., 53d Sess. ¶ 73, U.N. Doc. E/CN.4/1997/60 (1996); see also *Extrajudicial, Summary or Arbitrary Executions, Report of the Special Rapporteur,* U.N.E.S.C., Comm'n on Hum. Rts., 52d Sess. ¶¶ 507–17, 540–57, U.N. Doc. E/CN.4/1996/4.

51. *Extrajudicial, Summary or Arbitrary Executions, Report of the Special Rapporteur,* U.N.E.S.C., Comm'n on Hum. Rts., 53d Sess. ¶ 544, U.N. Doc. E/CN.4/1997/60/Add.1 (1996).

52. Id. ¶ 544(e).

of the United States provided nothing more than a reply in the form of a description of the legal safeguards provided to defendants in the United States in criminal cases.[53]

In his 1997 report, special rapporteur Bacre Waly Ndaye noted that "[a]s in previous years, the Special Rapporteur received numerous reports indicating that in some cases the practice of capital punishment in the United States does not conform to a number of safeguards and guarantees contained in international instruments relating to the rights of those facing the death penalty. The imposition of the death penalty on mentally retarded persons, the lack of adequate defense, the absence of obligatory appeals and racial bias continue to be the main concerns."[54] He said he "remains deeply concerned that death sentences continue to be handed down after trials which allegedly fall short of the international guarantees for a fair trial, including lack of adequate defense during the trials and appeals procedures. An issue of special concern to the Special Rapporteur remains the imposition and application of the death penalty on persons reported to be mentally retarded or mentally ill. Moreover, the Special Rapporteur continues to be concerned about those cases which were allegedly tainted by racial bias on the part of the judges or prosecution and about the non-mandatory nature of the appeals procedure after conviction in capital cases in some states."[55]

Ndaye had inquired on several occasions as to whether the United States would "consider extending him an invitation to carry out an on-site visit."[56] As a result of repeated initiatives, he received a written invitation from the government to visit the United States and conduct his investigation.[57] In October 1997, Ndaye conducted a two-week mission to the United States, where he attempted to visit death row prisoners in Florida, Texas, and California. At California's San Quentin Penitentiary, he was refused permission by authorities to meet with designated prisoners. Ndaye's visit provoked the ire of Senator Jesse Helms, chair of the Senate Foreign Relations Committee, who in a letter to William Richardson, United States permanent representative to the United Nations, described the mission as "an absurd U.N. charade." "Bill, is this man confusing the United States with some other country or is this an intentional insult to the United States and to our nation's legal system?" Helms asked. Ndaye replied: "I am very surprised that a country that is usually so open and has been helpful to

53. Id. ¶ 546.
54. Id. ¶ 543.
55. Id. ¶ 551.
56. Id. ¶¶ 547–48.
57. Id. ¶ 549.

me on other missions, such as my attempts to investigate human rights abuses in the Congo, should consider my visit an insult."[58]

Ndaye's successor as special rapporteur, Pakistani lawyer Asma Jahangir, has continued to pursue capital punishment issues. In her 1999 report, she said: "The Special Rapporteur's concerns as they relate to the United States are limited to issues pertaining to the death penalty. The increasing use of the death penalty is a matter of serious concern and particularly worrisome are the continued executions of mentally-ill and mentally-handicapped persons as well as foreigners who were denied their international right to consular assistance. The Special Rapporteur views the persistent application of the death penalty and subsequent executions of persons who committed crimes as minors as a very serious and disturbing practice that inherently conflicts with the prevailing international consensus."[59]

In 1997 the Commission on Human Rights began adopting a series of annual resolutions on the subject of capital punishment. The resolution affirmed the commission's conviction "that abolition of the death penalty contributes to the enhancement of human dignity and to the progressive development of human rights." It requested states to consider suspending executions and imposing a moratorium on the death penalty. The resolution was passed by a roll-call vote, twenty-seven in favor and eleven opposed, with fourteen abstaining.[60] Similar resolutions, with progressively sharper language, were adopted by the Commission on Human Rights in 1998, 1999, and 2000.[61] The resolution adopted at the commission's 2000 session called on states that still retain the death penalty to progressively restrict the number of offenses for which it may be imposed, to establish a moratorium on executions, with a view to completely abolishing the death penalty, and to make available to the public information with regard to capital punishment. All states were required to reserve the right to refuse extradition in the absence of assurances that the death penalty would not be imposed.[62]

58. John M. Goshko, "Helms Calls Death Row Probe 'Absurd U.N. Charade,'" *Wash. Post*, Oct. 8, 1997, at A7.

59. *Extrajudicial, Summary or Arbitrary Executions, Report of the Special Rapporteur*, U.N.E.S.C., Comm'n on Hum. Rts., 55th Sess. ¶ 257, U.N. Doc. E/CN.4/1999/39/Add.1 (1999).

60. U.N.E.S.C., Comm'n on Hum. Rts., Res. 1997/12, U.N. Doc. E/CN.4/RES /1997/12 (1997).

61. Id.; *The Question of the Death Penalty*, U.N.E.S.C., Comm'n on Hum. Rts., Res. 1998/8, U.N. Doc. E/CN.4/RES/1998/8 (1998); *The Question of the Death Penalty*, U.N.E.S.C., Comm'n on Hum. Rts., Res. 1999/61, U.N. Doc. E/CN.4/RES/1999/61 (1999).

62. *The Question of the Death Penalty*, U.N.E.S.C., Comm'n on Hum. Rts., Res. 2000/65, U.N. Doc. E/CN.4/RES/2000/65 (2000).

The Sub-commission on the Promotion and Protection of Human Rights, an expert body subordinate to the Commission on Human Rights, debated death penalty issues at its 1999 session. In August 1999 it adopted a resolution condemning the imposition of the death penalty for crimes committed by persons under the age of eighteen. A preamble to the resolution referred to six countries that had applied capital punishment in such circumstances over the past decade, namely Iran, Nigeria, Pakistan, Saudi Arabia, the United States, and Yemen. The resolution also called on states not to apply the death penalty for refusal to serve in or desertion from the military and called on states to commute all death sentences to at least life imprisonment on December 31, 1999, to mark the millennium.[63]

Use of the death penalty throughout the world, including the United States, has also been regularly denounced by the United Nations high commissioner for human rights, Mary Robinson. On February 4, 1998, she stated that she was "saddened to learn of the death by lethal injection last night of Karla Faye Tucker who was put to death for murders she committed fifteen years ago." Robinson also said that the "increasing use of the death penalty in the United States and in a number of other states is a matter of serious concern and runs counter to the international community's expressed desire for the abolition of the death penalty."[64]

The death penalty has also been debated within the General Assembly of the United Nations. Initially encouraged by the Commission on Human Rights, it took up the issue of capital punishment for the first time in 1968, with a resolution observing that "the major trend among experts and practitioners in the field is towards the abolition of capital punishment."[65] The resolution cited a series of safeguards respecting appeal, pardon, and reprieve and mandated the delay of execution until the exhaustion of such procedures, inviting governments to provide for a six-month moratorium before implementing the death penalty.[66]

63. U.N. Comm'n on Hum. Rts., Sub-Comm'n on the Promotion and Protection of Hum. Rts., 51st Sess., U.N. Doc. E/CN.4/Sub.2/1999/L.16 (1999); see also *The Death Penalty in Relation to Juvenile Offenders*, U.N. Comm'n on Hum. Rts., Sub-Comm'n on the Promotion and Protection of Hum. Rts., Res. 2000/17, U.N. Doc. E/CN.4/Sub.2/RES/2000/17 (2000).

64. U.N. Doc. HR/98/6 (Feb. 4, 1998).

65. G.A. Res. 2393, U.N. GAOR, 23d Sess., Supp. No. 18, at 41–42, U.N. Doc. A/7218 (1968). The General Assembly adopted the resolution by ninety-four votes to zero, with three abstentions. U.N. GAOR, 23d Sess., 1727th mtg. at 15, U.N. Doc. A/PV.1727 (1968).

66. *Report of the Commission on Human Rights*, U.N. ESCOR, 44th Sess., Supp. No. 4, at 132–36, 162–64, U.N. Doc. E/4475 (1968).

Many states favorable to capital punishment actually supported the resolution, noting that it confined itself to the "humanitarian" aspect of the question,[67] while some abolitionist states criticized its timidity, saying it would not "induce Governments to abolish the death penalty."[68] A few years later, a General Assembly resolution declared that "the main objective to be pursued is that of progressively restricting the number of offenses for which capital punishment may be imposed with a view to the desirability of abolishing the punishment in all countries."[69]

More than twenty years later, in 1994, capital punishment returned to the agenda of the General Assembly in the form of a draft resolution inviting states that had not abolished the death penalty to consider the progressive restriction of the number of offenses for which the death penalty might be imposed and to exclude the insane from capital punishment.[70] The final paragraph "encourage[d] states which have not yet abolished the death penalty to consider the opportunity of instituting a moratorium on pending executions with a view to ensuring that the principle that no state should dispose of the life of any human being be affirmed in every part of the world by the year 2000." The proposer, Italy, eventually obtained forty-nine cosponsors for the resolution. However, a skillful procedural gambit engineered by Singapore succeeded in blocking its adoption.[71] When the European Union again attempted to have a resolution put before the General Assembly in 1999, it was outmaneuvered by some retentionist states, even though these were very much in the minority. The whole business ended in the withdrawal of the resolution before it could be put to a vote.[72]

During the 1990s, with the dramatic expansion of its peacekeeping functions, the United Nations found itself organizing the civil administration of states in

67. U.N. GAOR 3d Comm., 23d Sess., 1557th mtg. ¶ 17, U.N. Doc. A/C.3/SR.1557 (1968) (statement of Mr. Li of China); U.N. GAOR 3d Comm., 23d Sess., 1558th mtg. ¶ 10, U.N. Doc. A/C.3/SR.1558 (1968) (statement of Mr. Paolini of France).

68. U.N. GAOR 3d Comm., 23d Sess., 1558th mtg. ¶ 2, U.N. Doc. A/C.3/SR.1558 (statement of Mr. Prohaska of Austria).

69. G.A. Res. 2857, U.N. GAOR, 26th Sess., Supp. No. 29, at 94, U.N. Doc. A/8429 (1971).

70. U.N. GAOR, 49th Sess., app. ¶ 4, U.N. Doc. A/49/234 (1994); U.N. GAOR, 49th Sess., U.N. Doc. A/49/234/Add.1 (1994); U.N. GAOR, 49th Sess., U.N. Doc. A/49/234/Add.2 (1994). The draft resolution was later revised in the Third Committee. U.N. GAOR 3d Comm., 49th Sess., U.N. Doc. A/C.3/49/L.32/Rev.1 (1994).

71. U.N. GAOR 3d Comm., 49th Sess., 61st mtg., U.N. Doc. A/C.3/49/SR.61 (1994).

72. See Ilias Bantekas and Peter Hodgkinson, "Capital Punishment at the Untied Nations: Recent Developments," 11 *Crim. L.F.* 23, 34 (2000).

post-crisis situations. In some cases, this involved the preparation and adoption of statutes in order to fill a legislative void. The United Nations has systematically abolished the death penalty in such countries. Accordingly, in 1992 capital punishment was prohibited by the United Nations Transitional Authority in Cambodia.[73] In Kosovo, when United Nations administration replaced the Yugoslav government following the NATO bombing campaign in 1999,[74] the special representative of the secretary-general, Bernard Kouchner, declared the death penalty abolished.[75] The United Nations transitional administrator in East Timor took the same step in late 1999.[76] Although it was not, strictly speaking, a United Nations initiative, in an essentially similar way the international community brought abolition to Bosnia and Herzegovina by including the Second Optional Protocol and the Sixth Protocol within the fundamental law of the new state, adopted at Dayton in November 1995. Subsequently, the Human Rights Chamber, also established by the Dayton Agreement, declared capital punishment to be against the constitution of Bosnia and Herzegovina.[77] It is a great irony that the abolitionist provisions of the Dayton Agreement were essentially imposed on the warring parties by the U.S. Department of State and in a jurisdiction, Ohio, that continues to apply the death penalty.

Death penalty issues have been frequently addressed by the various organs of the European Union, the fifteen-member organization dedicated to promoting economic and political integration within Europe. In October 1997, the European Union adopted the Treaty of Amsterdam, which amends the various conventions concerning the body and its components. The instrument is completed with a series of declarations, the first of which concerns the death penalty. It states: "With reference to Article F(2) of the Treaty on European Union, the Conference recalls that Protocol No. 6 to the European Convention for the Protection of Human Rights and Fundamental Freedoms signed in Rome on 4 November 1950, and which has been signed and ratified by a large majority of

---

73. S.C. Res. 745, U.N. SCOR, 3057th mtg., U.N. Doc. S/RES/745 (1992).

74. S.C. Res. 1244, U.N. SCOR, 4011th mtg., U.N. Doc. S/RES/1244 (1999).

75. *On the Authority of the Interim Administration in Kosovo*, U.N. Mission in Kosovo, U.N. Doc. UNMIK/REG/1999/1 (1999), available at http://www.un.org/peace/kosovo/pages/regulations/reg1.html.

76. *On the Authority of the Transitional Administration in East Timor*, U.N. Transitional Administrator in East Timor, ¶ 3.3, U.N. Doc. UNTAET/REG/1999/1, available at http://www.un.org/peace/etimor/untaetR/etreg1.html.

77. Damjanović v. Federation of Bosnia and Herzegovina, CH/96/30 Human Rights Chamber for Bosnia and Herzegovina, *Decisions and Reports 1996–1997*, at 147 (1997).

member states, provides for the abolition of the death penalty. In this context, the Conference notes the fact that since the signature of the above mentioned Protocol on 28 April 1983, the death penalty has been abolished in most of the member states of the Union and has not been applied in any of them." On June 29, 1998, the European Union's General Affairs Council stated: "The [European Union] will work towards the universal abolition of the death penalty as a strongly held policy now agreed by all [European Union] Member States." In December 2000, the European Union adopted a Charter of Fundamental Rights, article 2 of which, under the heading "Right to Life," proclaims: "1. Everyone has the right to life. 2. No one shall be condemned to the death penalty, or executed."[78]

The European Parliament, a European Union body of elected representatives from the member states, has adopted several resolutions on capital punishment over the years. As early as 1981 a resolution called for abolition of the death penalty in the European Community.[79] Following the coming into force of Protocol No. 6 to the European Convention on Human Rights, the European Parliament urged member states to ratify that abolitionist instrument.[80] In 1989 the European Parliament adopted the Declaration of Fundamental Rights and Freedoms, which proclaims the abolition of the death penalty.[81] More recently, the European Parliament has adopted several resolutions condemning the imposition of the death penalty within the United States. In 2000, for example, a resolution welcomed the worldwide trend toward the abolition of the death penalty. It said the parliament was "disturbed by Amnesty International figures which estimate that only China, the Democratic Republic of Congo and Iraq carried out more judicial executions than the United States in 1998," and the

78. Charter of Fundamental Rights of the European Union, done Dec. 7, 2000, art. 2, 2000 O.J. (C 364) 1, 9.

79. Abolition of the Death Penalty in the Community, 1981 O.J. (Annex 272) 116–29 (June 17, 1981) (Debates of European Parliament); E.C. Doc. 1-20/80; E.C. Doc. 1-65/81. The Northern Irish extremist Ian Paisley spoke against the proposal, as did some Greek members. The report was adopted on June 18, 1981. Votes, 1981 O.J. (Annex 272) 225–28 (June 18, 1981) (Debates of European Parliament); Abolition of the Death Penalty, 1986 O.J. (Annex 334) 300–303 (Jan. 17, 1986) (Debates of European Parliament); E.C. Doc. A 2-167/85, Doc. B 2-220/85.

80. Parliament Resolution on Abolition of the Death Penalty and the Accession to the Sixth Protocol to the Convention for the Protection of Human Rights and Fundamental Freedoms, 1986 O.J. (C 36) 214.

81. Fundamental Rights, 1989 O.J. (Annex 377) 56–58, 74–79 (Apr. 11, 1989) (Debates of European Parliament); Votes, 1989 O.J. (Annex 377) 151–55 (Apr. 12, 1989) (Debates of European Parliament); E.C. Doc. A 2-3/89.

resolution noted that even Attorney General Janet Reno admitted that no study so far has been able to prove the deterrent effects of the death penalty.[82]

Death penalty practice has also been a factor in assessing human rights within states whose recognition is being considered by the European Union. In its "opinion" on recognition of Slovenia, the Arbitration Commission presided over by French judge Robert Badinter took note of the abolition of the death penalty in that country's constitution.[83] It is clear that countries seeking membership in the Union—and there are now several throughout Central and Eastern Europe—must first abolish capital punishment.

The other European body concerned with human rights and therefore with capital punishment is the Council of Europe. Founded in 1949, it has a much larger membership than the European Union, being composed of forty-three member states covering virtually all of the European continent as well as much of northern Asia. New members of the council are required to abolish capital punishment. This has had the concrete effect of prompting abolition of the death penalty in the Russian Federation, Ukraine, and in several other countries within Central and Eastern Europe that have joined the council in recent years. On October 11, 1997, at the Second Summit of the Council of Europe, the heads of states or governments that are members of the Council of Europe adopted a series of declarations, including one dealing with capital punishment. The document calls for "the universal abolition of the death penalty and insist[s] on the maintenance, in the meantime, of existing moratoria on executions in Europe."

International Criminal Law

The first truly international trials were held in the aftermath of the Second World War and led, in many cases, to executions.[84] The Charter of the International Military Tribunal authorized the Nuremberg court to impose on a convicted war criminal "death or such other punishment as shall be determined

---

82. European Parliament Resolution on Abolition of the Death Penalty in the United States, April 13, 2000, B5-0341, 0354, 0359, 0370 and 0376/2000; see also European Parliament Resolution on Abolition of the Death Penalty in the United States, July 6, 2000, B5-0613, 0619, 0624, 0631 and 0638/2000.

83. Opinion No. 7 on International Recognition of the Republic of Slovenia by the European Community and Its Member States, 31 I.L.M. 1512, 1516 (Yugo. Arb. Comm'n 1992).

84. See William A. Schabas, "War Crimes, Crimes against Humanity and the Death Penalty," 60 *Albany L. Rev.* 733 (1997).

by it to be just."[85] Many of the Nazi defendants were condemned to death, although a few received lengthy prison terms and some were acquitted. The Soviet judge expressed, as an individual opinion, the minority view that all of those convicted should also have been sentenced to death. Those condemned to death were subsequently executed within a few weeks, with the exception of Hermann Göring, who committed suicide hours before he was scheduled to be executed.[86] A series of successor trials were held in Nuremberg pursuant to Control Council Law No. 10.[87] Again, large numbers were sentenced to death or to various lesser punishments, including life imprisonment or lengthy terms of detention. At the Tokyo Trial, seven defendants were sentenced to death and fifteen to life imprisonment.[88] The president of the Tokyo Tribunal penned a separate opinion that seemed to favor sentences other than death: "It may well be that the punishment of imprisonment for life under sustained conditions of hardship in an isolated place or places outside Japan—the usual conditions in such cases—would be a greater deterrent to men like the accused than the speedy termination of existence on the scaffold or before a firing squad."[89]

In answer to arguments that these sentences breached the rule against retroactive punishments, known by the Latin phrase *nulla poena sine lege*, it was said that "[i]nternational law lays down that a war criminal may be punished with death whatever crimes he may have committed."[90] The 1940 United States Army manual *Rules of Land Warfare* declared that "[a]ll war crimes are subject to the death penalty, although a lesser penalty may be imposed."[91] A postwar

85. Agreement for the Prosecution and Punishment of the Major War Criminals of the European Axis, Aug. 8, 1945, art. 27, 59 Stat. 1544, 1552, 82 U.N.T.S. 279, 300; see also Special Proclamation by the Supreme Commander for the Allied Powers at Tokyo, Jan. 19, 1946, art. 16, T.I.A.S. No. 1589, at 10, 4 Bevans 20, 26, amended by Apr. 26, 1946, T.I.A.S. No. 1589, at 16, 4 Bevans 27, 31.

86. In re Göring, 13 I.L.R. 203 (Int'l Mil. Trib. 1946). See generally Telford Taylor, *The Anatomy of the Nuremberg Trials: A Personal Memoir* (1992); *Les procès de Nuremberg et de Tokyo* (Annette Wieviorka ed., 1996).

87. Law No. 10, Punishment of Persons Guilty of War Crimes, Crimes against Peace and against Humanity, art. II(3), 3 *Official Gazette* (Control Council for Germany) 50, 51 (1946).

88. "Judgment," 20 *The Tokyo War Crimes Trial* 49, 854–58 (R. John Pritchard and Sonia Magbanua Zaide eds., 1981).

89. Separate Opinion of the President of the Tribunal, 21 *The Tokyo War Crimes Trial*, supra note 87, at 14; see also B. V. A. Röling, *The Tokyo Trial and Beyond: Reflections of a Peacemonger* (Antonio Cassese ed., 1993).

90. U.N. War Crimes Comm'n, *Law Reports of Trials of War Criminals* 200 (1949).

91. *Rules of Land Warfare*, Field Manual 27-10, ¶ 357 (Oct. 1, 1940).

Norwegian court answered a defendant's plea that the death penalty did not apply to the offense as charged by finding that violations of the laws and customs of war had always been punishable by death in international law.[92]

Early efforts to establish an international criminal justice system considered the appropriateness of the death penalty. A 1947 draft of the Convention on the Prevention and Punishment of the Crime of Genocide suggested that the maximum penalty for genocide should be capital punishment.[93] But only a few years later, a provision proposed by the International Law Commission for its "Draft Code of Offences against the Peace and Security of Mankind" avoided any categorical reference to capital punishment: "The penalty for any offense defined in this Code shall be determined by the tribunal exercising jurisdiction over the individual accused, taking into account the gravity of the offense."[94] A United Nations General Assembly committee subsequently recommended that the statute of the proposed international criminal court contain only the most general of texts dealing with sentencing; it suggested the phrase "the court shall impose such penalties as it may determine."[95] Moreover, the General Assembly committee even stated that the statute might exclude certain forms of punishment, such as the death penalty.[96]

The Cold War intervened to arrest further developments in international justice, and only in 1989 did the General Assembly revive the proposal to establish an international court. In the interim, international human rights law progressed from a somewhat benign tolerance of capital punishment to direct and outright opposition. When the issue of sentencing came before the International Law Commission in 1991, special rapporteur Doudou Thiam formally determined that capital punishment be excluded from the Code of Crimes

92. Public Prosecutor v. Klinge, 13 I.L.R. 262 (Nor. Sup. Ct. 1946).

93. *List of Substantive Items to Be Discussed in the Remaining Stages of the Committee's Session*, U.N. Ad Hoc Comm'n on Genocide, at 2, U.N. Doc. E/AC.25/11 (1948); see also *Draft Convention on the Crime of Genocide*, U.N.E.S.C., U.N. Secretary-General, Annex I, arts. 36–39, at 73–74, Annex II, arts. 30–33, at 82–83, U.N. Doc. E/447 (1948).

94. *Report of the International Law Commission*, U.N. GAOR, 6th Sess, Supp. No. 9, ¶ 59, art. 5, at 14, U.N. Doc. A/1858 (1951).

95. *Report of the Committee on International Criminal Jurisdiction*, U.N. GAOR, Comm. on Int'l Crim. Jurisdiction, 7th Sess., Supp. No. 11, ¶¶ 110–11, U.N. Doc. A/2136 (1952); id. Annex I, art. 32 ("The Court shall impose upon an accused, upon conviction, such penalty as the Court may determine, subject to any limitations prescribed in the instrument conferring jurisdiction upon the Court.").

96. Id. ¶ 111.

against the Peace and Security of Mankind and that a maximum sentence of life imprisonment be provided instead.[97] Although a few members of the commission argued that the supreme penalty should not be abandoned,[98] the vast majority felt it would be unthinkable, given the international trend in favor of abolition of the death penalty.

While the debate had been underway in the International Law Commission and the Preparatory Committee, the United Nations Security Council had also addressed the issue of sentencing when it set up the ad hoc tribunals for the former Yugoslavia and Rwanda. The Statutes of the two ad hoc tribunals contain brief provisions dealing with sentencing, proposing essentially that sentences be limited to imprisonment (thereby tacitly excluding the death penalty, as well as corporal punishment, imprisonment with hard labor, and fines) and that they be established with the "general practice" of the criminal courts in the former Yugoslavia or Rwanda taken into account.[99] The exclusion of the death penalty by the International Tribunal was a particularly sore point with Rwanda. In the Security Council, Rwanda claimed there would be a fundamental injustice in exposing criminals tried by its domestic courts to execution if those tried by the international tribunal—presumably the masterminds of the genocide—would only be subject to life imprisonment.[100] "Since it is foreseeable that the Tribunal will be dealing with suspects who devised, planned and organized the genocide, these may escape capital punishment whereas those who simply carried out their plans would be subjected to the harshness of this sentence," said Rwanda's representative. "That situation is not conducive to na-

97. *Ninth Report of the Draft Code of Crimes against Peace and Security of Mankind*, Int'l Law Comm'n, 43d Sess., ¶ 29, U.N. Doc. A/CN.4/435. For the discussion of this proposal by the International Law Commission, see Int'l Law Comm'n, 43d Sess., 2207th–2214th mtgs., U.N. Doc. A/CN.4/SR.2207-2214 (1991); U.N. GAOR, Int'l Law Comm'n, 46th Sess., Supp. No. 10, ¶¶ 70–105, U.N. Doc. A/46/10 (1991).

98. Int'l Law Comm'n, 43d Sess., 2211th mtg., ¶ 15, U.N. Doc. A/CN.4/SR.2211 (1991); Int'l Law Comm'n, 43d Sess., 2212 mtg., ¶¶ 19, 28, U.N. Doc. A/CN.4/SR.2212 (1991); Int'l Law Comm'n, 43d Sess., 2213d mtg., ¶ 55, U.N. Doc. A/CN.4/SR.2213 (1991). Special rapporteur Thiam promised that the commission's report would state that "two or three of its members" had expressed reservations about exclusion of the death penalty. Int'l Law Comm'n, 43d Sess., 2213d mtg., ¶ 59, U.N. Doc. A/CN.4/SR.2213.

99. *Statute of the International Criminal Tribunal for the Former Yugoslavia*, S.C. Res. 827, U.N. SCOR, 48th Sess., Annex, art. 24(1), U.N. Doc. S/RES/827 (1993); *Statute of the International Tribunal for Rwanda*, S.C. Res. 955, U.N. SCOR, 49th Sess., Annex, art. 23(1), U.N. Doc. S/RES/955 (1994).

100. U.N. SCOR, 49th Sess., 3453d mtg., at 16, U.N. Doc. S/PV.3453 (1994).

tional reconciliation in Rwanda."[101] But to counter this argument, the representative of New Zealand reminded Rwanda that "[f]or over three decades the United Nations has been trying progressively to eliminate the death penalty. It would be entirely unacceptable—and a dreadful step backwards—to introduce it here."[102] Since domestic trials began in Rwanda in December 1996 many hundreds have been sentenced to death.[103] Eventually, in April 1998, twenty-two individuals were executed by firing squad before thousands. Those who attended the public executions, held in municipal soccer stadiums, have told the author that the cathartic effect that had been promised and expected did not materialize. Since then, the Rwandan executioners have been silent, and the country has searched for original approaches to justice and accountability rooted in African traditions.

The death penalty is formally excluded from the Rome Statute of the International Criminal Court. The statute was adopted on July 17, 1998, and as of December 31, 2000, some 139 states had signed it, including many where the death penalty is still in effect. But the debate about capital punishment threatened to undo the Rome Conference when the statute was being negotiated. The campaign in favor of capital punishment was led by a persistent group of Arab and Islamic states, together with English-speaking Caribbean states, and a few others such as Singapore, Rwanda, Ethiopia, and Nigeria. The Rome negotiations were a perfect occasion for them to attempt to promote their position because adoption of the statute would require consensus. Desperate to resolve the issue and ensure support for the draft statute as a whole, the majority of delegates agreed to include a new article stating that the provisions for penalties in the statute are without prejudice to domestic criminal law sanctions,[104] as well as to authorize a declaration by the president at the conclusion of the conference pandering to the sensitivity of the death penalty states on the issue.[105] Nevertheless, the exclusion of the death penalty from the Rome Statute

101. Id.

102. Id. at 5.

103. William A. Schabas, "Justice, Democracy, and Impunity in Post-Genocide Rwanda: Searching for Solutions to Impossible Problems," 7 *Crim. L.F.* 523 (1996).

104. *Rome Statute of the International Criminal Court*, U.N. GAOR, 53d Sess., art. 80, U.N. Doc. A/CONF.183/9 (1998).

105. The agreed-upon declaration reads as follows: "The debate at this Conference on the issue of which penalties should be applied by the Court has shown that there is no international consensus on the inclusion or non-inclusion of the death penalty. However, in accordance with the principles of complementarity between the Court and national jurisdictions, national jus-

can be nothing but an important benchmark in an unquestionable trend toward universal abolition of capital punishment.[106]

Extradition

Extradition has become an important indirect way in which international law promotes the abolition of the death penalty. Since the late nineteenth century, many extradition treaties have contained clauses by which states parties may refuse extradition for capital offenses in the requesting state unless a satisfactory assurance is given that the death penalty will not be imposed. Such provisions can be found as early as 1889, in the South American Convention, in the 1892 extradition treaty between the United Kingdom and Portugal, in the 1908 extradition treaty between the United States and Portugal, and in the 1912 treaty prepared by the International Commission of Jurists.[107] These clauses have now become a form of international law "boilerplate" and are contained in model extradition treaties adopted within international organizations, including the United Nations.[108]

---

tice systems have the primary responsibility for investigating, prosecuting and punishing individuals, in accordance with their national laws, for crimes falling under the jurisdiction of the International Criminal Court. In this regard, the Court would clearly not be able to affect national policies in this field. It should be noted that not including the death penalty in the Statute would not in any way have a legal bearing on national legislations and practices with regard to the death penalty. Nor shall it be considered as influencing, in the development of customary international law or in any other way, the legality of penalties imposed by national systems for serious crimes." Press Release, United Nations, "U.N. Diplomatic Conference Concludes in Rome with Decision to Establish Permanent International Criminal Court (July 17, 1998)," U.N. Doc. L/ROM/22.

106. *The Question of the Death Penalty*, U.N.E.S.C., Comm'n on Hum. Rts., Res. 1999/61, pmbl., U.N. Doc. E/CN.4/RES/1999/61 (1999).

107. Geoff Gilbert, *Aspects of Extradition Law* 99–100 (1991); Am. Inst. of Int'l Law, "Project No. 17: Extradition," 20 *Am. J. Int'l L.* 331 (Spec. Supp. 1926); "Draft Convention on Extradition," 29 *Am. J. Int'l L.* 21, 228 (Supp. 1935); P. Leboucq, "Influence en matière d'extradition de la peine applicable dans le pays requérant," 38 *J. du Droit Int'l* 437 (1911); J. S. Reeves, "Extradition Treaties and the Death Penalty," 18 *Am. J. Int'l L.* 298 (1924); Sharon A. Williams, "Extradition to a State That Imposes the Death Penalty," 28 *Can. Y.B. Int'l L.* 117 (1990); Sharon A. Williams, "Nationality, Double Jeopardy, Prescription and the Death Sentence as Bases for Refusing Extradition," 62 *Int'l Rev. Penal L.* 259 (1991); Sharon A. Williams, "Human Rights Safeguards and International Co-operation in Extradition: Striking the Balance," 3 *Crim. L.F.* 191 (1992).

108. "Model Treaty on Extradition," in U.N. 8th Congress on the Prevention of Crime and the

Several important cases have been heard by courts in Europe and Canada concerning extradition to the United States. Extradition to the United States from Europe is now contingent on such assurances, the result of the case law of the European Court of Human Rights and the new Charter of Fundamental Rights of the European Union. Canada was more compliant with extradition for many years until a February 2001 judgment of its Supreme Court declared unconstitutional extradition without assurances that the death penalty would not be imposed, except in "exceptional cases."[109]

In a celebrated judgment (*Soering v. United Kingdom*) issued on July 7, 1989,[110] the European Court of Human Rights confirmed that circumstances relating to a death sentence could give rise to issues respecting the prohibition of inhuman and degrading treatment or punishment. Specifically, it ruled that extradition of an offender to the United States for a crime subject to capital punishment breached article 3 of the European Convention on Human Rights,[111] which prohibits torture and "inhuman or degrading treatment or punishment." Because the European Convention's archaic right to life provision specifically recognizes capital punishment as an exception, the European judges found the violation in the "death row phenomenon," by which protracted detention prior to execution is itself a human rights violation, rather than in the death penalty per se. Since then, the prohibition has become more general. Subsequent decisions of the European Commission of Human Rights have taken the approach that extradition without an assurance that capital punishment would not be imposed is contrary to the European Convention of Human Rights.[112] There are no more cases of this nature before the European Court because national courts within Europe routinely insist on such assurances. Thus the litigation never reaches the international court in Strasbourg. On at least two occasions, the French Conseil d'Etat has refused to extradite, expressing the view that Protocol No. 6 to the European Convention on Human Rights establishes a

Treatment of Offenders, *Report*, art. 4(d), at 71, 75, U.N. Doc. A/CONF.144/28 (1990); Inter-American Convention on Extradition, adopted Feb. 25, 1981, art. 9, O.A.S.T.S. No. 60; European Convention on Extradition, done Dec. 13, 1957, art. 11, 359 U.N.T.S. 273. The Italian Constitutional Court has ruled that article 11 of the European Convention on Extradition does not codify a customary rule of international law. In re Cuillier, 78 I.L.R. 93 (Italy Corte cost. 1988).

109. United States v. Burns, 2001 SCC 7, No. 26129 (Can. Feb. 15, 2001).

110. Soering v. United Kingdom, 161 Eur. Ct. H.R. (ser. A) (1989).

111. Supra note 18.

112. Supra note 42.

European *ordre public* that prohibits extradition in capital cases.[113] The Supreme Court of the Netherlands has taken the same view, invoking the Protocol in refusing to return a United States serviceman,[114] although the Netherlands was required to do so by the NATO Status of Forces Agreement.[115] The Dutch court found that the European Convention and its Protocol No. 6 took precedence over the other treaty. In June 1996, Italy's Constitutional Court took judicial opposition to extradition for capital crimes one step further when it refused to send Pietro Venezia to the United States, despite assurances from American prosecutors that the death penalty would not be sought or imposed. Referring to the mechanism by which the Italian authorities consider the sufficiency of the undertaking by U.S. authorities not to impose capital punishment, the Constitutional Court stated:

> Such a solution has the advantage of providing a flexible solution for the requested State, and allows for policy to be developed over time based on considerations of criminal law policy; but in our system, where the prohibition of the death penalty is enshrined in the Constitution, the formula of "sufficient assurances"—for the purpose of granting extradition for crimes for which the death penalty is provided in the legislation of the requesting State—is not admissible from the standpoint of the Constitution. The prohibition set out in paragraph 4 of article 27 of the Constitution and the

113. Fidan, Conseil d'Etat, Feb. 27, 1987, Lebon 1987, 81, D. 1987, 305; Gacem, Conseil d'Etat, Feb. 27, 1987, Lebon 1987, 733, JCP 1988, IV, 86. *Fidan* was cited by Judge De Meyer in his concurring opinion in *Soering*, 161 Eur. Ct. H.R. at 51.

114. Netherlands/Short, HR 30 maart 1990, NJ 249, 29 I.L.M. 1375; see Steven J. Lepper, "Short v. The Kingdom of the Netherlands: Is It Time to Renegotiate the NATO Status of Forces Agreement?," 24 *Vand. J. Transnat'l L.* 867 (1991); John E. Parkerson Jr. and Steven J. Lepper, "Commentary on Short v. Netherlands," 85 *Am. J. Int'l L.* 698 (1991).

115. Agreement between the Parties to the North Atlantic Treaty Regarding the Status of Their Forces, June 19, 1951, 4 U.S.T. 1792, 199 U.N.T.S. 67. Note that on June 19, 1995, the states parties to the NATO treaty finalized the Agreement among the States Parties to the North Atlantic Treaty and the Other States Participating in the Partnership for Peace Regarding the Status of Their Forces Together with an Additional Protocol. Article 1 of the Additional Protocol states: "Insofar as it has jurisdiction according to the provisions of the agreement, each State party to the present additional protocol shall not carry out a death sentence with regard to any member of a force and its civilian component, and their dependents from any other State party to the present additional protocol." Additional Protocol to the Agreement among the States Parties to the North Atlantic Treaty and the Other States Participating in the Partnership for Peace Regarding the Status of Their Forces, done June 19, 1995, art. 1, http://www.nato.int/docu/basictxt/b950619b.htm.

values that it expresses—foremost among them being life itself—impose an absolute guarantee.[116]

When the European Union adopted the Charter of Fundamental Rights in December 2000, it also took an intolerant view of extradition requests that did not include an assurance that capital punishment would not be imposed. The Charter affirms that "[n]o one may be removed, expelled or extradited to a State where there is a serious risk that he or she would be subjected to the death penalty."[117] This is far more than *Soering* ever stated, of course, but it testifies to the influence of that innovative decision. Intriguingly, the explanatory notes that accompany the Charter say the provision "incorporates case law from the European Court of Human Rights," citing the *Soering* judgment.[118] In effect, then, the *Soering* precedent reaches considerably further than it was intended, or at any rate further than a reasonable construction of the decision can bear. The result is that most extradition requests made by the United States will now require assurances that capital punishment will not be imposed. This creates, in effect, a two-tier system within the United States, whereby those who manage to flee the jurisdiction will ensure that they are not executed, even if they are caught abroad and their extradition is effected.

Canadian courts were initially reluctant to follow European precedents.[119] Article 6 of the Extradition Treaty between Canada and the United States declares: "When the offense for which extradition is requested is punishable by death under the laws of the requesting State and the laws of the requested State do not permit such punishment for that offense, extradition may be refused unless the requesting State provides such assurances as the requested State considers sufficient that the death penalty shall not be imposed, or, if imposed, shall not be executed."[120] As noted above, the Supreme Court of Canada held in a unanimous decision on February 15, 2001, that extradition without assurances in capital cases was contrary to the Canadian Charter of Rights and Freedoms, except in "exceptional cases." Relying largely on the international

116. "Venezia v. Ministero di Grazia e Giustizia, Corte cost., 27 June 1996," 79 *Rivista di Diritto Internazionale* 815, 821 (1996).

117. Charter of Fundamental Rights of the European Union, supra note 78, art. 19(2), at 12.

118. Draft Charter of Fundamental Rights of the European Union, at 21, CHARTE 4473/00, CONVENT 49 (Oct. 11, 2000), available at http://www.europarl.eu.int/charter/pdf/text_en.pdf.

119. Kindler v. Canada, [1991] 2 S.C.R. 779 (Can.).

120. Extradition Treaty between Canada and the United States of America, Dec. 3, 1971, U.S.-Can., art. 6, 27 U.S.T. 983, 989, amended by S. Treaty Doc. 101-17 (1990).

debate, the court noted that the abolition of the death penalty was a major Canadian initiative in international law and reflected a "concern increasingly shared by most of the world's democracies." In support, the court referred to the various treaties and resolutions that have advanced the cause of abolition and to the prohibition of capital punishment in cases of war crimes, crimes against humanity, and genocide tried before international criminal tribunals. According to the Supreme Court:

> The existence of an international trend against the death penalty is useful in testing our values against those of comparable jurisdictions. This trend against the death penalty supports some relevant conclusions. First, criminal justice, according to international standards, is moving in the direction of abolition of the death penalty. Second, the trend is more pronounced among democratic states with systems of criminal justice comparable to our own. The United States (or those parts of it that have retained the death penalty) is the exception, although of course it is an important exception. Third, the trend to abolition in the democracies, particularly the Western democracies, mirrors and perhaps corroborates the principles of fundamental justice that led to the rejection of the death penalty in Canada.[121]

The Canadian court also attached significance to the evolving debate within the United States itself, citing recent studies raising the issue of whether innocents may be in danger of conviction and execution and showing that racial bias and poverty continue to play too great a role in determining who is sentenced to death.

Conclusion

The classic weakness of international human rights law lies in its means of implementation. Increasingly, however, international human rights law is being applied by domestic courts, and this contributes immensely to its effectiveness. In some countries, it is given primacy over incompatible domestic legislation. In others, it has been used by courts to assist in interpreting the scope of constitutional norms that have usually been inspired by the international instruments. Death penalty jurisprudence provides one of the most dramatic examples of this synergy between international and domestic human rights law.

121. United States v. Burns, 2001 SCC 7, No. 26129, ¶ 92 (Can. Feb. 15, 2001).

Courts of several states, including South Africa,[122] Zimbabwe,[123] Canada,[124] Hungary,[125] Tanzania,[126] Bosnia and Herzegovina,[127] and the United Kingdom[128] have found international law to be particularly helpful in interpreting concepts such as the right to life and the protection against cruel, inhuman, and degrading punishment. In a 1995 judgment of the South African Constitutional Court, which ruled that capital punishment was incompatible with the right to life and the protection against cruel, inhuman, and degrading punishment, President Arthur Chaskalson wrote: "The international and foreign authorities are of value because they analyze arguments for and against the death sentence and show how courts of other jurisdictions have dealt with this vexed issue. For that reason alone they require our attention."[129] He provided a detailed analysis of the international instruments as well as the case law of such bodies as the Human Rights Committee and the European Court of Human Rights.

This chapter has highlighted international developments, but with a special emphasis on their impact on the United States. The last great democracy to retain capital punishment, it remains peculiarly attached to a harsh and repressive criminal justice system and to concepts of sentencing, particularly "just deserts," that are in dramatic decline elsewhere. With respect to international developments, the United States seems to have a studied indifference, possibly the consequence of its long isolationist traditions but more likely attributable to the arrogance associated with its status as the last remaining superpower. Can it be without irony that the same politicians who shrilly condemn the world's "rogue states," like Iran and Iraq, share with them a devotion to the death penalty deemed unacceptable to the majority of nations? Unlike their counterparts in other parts of the world, judges and legislators in the United States have given short shrift to the growing body of declarations, treaties, and

---

122. S. v. Makwanyane, 1995 (3) SALR 391 (CC).

123. Catholic Comm'n for Justice and Peace in Zimb. v. Attorney-General, Zimbabwe, 1993 (1) ZLR 242 (Zimb.).

124. *Burns*, 2001 SCC 7.

125. Ruling 23/1990 (X.31) AB, Alkotmánybíróság [Constitutional Court], Oct. 24, 1990, MK Oct. 31, 1991 (Hung.).

126. Republic v. Mbushuu, [1994] T.L.R. 146 (Tanz.).

127. Damjanović v. Federation of Bosnia and Herzegovina, CH/96/30 Human Rights Chamber for Bosnia and Herzegovina, *Decisions and Reports 1996-1997*, at 147 (1997).

128. Pratt v. Attorney-General for Jamaica, [1994] 2 A.C. 1 (P.C. 1993) (appeal taken from Jam. CA).

129. S. v. Makwanyane, 1995 (3) SALR 391, ¶ 34 (CC).

judgments described in this chapter. This seems true even when the judgments directly target the United States.

Can the international context influence the course of abolition within the United States? Certainly, there is a very direct impact when countries refuse to extradite alleged murderers to the United States without assurances that capital punishment will not be imposed. In the long run, its growing status as an international pariah on the subject should contribute to the debate within the United States, with an additive and synergistic effect on other factors, such as the danger of wrongful conviction. There is a strong constituency within the United States that desires it to play a full role in the international human rights systems. This can be seen in the ratification of certain human rights treaties during the early years of the Clinton administration and in the signing of the Rome Statute of the International Criminal Court on December 31, 2000. There are also, unfortunately, vocal and influential elements who attack international human rights law as an encroachment on U.S. sovereignty. The changing dialectic of these two currents with respect to international law and practice may well make an important and possibly even decisive contribution to the survival or defeat of capital punishment within the United States in the first decades of the twenty-first century.

POSTSCRIPT: THE PECULIAR PRESENT OF AMERICAN CAPITAL PUNISHMENT

Franklin E. Zimring

My aim here is not to summarize or to critique the materials assembled in this volume, but instead to use the book's contributions as a foundation for my own interpretation of recent history and current conditions in the United States. Can we add up the insights in this volume on international legal trends, racial patterns, habeas corpus, jury competence, and the risk of executing defendants innocent of their crimes into a coherent account of how the conditions described in this book have come about and forecast what is likely to happen next?

My attempt to comprehend the special character of American capital punishment is organized under four headings: (1) the exceptionalism of current American capital punishment policy; (2) the wide range of capital punishment policies throughout the United States; (3) the paradox of continuity in execution pattern after a change in law when compared to earlier times; and (4) the fundamental conflict between the operational requirements of a functioning execution system and American legal values.

American Exceptionalism: A Profile

At the turn of the twenty-first century, the contrast between the United States and all other Western democracies on the issue of execution as state policy is extraordinary. In the United States, thirty-eight states and the federal government authorize death as a criminal punishment, and twenty-nine states have conducted at least one execution. In contrast, most Western European nations consider rejection of capital punishment a fundamental aspect of a government commitment to human rights. This means that the American embrace of executions divides us at this moment from our Western peers as does no other issue.

While this current contrast is extreme, much that separates American and European practice is the result of recent policy shifts. Executions declined in the United States from about 100 per year in the early postwar period to fewer than ten per year in the mid-1960s, and they then stopped completely after mid-1967 for a decade. Only after the Supreme Court rulings in 1976 in *Gregg v. Georgia*,[1] *Proffit v. Florida*,[2] and *Jurek v. Texas*[3] did capital punishment become a legal possibility. Up to 1976, the declining rates and heightened conflict surrounding the death penalty in the United States was typical of a nation on the way to abolition.[4] The resurgent enthusiasm for executions in the United States is the product of the last twenty-six years.

Although Europe is now the world capital of abolitionist evangelism, the great majority of abolitions in Europe occurred after the Second World War. As recently as 1977, when Gary Gilmore became the first person executed in the United States in a decade, two French prisoners were sent to the guillotine. That 1977 witnessed not only the first of the new wave of United States executions but also the last of the Western European uses of an instrument more commonly associated with Robespierre is a stunning demonstration of how quickly after changes in conduct the moral judgments about that conduct can harden into orthodoxy. A good history is waiting to be written on how and why the Western democracies created this orthodox stance so very quickly after their initial abolition of the death penalty. Part of their swiftness no doubt reflects uneasiness about execution for many decades before abolition took hold.

Whatever might explain the divergent paths of policy toward the death penalty in Europe and the United States over the past quarter-century, differences in public opinion about the punishment of killers was not a significant factor. British public opinion was just as opposed to abolition in the late 1960s when executions were prohibited as American public opinion was when *Furman v. Georgia* was announced.[5] In France, in September 1977, Hamida Djandoubi, a one-legged Tunisian farm worker who killed a female friend, was beheaded despite the opposition of the French president to capital punishment. The *New*

1. Gregg v. Georgia, 428 U.S. 153 (1976).

2. Proffitt v. Florida, 428 U.S. 242 (1976).

3. Jurek v. Texas, 428 U.S. 262 (1976).

4. Franklin E. Zimring and Gordon Hawkins, *Capital Punishment and the American Agenda* ch.2 (1986).

5. See id. at ch.1.

York Times reported, "The president has said he is personally opposed to the death penalty, but according to a poll in the latest edition of the magazine *Paris Match*, he is supported in this view by only 27% of French people. The poll found 61% in favor of retaining the guillotine."[6] Yet this was the last Western European execution in the twentieth century.

However suggestive the parallels between public opinion in Europe and the United States during the 1970s may be, the contrast in governmental approach to the death penalty in Western Europe and the United States at the turn of the twenty-first century is quite sharp. The Europeans regard the question of having a death penalty as a human rights issue, a test of the proper limits of governmental power, and a fundamental concern rather than an isolated or incidental policy. In the United States, the question is regarded as an issue of criminal justice policy, a matter for provincial governments to determine rather than a basic question for the central government. So, it is not merely that the Europeans and the Americans reach different answers to the same question; there are profound differences as well on what the key issues to be addressed are.

One further measure of the gulf between other Western democracies and the United States on the death penalty is the willingness of our democratic peers to object to the American practice of capital punishment. Along with political repression, official racism, systematic persecution of ethnic minorities, and governmental abuse of children, execution is on the short list of governmental practices that inspire protests from the citizens of other Western democracies no matter where such practices are found. But only the death penalty on this short list of condemned forms of conduct separates the United States from European Union and developed Commonwealth nations. It is no longer unusual for a pending execution in an American state to attract appeals and protests not only from the pope but also from civil authorities and politicians in Italy, Mexico, France, Panama, and Germany. Rejecting the hangman has become an orthodox belief in advanced democracies, a value worthy of export to nations hoping to join the European Union.

Only twenty-five years removed from the guillotine, the community of Western nations other than the United States displays remarkable unanimity and conviction on the wrongness of execution as state policy. There is every bit of the ardor often found in religious converts in the passion of European governments and nongovernmental organizations on the subject of executions. And the willingness of critics from other nations to make invidious moral judg-

---

6. "Convicted Murderer Hamida Djandoubi, Tunisian, Executed by Guillotine," *N.Y. Times*, Sept. 11, 1977, at 6.

ments about capital punishment has surfaced surprisingly in the 1990s. There is consensus not only on the proper moral stand about capital punishment but also on the importance of the issue.

The dissolution of the Soviet Union and the end of its hegemony in Central and Eastern Europe has added to the status of non-execution as a human rights orthodoxy in two ways. First, a number of Central and Eastern European nations were quick to abolish capital punishment when liberated from Soviet domination. From 1987 to 1992, nations like East Germany, Czechoslovakia (and later both of the republics that emerged from it), Hungary, and Romania were quick to reject the death penalty as an instrument of state power. In Romania, those who overthrew the regime shot Nicolai and Elena Ceauşescu and abolished capital punishment in the same month! Both steps could be seen as emphatic rejections of the abuses associated with unlimited governmental power in the immediate past.[7] In less bloodthirsty environments like Hungary and the Czech Republic of Vaclav Havel, the association of abolition of the death penalty with the political liberation of oppressed populations powerfully reinforced the sense that opposition to execution is a moral and political imperative.

The second contribution of the Soviet implosion to the European consensus on capital punishment was to provide a demonstration project of how multinational European incentives and pressure could hasten policy change in nation-states hungry for European aid and recognition. Since the Iron Curtain fell, all twelve of the Central European nations that retained a death penalty in the Soviet era have abolished the death penalty. The Ukraine abolished its death penalty in 2000 and Russia suspended executions in mid-1999, both in response to organized European pressure.[8]

From a European perspective in 2002, abolition is a policy imperative for a developed nation. The United States and Europe do not merely have policy differences on this subject: the American position is regarded as deviant in a morally important way.

Governments That Execute

Whatever the orthodoxy in the developed West may be at this point, it is certainly not exceptional in 2002 for a sovereign nation to execute criminal offenders. While more than 100 nations have abolished the death penalty de facto or de

7. See Franklin E. Zimring, "Inheriting the Wind: The Supreme Court and Capital Punishment in the 1990s," 20 *Fla. St. U. L. Rev.* 1, 9 (1992).

8. See generally Amnesty International, *Annual Report 2001* (2001).

jure, about ninety nations retain a death penalty and many of them execute prisoners with regularity. The death penalty remains standard policy in Islamic nations, in most of Asia, and in many parts of Africa.

What separates the United States from every other nation that executes regularly is the long-standing commitment in the United States to due process protections in criminal trials and plenary opportunities for appellate reviews. The combination of a large-scale death penalty and a large-scale appellate review framework has generated a substantial and cumbersome death penalty appeal process in the United States without precedent in American history or equal in any other nation.

One other characteristic sets the United States apart from other nations that regularly resort to execution, and that is a respectable record on other topics involving human rights. With the exception of the United States, none of the top twenty executing nations has an above-average record in human rights matters. Instead, the most frequent executing nations on Amnesty International's lists include notorious human rights abusers like China, Iraq, and Iran. Only Japan, with a trickle of death sentences and sporadic, infrequent, and secret executions, has any pretensions to a decent human rights/civil liberties reputation. So, when executions happen in the United States (and in Japan as well), they generate the appearance of dissonance with other professed values and legal standards, a problem that Syria, Sudan, Afghanistan, and Iraq never confront.

It is difficult to overstate the degree to which the United States finds itself, in 2002, isolated and morally judged on capital punishment policy. While none of the economic incentives that pushed Eastern Bloc nations toward ending execution can ever be effectively employed to influence the world's preeminent economy, there is now almost no comfort that a supporter of American execution can take from international trends in policy or judgments about the moral claims of American governments to execute. The American government has seldom been judged so harshly on elements of domestic governmental policy. Slavery and racial segregation are the only other examples that quickly come to mind where domestic policy in the United States was regarded as well below the then-applicable moral standards of the developed nations. This is not a comfortable position for a nation that regards itself as a moral leader.

Interstate Variations and Their Implications

In one important sense, the notion most foreign critics have of a national policy about capital punishment in the United States is misleading. While the constitutional standards that govern death penalty administration are a matter of federal law, more than 99 percent of all death sentences and all of the executions during the first quarter-century after *Gregg v. Georgia* have been the product of individual state governments in the United States, and the state governments in the United States vary widely in both the theory and practice of capital punishment. The variation in death penalty practice among the U.S. states is so very wide that it both invites careful inquiry about the causes of different policies and casts doubt on the importance of federal constitutional standards as a significant control over variation in state capital punishment policy.

Documentation of the variation in death penalty policy begins with the division on the basic issue of death as a criminal punishment. Thirty-eight states provide for some form of capital punishment, while twelve states do not. Many of the latter group of states in the United States abolished the penalty long ago, and the great majority of those U.S. states that abolished death as a punishment before 1960 have never reintroduced it. The state of Michigan abolished the death penalty more than a century before France and England took any serious steps toward that goal. Populous states like Wisconsin and Minnesota are stable in abolition policy even though their publics share the concerns about crime and other social trends that are believed to have provoked the revival of American executions. Abolition of the death penalty has a longer pedigree in the history of American state government than in Europe and the British Commonwealth.

Further, seven of the states in the United States that provide a death sentence in their statutes have not conducted any executions in the first quarter-century after *Gregg v. Georgia*. South Dakota and New Hampshire have not had executions in over half a century. The populous state of New Jersey legislated a death penalty in 1980, but no executions have followed in more than two decades.

At the other extreme are several states in the American South. In the year 2000, seventy-six of the eighty-five executions carried out in the United States (89 percent of the total) took place in the South, even though that region accounts for about one-third of the U.S. population and about 40 percent of the American states that authorize a death penalty.[9] Two-thirds of all American executions in 2000 were conducted in just three of the thirty-eight American states that authorize executions: Texas, Oklahoma, and Virginia. The state of Texas alone currently executes more people (forty in 2000) *every year* than were executed in the *quarter-century prior to 2001* in the four most populous states

9. Execution totals are from the Death Penalty Information Center, whose Web site is located at http://www.deathpenaltyinfo.org.

outside the South that have conducted executions: California (nine), Pennsylvania (three), Illinois (twelve), and Ohio (one).

The huge interstate variations in rates of execution are even more curious when the penal codes and death row populations of low-execution and high-execution states are compared. There is, for example, no great difference in the definition of capital murder in the penal codes of Texas and California. Texas had a death row population of 392 in January of 1995 while California had a nearly identical population of 398. Over the six years from January 1995 through December 2000, however, Texas executed a total of 154 prisoners while California executed six. The ratio in raw execution numbers was 27 to 1; when controlling for state population, the ratio was 42 to 1. When expressed as an execution rate based on the 1995 death row population, the difference in execution rates was 26 to 1.[10]

The contrast in execution rates for states with nearly identical 1995 death row populations is staggering. In Texas the cumulative execution risk for six years was more than 1 in 3, and in California the cumulative risk was less than 1 in 65. Even though the homicide statutes are similar and the same federal constitutional doctrines and procedures govern the cases, these enormous gaps in execution risk suggest very different actual standards for enforcing a penalty of death. While the Texas record is an extreme case, the California statistics are typical of northern states like Pennsylvania, Ohio, and New Jersey. As we shall soon see, southern jurisdictions such as Virginia and South Carolina generate execution numbers and risks that are an order of magnitude greater than those in the large northern states that sentence offenders to death on a regular basis.

A Systematic Analysis of State Execution Rates

In an effort to construct a systematic measure of the state-to-state variation in death penalty policy, it is possible to compare the history of every U.S. state that had fifty or more prisoners on death row at the start of 1995 and determine how many prisoners each of these states executed in the six years from 1995 through 2000. The comparison was limited to the seventeen states with large death row populations in 1995 so that the variations we observe are based on substantial samples of death cases. Figure 1 reports on the rate of executions from 1995 through 2000 for every 100 death-sentenced prisoners in 1995. For example, Georgia had a death row population of 106 in January 1995 and a total of five executions during the six-year period of 1995–2000; thus the rate per 100

10. The data sources for the death row and execution totals are reported in figure 1.

Figure 1. Executions in Six Following Years per 100 Offenders on Death Row in January 1995, for Seventeen Large Death Row States. Sources: Death Penalty Information Center, http://www.deathpenaltyinfo.org; NAACP Legal Defense and Education Fund, Death Row USA (1995).

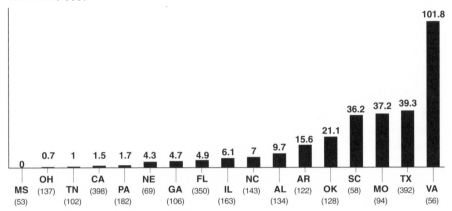

Note: 1995 death row population given in parentheses.

reported in figure 1 is 4.7. Because a very small number of prisoners who joined death row later and dropped appeals might be found in the 1995–2000 executions, the risk per 100 that we compute is not a perfect measure of execution risk over the period of those with pre-1995 death sentences. But the variance can only be tiny, and the measure is the best operational expression of variations in execution policy.

Even excluding Mississippi's zero execution record, the variation in execution rate per 100 death row prisoners is greater than 100 to 1, with Ohio killing fewer than 1 in 100 prisoners and Virginia's executions during the study period exceeding its death row population at the outset. The major eastern and midwestern states are clustered in the low end of the distribution, while all the high-risk states except Arizona are in the South. But southern states like Georgia and Florida have execution risks less than a sixth of the risk found in Texas and South Carolina and less than 5 percent of the Virginia measure; so the variation within the region is very substantial. The Illinois execution risk runs between four and six times that of the other large death row Northern states, even though the scandals profiled in earlier chapters halted executions there in 1999.

When reviewing the very substantial range of risks reported in figure 1, it should be remembered that my focus on the death row population as the beginning of the analysis means that interstate differences in homicide rates, death penalty prosecutions, statutory coverage, and jury willingness to sentence to death do not have any direct influence on the different rates of execution reported. Figure 1 only shows the state-to-state differences in transforming death sentences into executions. Further, both the substantive standards and the court system that provides the ultimate review of all these cases are federal—so the same law and the same courts are governing outcomes. Under such circumstances, a range of risks that covers two orders of magnitude should be quite surprising. And the wide range is not the result of one or two states at the far end of an execution risk distribution. Twenty-five percent of states executed fewer than 1 in 50 of their condemned prisoners, and 25 percent of the states listed in figure 1 executed more than 1 in 3; thus the fourth-highest state (South Carolina) had an execution risk 24 times greater than the fourth-lowest state (California).

While the operating elements that produce these huge differences are not well understood, the significance of the degree of variation is beyond controversy. And the next section will show that these patterned variations, with much higher rates in the South, are not diminishing with the passage of time. While the number of states that have ever executed goes up over time, the clustering of executions in a relatively small number of jurisdictions does not yield to a more even spread over time. I have already noted that only three of the thirty-eight states with death penalties executed two-thirds of the prisoners put to death in year 2000.

The wide variation and the clear regional pattern of death penalty policies among U.S. states suggest two substantive conclusions of potential importance. First, rather than simply attempting to test theories of American particularity in capital punishment by comparing the United States as a whole to other nations, those who would investigate the roots of policy in the United States should also test their theories against the stable differences among American states. What separates Michigan and Wisconsin and Minnesota from Ohio and Pennsylvania? Why are states like Virginia, Texas, and Missouri so much more execution-prone than New Jersey, Ohio, and Pennsylvania? Neither rates of crime nor fear of violence are distributed in anything like the peculiar pattern of American executions. Learning what causes different execution risks in Virginia as opposed to Maryland will probably help establish what kind of factors separate most American states from the governments of other Western democracies.

The second lesson of the huge range of rates of execution is that the law in action on capital punishment differs widely from state to state regardless of the similarity of statutes and procedures. When states like California, Ohio, Pennsylvania, and New Jersey have execution rates that are a tiny fraction of those found in Texas and Virginia, it is obvious that different standards of review are in fact being used both in state courts and in the various federal circuits. The implication of this wide variety of standards-in-fact is that the safeguards that were supposed to accompany the guidelines and appellate scrutiny of the post-*Gregg* death penalty are nowhere in evidence. The rate at which death sentences are affirmed in state high courts varies from 1 in 10 to more than 8 in 10 under identical federal constitutional standards.[11] The reversals by federal courts in death cases do not begin to correct for these wide differences. What is considered harmless error and leads to execution in Virginia is obvious ground for reversal in New Jersey. And the size of the variation between systems makes it difficult to detect any differences between the capital punishment regimes that *Furman v. Georgia* struck down and those that *Gregg v. Georgia* launched. The result may be a triumph of federalism, but it cannot be viewed as a system in which the difference between life and death is governed by consistent national principle.

Continuity and Change in State-Level Execution Policy

This section reports a paradox that is evident when execution trends over time are compared with legal trends. The legal revolution in standards for capital punishment that was supposed to lead to principled administration of the death penalty has produced a larger concentration of executions in the capital punishment confederacy than ever before in American history. The regional pattern of concentrated executions in the South when state policy was not closely regulated by federal standards has continued and intensified in the post-*Gregg* era even though the dominant role of federal rules and federal courts should have evened such differences out. The degree to which past patterns of capital punishment policy are reflected in current patterns is remarkable despite the significant time gaps and the change in legal standards that interrupted the administration of the death penalty in the 1960s and 1970s.

Changing Legal Standards

The legal standards for the administration of capital punishment changed markedly in the 1970s. The watershed event was the U.S. Supreme Court's decision in *Furman v. Georgia* in 1972 that leaving the choice of imprisonment or execu-

11. See Sam Kamin, "The Death Penalty and the California Supreme Court: Politics, Judging and Death" ch.2 (2000) (unpublished Ph.D. dissertation, University of California, Berkeley) (on file with author).

tion to jury discretion is a violation of the Eighth Amendment prohibition of cruel and unusual punishment. Since only nonarbitrary patterns of outcome are allowed under the *Furman* precedent, federal law and federal courts now generate the authoritative judgments about the offenses and procedures that are necessary to legitimate a death sentence. Further, because the federal courts wait for the exhaustion of all primary processes of state court review before allowing federal trial courts to exercise habeas corpus jurisdiction, it takes years before the state court review process ends and the federal court process may begin. Yet if federal law is primary, federal review must be a critical step in trying to render the process less arbitrary in its selections for execution. As we shall soon see, the federalization of capital punishment issues has produced tremendous delay and generated huge populations on state death rows.

Executions over Time

Figure 2 shows the pattern of executions in the United States as a whole over the period from 1950 to 2000. The aggregate total of U.S. executions starts at about 100 per year and declines steadily until halted by a ten-year moratorium in 1967; then it builds back up starting in the late 1970s. By the late 1990s the totals are close to those observed in the early 1950s. But this apparent return to a previous equilibrium is misleading. The population of condemned prisoners from which executions were drawn in the 1950s was never as much as one-tenth the size of the death rows of the late 1990s. In 1960 there were 220 prisoners under sentence of death in the United States. In 2002 there are over 3,700.

The concentration of executions in southern states has actually intensified. Table 1 compares the regional concentration of executions in the 1950s with that observed in the 1980s and 1990s.

The three five-year periods omitted from table 1 between 1965 and 1980 had a cumulative total of thirteen executions, too small for any meaningful analysis of the geographical distribution of execution. The geography of executions in the 1950s and early 1960s was dominated by southern states, with about six out of ten executions in each of the five-year periods. This overrepresentation was balanced by an underrepresentation of the populous northeastern and the north-central states.

After executions resumed in the late 1970s, the pattern of concentration noted in the earlier period not only continued; it intensified. The southern states went from six out of ten to eight out of ten U.S. executions, leaving for the other three regions only half the proportion of completed death sentences they

Figure 2. U.S. Executions by Year, 1950–2000. Source: Bureau of Justice Statistics, U.S. Department of Justice, *Capital Punishment 1999*.

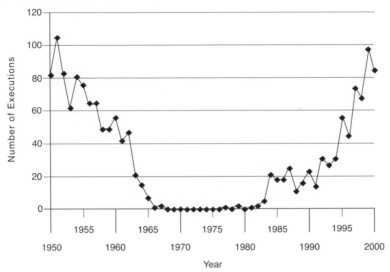

had carried out in earlier years. The Northeast disappeared from the distribution, and the other two regions split the remainder.

All during the postwar period, the southern dominance of execution statistics demonstrates the important difference between the formal and operational significance of the death penalty. The majority of the death penalty states in the United States were always outside the South, while the majority of the executions were always in the South.

But the ratio of southern to nonsouthern executions was 1.5 to 1 before *Furman v. Georgia* and has been 4 to 1 in the years since executions resumed. There is nothing in the changing distribution of death penalty states or in the population demography of the United States that would explain this greater intensity of concentration. Two populous states can pass similar laws providing death penalties for selected homicides. The same federal constitutional rules can govern. But one state will average more than thirty executions every year and the other will average none or one.

What this must mean is that the gap between the formal classification and the operational execution status of a state is greater now than prior to *Furman v. Georgia*. In this important sense, there is more of a gap between the formal and operational status of state systems and much more variation within the death penalty category of states than in earlier times.

Table 1. Percent Distribution of Executions in the United States by Region, Five-Year Intervals

	Northeast	North Central	West	South	Total
1950–54	14	10	16	60	100% (407)
1955–59	17	5	17	61	100% (301)
1960–64	9	9	25	57	100% (180)
[1965–79]					
1980–84	–	3	–	97	100% (29)
1985–89	–	2	6	92	100% (88)
1990–94	–	10	8	82	100% (139)
1995–99	1	14	9	76	100% (341)

Note: In the Total column the number in parentheses indicates the actual number of executions for the given five-year period.
Sources: Death Penalty Information Center (Washington, D.C.), Web site located at http://www.deathpenaltyinfo.org; Franklin E. Zimring and Gordon Hawkins, *Capital Punishment and the American Agenda* (1986).

One other conclusion seems likely: when nonlegal variables such as region and state determine so much of a variation within the death penalty category, the residual implication is that legally relevant elements such as homicide rates or death sentence volume are of diminished significance in explaining execution rates. That is certainly the inference I draw from the individual-state analysis presented earlier in figure 1.

What has federal review generated other than substantial delay between sentence and execution while appeals are pursued? Statistical profiles suggest that the aggregate reversal rate when state and federal processes are combined runs about 70 percent.[12] And no doubt the federal appellate process has identified many cases where prejudicial errors would be ignored except for federal review. But there are few indications that federal review creates a substantial evening-out of the degree of scrutiny that death cases receive when federal and state review are combined. And the huge state-to-state differences in execution risk for prisoners under sentence of death that survive the current federal and state review system undermine the assumptions of *Gregg v. Georgia*. Using gross indicators like the regional concentration of execution and the range of variation in execution risk, the circumstances of death penalty administration appear to differ more from state to state in the 1990s than they did in the 1950s and 1960s. Federal review of the kind practiced in the 1990s identifies injustices in

12. See James S. Liebman et al., "Capital Attrition: Error Rates in Capital Cases, 1973–1995," 78 *Tex. L. Rev.* 1839, 1850 (2000).

individual cases, but it does not provide any systemic quality control creating unified standards of review in death cases.

The Assault on Legal Values

Trying to administer the death penalty on a recurrent basis creates an unprecedented tension between the willingness of a legal system to investigate allegations of illegality and the prompt administration of the prescribed punishment for crimes. When imprisonment is the punishment imposed, the defendant can pursue appeals at great length without frustrating the state's desire that the punishment be meted out, because the defendant can be punished while the legal system's examination of the case continues. The endless habeas corpus filings of a life prisoner might be an inconvenience to the prosecutor or the state attorney general, but this litigation does not frustrate the state's penal purpose because the punishment is not postponed.

Death is different, however, because any meaningful legal appeal must postpone the execution of the prescribed punishment. This makes a lengthy appellate and collateral review process a viable method of putting off execution for the defendant who wants to avoid it. For the prosecutor, this linkage makes the process of legal review into a resented postponement of the punishment. The review itself, not merely the chance of reversal, becomes the object of hostility. As long as the defendant's access to judicial review has not ended, he can escape death, and in this sense he is winning his struggle with state power. This is how the judiciary becomes identified as an adversary by legal officers of the state.

This resentment of judicial review is exacerbated by the genuine dilemmas of federalism in the enforcement of constitutional standards in state death cases. The standard method of deference to state interests in the federal system is to require defendants to exhaust all state remedies prior to requesting federal court review. This means, however, that it can take many years before the preconditions to federal review of a state death case are met. In California, where appointment of counsel to pursue an initial state appeal can take five years, the delay until federal courts can begin to conduct a review may be a decade or more. With a high volume of death cases, the only way that state courts can speed up review of death cases would be to lower the standard of review, which in turn should make death sentences more vulnerable once federal review is launched.

All these pressures have created hostility toward federal court review of state death cases and have encouraged judicial and legislative efforts to cut off federal

by using a wide variety of procedural waivers and time limits. In ·eme Court in the 1980s and 1990s, many of the justices grew to cesses of "last-minute appeals" that make the Court the last stop cutioner.[13] The Court also crafted doctrines placing high burdens on prisoners to demonstrate errors before federal courts are entitled to hold hearings to review state death sentences.[14]

I believe that the fear of long delays and last-minute litigation has also influenced the choice of some constitutional standards for death cases that otherwise defy easy justification. Consider, for example, the problem of mental retardation. While the U.S. Supreme Court appears to hold that the execution of a prisoner for a crime committed under age sixteen violates the Eighth Amendment, the Court stopped short of extending this reasoning to mentally retarded adults.[15] Why the distinction between chronological and cognitive immaturity?

The reason may be the fear that mental ability is a softer and more open-ended concept susceptible to disputes that provide ammunition for dreaded episodes of last-minute litigation. Many hundreds of condemned prisoners are close enough to the boundaries of mental retardation to make colorable claims for such a status. But procedural vulnerability is one thing, and the moral persuasiveness of the analogy between youth and retardation is quite another. To allow the obviously cognitively impaired to be executed because other condemned prisoners might exploit an exception for the retarded is a morally challenged reading of the Eighth Amendment that a majority of the U.S. Supreme Court has been reluctant to endorse. So the issue has stymied the Court for over a decade.

A second area where litigation fears may have distorted constitutional doctrine concerns the presentation of evidence of innocence in the federal courts. To the layman's sense of justice, the most obvious mistake that any capital punishment system could ever make would be to execute an innocent person. The claim of innocence is so compelling that procedural barriers to hearing claims of innocence seem especially small-minded. But this means the claim of innocence becomes a particular threat for those who hate "last-minute litigation," whether or not many defendants will actually prevail on the merits, because of its potential for generating delays while new alibi witnesses are

13. See Zimring, supra note 7, at 13–17.
14. See Yackle, ch.2 in this volume.
15. Compare Thompson v. Oklahoma 487 U.S. 815 (1988), with Penry v. Lynaugh 492 U.S. 301 (1989).

heard or accounts of the confessions of others reopen cases after other appeals have been exhausted.

This special vulnerability of the system to claims of innocence explains why such claims have become a particular target for reforms to speed up the execution process, and why judges and legislatures end up saying embarrassing things when seeking to minimize the threat of disruption by exculpatory claims to scheduled executions. I suspect that Chief Justice William Rehnquist's phrase in *Herrera v. Collins* will be remembered a century after its 1993 publication: "We may assume, *for the sake of argument* . . . , that in a capital case a truly persuasive demonstration of 'actual innocence' made after trial would render the execution of a defendant unconstitutional."[16]

One obvious problem with the refusal to hear claims of innocence is aesthetic: it just does not look good for a legal system to put to death persons whose claims to evidence of innocence have not been fully heard. A second problem is functional: requiring that condemned prisoners prove their innocence by clear and convincing evidence will generate greater risks of execution of innocents than a less grudging standard for allowing a claim to be heard. The only rules rigid enough to cut delay will increase the chances of erroneous execution.

As the level of conflict about the death penalty increased in the United States during the 1990s, the two most common complaints about the modern death penalty launched law reform movements that operated at cross-purposes. Frustration about delays in carrying out executions created the Anti-Terrorism and Effective Death Penalty Act of 1996, which attempts to reduce the time to execution by not permitting the presentation of federal constitutional claims unless strict time limits are met after state proceedings and by creating strong presumptions for the validity of state court decisions in capital cases.

Just as this attempt to "streamline" the death penalty process was being passed in the wake of the Oklahoma City bombing, a scandal in Illinois was launched by the disclosure that several innocent men had been sentenced to death and some came close to execution. The result of this cause célèbre was a moratorium on executions in Illinois and legislative efforts to generate similar pauses in the execution machinery in a number of states, mostly in the north.

The problem, of course, is that any attempt to "streamline" the process to facilitate more and faster executions will increase the chances that wrongly convicted persons are executed, and any serious attempt to identify and protect the wrongly convicted will add delay and additional judicial inquiry to the

16. Herrera v. Collins, 506 U.S. 396, 417 (1989) (italics added).

process of appellate review. A nation can have full and fair criminal procedures, or it can have a regularly functioning process of executing prisoners; but the evidence suggests it cannot have both.

The rhetorical posture of those who advocate the streamlining process is to assume the guilt of all participants in the death penalty appeal process or at least of all those who do not receive relief in state courts. With a state court reversal rate that varies from 1 in 10 in Virginia to more than 8 in 10 in New Jersey,[17] however, the accuracy and fidelity to national standards of state court systems is open to serious question.

The clustering of known innocence cases in a northern state like Illinois makes it hard to believe the allegation of then–presidential candidate George W. Bush that a state like Texas with no public defender services and twenty-five times the number of executions has not risked putting an innocent convict to death. Yet the architects of streamlining cannot admit to an increased chance of wrongful execution because such an acknowledgment would undermine public support for the enterprise. The public demands two attributes in a death penalty system: speed and infallibility. Since an execution system that produces quick and unfailingly correct results cannot happen, the conflicts generated by executions will only grow larger with the passage of time—either of the chronic problems of a high-volume death penalty regime can only be addressed by making the other problem worse.

The 1996 federal legislation, with its procedural forfeitures and heavy presumptions of state court validity is an all-but-explicit admission that meticulous due process and full federal judicial inquiry cannot coexist with an "effective death penalty." The decline in federal oversight was no accident, of course. For some of the hard-right sponsors of the legislation, the diminished power and role of the federal courts and constitutional standards is marvelous news.

But a much larger middle segment of American public opinion would be deeply disturbed by having to choose between protections against wrongful executions and systemic efficiency. The death penalty system the public really wants cannot happen now and never was achievable in the reality of state criminal procedure. With 3,700 condemned prisoners, an error-proof system would be all but paralyzed. A smoothly functioning system would make deadly mistakes. Neither alternative is acceptable to broad segments of American opinion.

These inherent conflicts are a fault line under the superficial stability of citizen support for the death penalty in the United States. The execution system

17. See Kamin, supra note 11, at ch.2.

can never live up to the public's standards for a death penalty worthy of support. It will be either too cumbersome and halfhearted when appeals are allowed or arbitrary and unjust when they are restricted. The death penalty in the United States is destabilized by the inherent limits of mass criminal justice. The only clear path out of the impasse is an end to executions.

CONTRIBUTORS

KEN ARMSTRONG is a legal affairs writer for the *Chicago Tribune*.

JOHN H. BLUME is Visiting Professor of Law, Cornell Law School, and Director, Cornell Death Penalty Project, Cornell Law School.

THEODORE EISENBERG is the Henry Allen Mark Professor of Law, Cornell Law School.

PHOEBE C. ELLSWORTH is the Kirland and Ellis Professor of Law, University of Michigan Law School, and the Robert B. Zajonc Collegiate Professor of Psychology, University of Michigan.

STEPHEN P. GARVEY is Professor of Law, Cornell Law School.

SAMUEL R. GROSS is the Thomas G. and Mabel Long Professor of Law, University of Michigan Law School.

SHERI LYNN JOHNSON is Professor of Law, Cornell Law School.

STEVE MILLS is a metro reporter for the *Chicago Tribune*.

WILLIAM A. SCHABAS is Professor of Human Rights Law, National University of Ireland, Galway, and Director, Irish Centre for Human Rights, National University of Ireland, Galway.

LARRY W. YACKLE is Professor of Law, Boston University School of Law.

FRANKLIN E. ZIMRING is the William G. Simon Professor of Law, University of California, Berkeley, School of Law, and Director, Earl Warren Legal Institute, University of California, Berkeley, School of Law.

INDEX

Charter of Fundamental Rights, 206, 208

Charter of the International Military Tribunal, 200–201

Chaskalson, Arthur, 209

Chessman, Caryl, 40

Chicago Conference on Wrongful Convictions in Capital Cases, 40–41

Chicago Tribune, 3, 22–23, 95, 98, 105, 110–13, 117–20

China, human rights abuses in, 216

Christian Coalition, 26

Christie, John Reginald Halliday, 101–2

circuit courts, multiple federal petitions and, 92 n.95

Civil War, 124

"clear break" decisions, habeas corpus and, 75

Clinton, William, 42, 95, 122–23, 211

CNN–*USA Today*–Gallup poll, 103–4

Code of Crimes against the Peace and Security of Mankind, 202–3

cognitive science research, psychology of moratorium support and, 46–53

Coke, Edward (Lord), 63 n.17

Coker v. Georgia, 150 n.9

Cold War, international laws on capital punishment and, 202–3

Collins, Susan, 114

Columbine High School, 36

Commission on Human Rights, 178, 192–93, 195–96

Congress (U.S.): habeas corpus principle and, 67–68, 78–80; limits on federal courts by, 60–61, 68–74, 89–91; moratorium proposals in, 95; multiple federal petitions, 91–93

Constitutional Court of Italy, 207

constitutional criminal procedure, habeas corpus principle and, 74–79

Constitution of the United States: aggravating circumstances rules, 153–56; capital punishment debate and framework of, 1–2, 18–20, 41–42; habeas corpus principle and,

58–59; jurors' comprehension rules, 153–54; mitigating circumstances rules, 157–59

Constitution Project, 113–15

Control Council Law No. 10, 201

Convention against Torture and Other Cruel, Inhuman, and Degrading Treatment or Punishment, 184

Convention on the Prevention and Punishment of the Crime of Genocide, 183, 202

Convention on the Rights of the Child, 183–84

Convicting the Innocent, 99

Cornyn, John, 113

Council of Europe, 184, 186–87, 200

Court of Human Rights, 180

crime rates: moratoriums on capital punishment and changes in, 52–53; as political issue, 41–43; public perception of, 12–18, 31, 41–42; time lag in data on, 15–16

Criminal Cases Review Commission, 100

criminal justice, capital punishment as, 214

criminal prosecutions, errors in, 69

Criner, Roy, 112

cross-racial identification errors, 132–33

"cruel and unusual punishment" principle, abolition of death penalty on grounds of, 187

"cultural truism," death penalty as, 20–21, 43

Cuomo, Mario, 43

Czechoslovakia, capital punishment issues in, 215

Dabney, Condy, 97

Daniels, Gail Lewis, 133

Dayton Agreement, 198

Dead Man Walking, 24

death penalty. *See* capital punishment

Death Penalty Information Center, 95 n.3

Death Penalty Postconviction Representation Project, 72

"death-qualification," jury selection based on, 149–50

"death row phenomenon," 206

Declaration of Fundamental Rights and Freedoms, 199

defendant: future dangerousness of, 165–68; remorse of, 164–65

defense attorneys: habeas corpus filing deadlines and, 84–85; incompetency of, 105–13; limits on performance of, 69–74; minimum standards for, 114; multiple federal petitions and, 91–93; state court procedural defaults and, 85–88

"deliberate bypass" rule, 91–93

Demps, Bennie, 119–20

Detroit Free Press, 116

Devine, Dick, 106

Diamond, Shari, 50

"diligence" test, habeas corpus and, 90–91

Djandoubi, Hamida, 213–14

DNA technology: capital punishment debate and, 3, 41; exonerations based on, 114, 123; Ford Heights 4 case and, 110–11; hair analysis and, 107, 109 n.12; media focus on, 118; moratoriums on death penalty and, 45, 53, 97; public opinion concerning, 29, 37, 39–40; reopening of cases and, 100–102; wrongful convictions and impact of, 98–99

"dominative" racists, 135–36

Douglas, William O. (Justice), 124

"Draft Code of Offences against the Peace and Security of Mankind," 202

Drayton, Ricky, 134–35

due process: for foreign nationals, 191–92; habeas corpus principle and, 61–68; origins of, 63 n.17

Dukakis, Michael, 11, 42, 44

Duncan v. Walker, 85 n.77

Dwyer, Jim, 98–99, 115 n.17, 123

East Timor, 198

Eighth Amendment: abolition of death penalty and, 187; "cruel and unusual punishment" provision, 150, 222, 226; habeas corpus principle and, 62, 67; racial bias in capital punishment and, 127–28

Eisenberg, Thomas, 4

Ellsworth, Phoebe, 2

Engler, John, 27, 45

English Habeas Corpus Act of 1679, 64 n.17

Equal Protection Clause, 127–28

equal protection principle, race and capital punishment and, 121–22, 127–28

European Commission of Human Rights, 190, 206

European Convention on Human Rights, 184–86, 199, 206–7

European Court of Human Rights, 180, 187, 190, 206, 209

European Parliament, 199–200

European Union, 197–99, 206, 208, 214–15

Evans, Timothy John, 101–2

"exclusionary rule," habeas corpus and, 73, 75

executions: analysis of state execution rates, 218–21; of foreign nationals, 191–92; imposition of death sentence and waiting period for, 60 n.1; of innocents, 22–37, 116–30; international law concerning, 188–89; international patterns of, 215–16; interstate variations in, 217–21; moratorium on, 2–3, 23–27; patterns of concentration in, 222–25; reform proposals for, 227–28; in Rwanda, 203–4; statistics on, 1, 44–45, 94–95, 213, 218–21; in Texas, 3, 22–23, 95, 98, 105, 110–11

"exhaustion doctrine," 80–85

exonerations: cross-racial identification errors and, 132–33; defense attorney incompetence and, 108 n.10; historical cases of, 97–98; reopening of cases and, 100–102; statistics on, 94–95; in Texas, 112–13

Ex parte Royall, 80–81

extradition, capital punishment and, 205–9

eyewitnesses, fallibility of, 115

hair analysis, wrongful conviction and errors in, 107, 109

Hand, Learned (Justice), 3, 96–98

Hanratty, James, 100

"harmless" error standard, 79 n.63

Harris polls: on capital punishment, 8–9, 31–32; on public perception of crime, 14; on wrongful executions, 30

Havel, Vaclav, 215

Helms, Jesse, 194

Henderson, Wilburn, 118–20

Herrera v. Collins, 73, 74 n.45, 227

Hill, Herbert, 106

Hillard, Jerry, 120

Hogue, Jerry Lee, 116–17

Holmes, Oliver Wendell (Justice), 65–66

homicide rates: death penalty as deterrent to, 34–37, 223–24; public attitudes on death penalty and, 13–18

Hoop Spur, Arkansas, 65–66

Human Rights Chamber, 198

Human Rights Committee, 180, 188–90, 193, 209

human rights conventions, abolition of capital punishment and, 178–211, 214, 216

Hungary, capital punishment issues in, 209, 215

Illinois Supreme Court, 83, 87–88, 94, 102, 105–11, 120; capital punishment reforms and, 113–15; executions ordered by, 218–21, 227–28

information: role of, in moratoriums on death penalty, 45–53

innocence: capital punishment and issue of, 3, 28–37, 226–29; erroneous death sentences and, 22–27, 38–40

Innocence Protection Act, 114

Inter-American Commission of Human Rights, 180, 191

Inter-American Court of Human Rights, 192

International Court of Justice, 191–92

International Covenant on Civil and Political Rights, 183–85, 188–90, 192–93; Optional Protocols, 186, 189, 193, 198–99

International Criminal Court, 204–5

international law: capital punishment and, 4, 178–211; criminal law, 200–205; exceptionalism of U.S. and, 212–16; extradition and, 205–9

International Law Commission, 202–3

Iran, capital punishment in, 196, 216

Iraq, human rights abuses in, 216

Italy, capital punishment issues in, 197, 207, 214

Jackson, David, 109

Jackson, Jesse, 104

Jagger, Bianca, 104

Jahangir, Asma, 195

jailhouse informants, 106–11; limits on use of, 115

Jamaica, capital punishment in, 188–89

Jimerson, Verneal, 110

John Paul II (Pope), 25–26

Johnson, Lyndon Baines, 41 n. 128

Johnson, Sheri Lynn, 4

Jones, Leo, 119–20

judicial review, state hostility toward, 225–29

Jurek v. Texas, 213

juries: aggravating circumstances rules, 153–56; capital juries, 4; Capital Jury Project study of, 145–77; comprehension rules for, 153–54; demographic variables in, 168–69; habeas petitions and, 74 n.45; instruction guidelines for, 175–76; misconduct claims against, 133; mitigating circumstances rules, 153, 156–59; qualification limitations of, 150–53; racial bias in guidance of, 139–40; racial composition of, 107–10, 142–43, 162–63; role of, in capital punishment cases, 62; selection criteria, 174–75;

Posey, Leroy, 109–10

postconviction proceedings, habeas corpus principle and, 62–63; federal court hearings and, 89–91; "mixed" petitions of prisoners, 81–85; multiple federal petitions, 91–93; procedural barriers to, 79–80; Rehnquist Court limits on, 71–79; state court procedural defaults and, 85–88; timing rules, 80–85

Powell, Lewis (Justice), 126–27

Prejean, Sister Helen, 24

Preparatory Committee, 203

"probable innocence" standard, 87 n.83, 89 n.87

pro bono legal services, state provision of, 72–74

procedural default: defined, 121 n.1; equal protection principle and, 121–22; habeas corpus and, 85–88

Proffitt v. Florida, 213

Promise of Justice, A, 108 n.10

prosecutors: biased conduct of, 133–35; death penalty sought by, 131–32

Protess, David, 94–95, 108 n.10

psychiatric testimony: validity of, in capital cases, 112, 121–22

psychological research, moratoriums on death penalty and, 46–53

public defender system, 69–72

public opinion: on capital punishment, 2, 7–57; on crime rates, 12–18; European and U.S. attitudes on death penalty compared, 213–16; reliability of data on, 9–11; surveys on general death penalty attitudes, 53–58; on wrongful convictions, 103–4

Purvis, Will, 99

"*p*" value, 155–56; seriousness of crime research, 163–64

Queen Elizabeth II, 102

race: biased conduct of trial participants, 133–35; capital punishment and issues of, 3–4, 24, 27, 121–43; charging practices and, 141; crime and, 41 n.128; cross-racial identification errors, 132–33; denials of bias based on, 138–39; forms and manifestation of prejudice, 135–36; future dangerousness predictions based on, 132; future of discrimination based on, 143; GAO study of bias based on, 129–30; history of discrimination based on, 124–28; jurors' guidance and, 139–40; jury composition and issues of, 107–10, 142–43, 162–63, 177; jury misconduct claims and, 133; jury selection based on, 107–11, 142–43; limits of law on, 141; neutrality as tool against, 143; nonstatistical evidence of bias based on, 132; persistence of discrimination in capital cases, 135–43; prevalence of discrimination in capital cases and, 128–35; prohibition against arguments based on, 142; sentencing decisions of jurors and, 139, 163, 168–74; verdict impeachment rules, 141–42; victim impact testimony and, 140–41

race-of-defendant effects, research on, 130–31, 136–37

race-of-victim effects, research on, 131, 137–38

Radelet, Michael, 105

Raines, Willie, 109

rape, capital punishment for, 125, 153 n.12

Reagan, Ronald, 67–68

regression coefficient, statistical modeling of jurors and, 171–74

"regressive" racism, 138

Rehnquist, William (Chief Justice): habeas corpus rulings in court of, 67–93; on innocence claims, 227

religion, of jurors, 168–69, 173–74

Reno, Janet, 200

Republican Party, death penalty as political issue for, 41–43

Research and Forecasts polls, 14

"residual doubt" principle, 115

"Rethinking the Death Penalty," 2
retribution, support for capital punishment based on, 33
retroactive punishment: habeas corpus and, 74–79; international law and, 201–2
Rezin v. Wolff, 87 n.84
Richardson, William, 194
right to counsel, habeas corpus rulings and, 69–74
"right to life" provisions, international covenants on capital punishment, 184
Robertson, Pat, 26, 45, 96
Robinson, Mary, 196
Romania, capital punishment issues in, 215
Rome Statute of the International Criminal Court, 204–5, 211
Roosevelt, Eleanor, 178–79
Roosevelt, Franklin D., 178
Roper Center for Public Opinion Research, 8 n.4, 9
Rose (Lord Justice), 101
Rose v. Lundy, 81–82
Ross v. Moffitt, 72 n.38
Rules of Land Warfare, 201–2
Russian Federation, death penalty in, 200
Rwanda, genocide in, 203–4
Ryan, George, 2–3, 23–24, 26–27, 30–31, 40–41, 45, 95–96; Constitution Project and, 113

Saldano, Victor, 121–23, 132, 143
San Jose Conference, 185
Saudi Arabia, capital punishment in, 196
Sawyer v. Smith, 77
Scalia, Antonin (Justice), 5, 128
Schabas, William, 4
Scheck, Barry, 29, 98–99, 107, 115 n.17, 123
Schlup v. Delo, 87 n.83
Schmal, Carol, 109–10
Selden, John, 63 n.17
sentencing decisions: future dangerousness of defendant and, 165–68; life vs. death deci-

sions, 161–74; mandatory death sentences and, 159–61; parole eligibility as factor in, 166–68; remorse of defendant as factor in, 164–65; seriousness of crime and, 163–64; statistical modeling of, 162–63, 169–74
seriousness of crime measurements, sentencing decisions based on, 163–64
sex, of jurors, 168–69
Shafir, Eldar, 45–48
Simpson, O.J., 29
Singapore, 197
"60 Minutes," 116
Slovenia, 200
Smith, Gordon, 114
Smith, James, 97
Soering v. United Kingdom, 206, 208
South African Constitutional Court, 185, 209
South American Convention, 205
South Carolina: aggravating circumstances rules, 154–56; executions rates in, 219–21; juror sentencing decisions in, 162–63, 173 n.47; mandatory death sentences rules, 159–61; mitigating circumstances rules, 156–59; racial bias in capital cases in, 134
South Dakota, abolishment of death penalty in, 217
Soviet Union, dissolution of, 215
standards-in-fact, interstate variations in, 220–21
state court systems: aggravating circumstances guidelines, 153–56; analysis of execution rates in, 218–21; capital punishment laws and, 18–19, 37–40; counsel appointments by, 72 n.39; formal vs. operational status of, variations in, 222–25; habeas corpus issue and, 3, 60–68, 73–74; hostility to judicial review in, 225–29; juror instruction guidelines for, 175–76; legal trends in, 221–25; procedural defaults in, 85–88; racial bias in, 124–28; Rehnquist Court habeas corpus rulings and, 76–78; timing rules for habeas corpus and, 83–88;

Library of Congress Cataloging-in-Publication Data

Beyond repair? : America's death penalty / edited by Stephen P. Garvey.

p. cm. — (Constitutional conflicts)

Includes index.

ISBN 0-8223-2960-3 (cloth : alk. paper) —

ISBN 0-8223-3043-1 (pbk. : alk. paper)

1. Capital punishment—United States. I. Garvey, Stephen P.

II. Series.

KF9227.C2 B49 2002

345.73'0773—dc21   2002008170